THE HISTORY OF
JAPANESE PRINTING
AND
BOOK ILLUSTRATION

THE HISTORY OF
JAPANESE PRINTING
AND
BOOK ILLUSTRATION

DAVID CHIBBETT

KODANSHA INTERNATIONAL LTD.
TOKYO, NEW YORK AND SAN FRANCISCO

Distributed in the United States by Kodansha International/USA Ltd., through Harper & Row, Publishers, Inc., 10 East 53rd Street, New York, New York 10022.

Published by Kodansha International Ltd., 2–12–21 Otowa, Bunkyo-ku, Tokyo 112 and Kodansha International/USA Ltd., 10 East 53rd Street, New York, New York 10022 and 44 Montgomery Street, San Francisco, California 94104.
LCC 76–9362
ISBN 0–87011–288–0
JBC 1070–784489–2361
First edition, 1977

For Judith

CONTENTS

PREFACE

In the West in recent years there has been an enormous upsurge of interest in the Japanese illustrated book both as a creative art form and as a vehicle reflecting the achievement of Japanese genius in painting. This is due to the fact that nearly all the great Japanese artists of the major schools of painting either turned to book illustration at some stage in their careers or had their work reproduced in books after their death. Surprisingly though, it is Western scholars who have written more extensively on this than Japanese scholars, who have devoted more attention to the history of Japanese printing. The names of Louise Norton Brown, Jack Hillier, C. H. Mitchell and Toda Kenji readily spring to mind in the former connection, while Kawase Kazuma, Nagasawa Kikuya and Sorimachi Shigeo have been particularly drawn to Japanese printing history.

Although the history of printing and printed book illustration are closely related, they are also vastly different subjects which should perhaps be treated separately. However, it did not seem fair to ignore one at the expense of the other. Rather, I have attempted to draw together the threads of Japanese printing and printed book illustration in a general introduction to the whole subject, which, I hope, will be of use both to those with a professional and an amateur interest.

As none of the previously mentioned authors in the West have devoted much attention to the history of Japanese printing, and as this particular subject has never been extensively treated in any Western language, I have, therefore, devoted the first section of this book to that alone, drawing largely on facts derived from Japanese language sources.

Book illustration, an enormous subject in itself, is much better covered by Western authorities, and I have confined myself in the second section to a factual recording of the names of the most important artists who illustrated books as well as their most celebrated works. In the space available, no attempt has been made to consider the aesthetics of Japanese art, and it is hoped that any such lack will be compensated for by the amount of information and material presented.

The very nature of an introductory work is a restricting one, and subjects are dealt with in paragraphs when they really deserve chapters, and in chapters when they really deserve books. If, however, I have succeeded in presenting a coherent account of the development of Japanese printing and book illustration up to 1868, my purpose will have been served.

My thanks are due to the Director-General of the Reference Division of the British Library for his kind permission to reproduce the illustrations contained in this work; to my friends and colleagues Mr. Kenneth Gardner of the Department of Oriental Manuscripts and Printed Books, the British Library; Mr. Brian Hickman of the School of Oriental and African Studies, the University of London; Mr. Charles Harris of the British Library; and most of all to my wife Judith, to whom this book is dedicated.

DAVID CHIBBETT

London,
January 1977

PART ONE

THE HISTORY OF
JAPANESE PRINTING

1 | THE PRINTED BOOK

In the history of the human race, there can be no doubt that printing has proved to be one of man's most significant and beneficial inventions, providing the opportunity for thoughts on all subjects to be recorded and communicated to a wide audience throughout the ages. The history of the printed book in Japan, as elsewhere, is basically two subjects: it is the history of how the book was printed, its physical constituents and characteristics; and it is the history of what was printed and why. In the final analysis, what was printed is more important than how it was done, but in Japan, particularly, such attention was paid to the overall appearance of the book that the finished product was often a work of art in itself, quite apart from the value of its contents. This tradition of excellence inherent in book production continues to the present day, and the Japanese are not only one of the world's most prolific producers of books but also one of those most dedicated to quality. The tradition of printing in Japan dates back at least to the eighth century, further than in any other country except China and Korea, and this book endeavors to examine the history of that tradition as applied to books and the illustrations used in them.

Before turning to the history of what was printed, it is necessary to examine in some detail the physical constituents of the printed book in Japan as it developed through the centuries. As none of the principal ingredients of the book—a written language, paper, binding, printing—originated in Japan itself, it would be inappropriate to begin a history of the printed book anywhere else than in China.

THE INTRODUCTION OF WRITING

Throughout most of the period with which this book deals, China was the dominant presence in the Far East both militarily and culturally. During the Chinese Han dynasty (206 B.C.–A.D. 220), when China and Japan probably first made contact, Chinese civilization was one of the most advanced in the world while Japan was still in the throes of the Stone Age. From Han times onward, Japan received a wave of beneficial imports from China through Korea, which included the foundations of a civilization—science, art, literature and religion. By the end of the Nara period (A.D. 710–784), Japan, in the outward lifestyle of its inhabitants, was seemingly Chinese, with a religion borrowed from China and a system of government consciously modeled on that of China. Even native works of literature were written in the Chinese language, and it was the latter which contributed the first essential element needed toward the production of a printed book.

The early Japanese had no written language of their own, and although spoken Japanese had no relation whatsoever to spoken Chinese, it was due to China's dominating influence that Japan came to adopt the Chinese writing system. The cultural pressure exerted by China during those times can be compared to that of the Catholic Church in medieval Europe, when Latin became the official language of the countries concerned regardless of the spoken language of the inhabitants.

Tradition ascribes the invention of Chinese writing to the semilegendary Yellow Emperor, or Huang-ti, who is supposed to have lived during the third millennium B.C. Legends of this kind are not uncommon in both China and Japan, and aside from the impossibility of one man inventing a complete writing system, Huang-ti's contribution should be taken to mean no more than that during the time he is supposed to have lived, some form of written language was in existence. To some extent this hypothesis is borne out by the evidence of the earliest known form of writing, the oracle bone inscriptions of the Shang dynasty (c. 1401–1123 B.C.). The Shang people were certainly not the first Chinese to make use of bones and shells for divination, but they do seem to have been the first to record the results of the divination on the bones and shells they used. According to Tsuen-hsuin Tsien's *Written on Bamboo and Silk: The Beginnings of Chinese Books and Inscriptions*, these inscriptions indicate that the Shang had a written vocabulary of some 2,500 characters, ample for simple literary use, but the significant point is that these characters were already rather sophisticated in form.

Written Chinese is popularly described as a pictographic language, but this is somewhat misleading. Certainly, many of the basic characters are derived from pictographic origins: words such as "tree" (木), "sun" (日), "large" (大—a man standing with his arms outstretched), "small" (小—a man standing with arms at his side) clearly stem from simplified pictures. However, pictographs alone would be inadequate to convey more complex thought concepts without the aid of ideographs, which combined with the pictographic element to convey an association of ideas. The character for "west," for example (西), is a simplified picture of a bird sitting on its nest, the idea association being that birds go to their nests when the sun goes down and the sun goes down in the west. Other characters are neither pictographic nor ideographic, but combine a pictograph with a phonetic element. For example, add the phonetic element 公 to the character for "tree," and you have the combination 松 which means "pine tree." In such cases the phonetic element does not contribute to the meaning either pictographically or ideographically. T. H. Tsien's examination of characters found on Shang oracle bones and shells indicates that those which have been deciphered (about half) show the presence of all three forms mentioned above. This argues strongly in favor of a considerable sophistication in the written language of the Shang, one that must have developed over a very long period.

The 2,500 Shang characters increased to 9,000 by A.D. 100, to about 18,000 by A.D. 500, to about 27,000 by A.D. 1000; the largest dictionary today in number of characters has some 50,000. Certainly, by the time written Chinese reached the Japanese islands it was more than sophisticated enough to convey the relatively simple Japanese language. The question is, however, when did Chinese writing reach Japan? Consultation of archaeological evidence and of Chinese and Japanese historical chronicles points toward the Chinese Han dynasty (206 B.C.–A.D. 220) as the period in which the Japanese first became acquainted with written Chinese. In antiquity there seems to have been no direct sea traffic between the two countries, and the limited communication between them was carried out through Korea. In 109 B.C. Emperor Wu-ti conquered most of Korea apart from the far south, and this led to many Chinese emigrating to Korea, taking their advanced culture with them. By 75 B.C., however, Korean resistance forced the Chinese out of all but the Lo-lang district, which continued to thrive as a center of Chinese culture. Evidence of Japanese contact with Korea at this early date is established by the numerous examples of Han bronze mirrors that have been excavated in Japan. Significantly, some of these mirrors bear inscriptions in Chinese, a sure sign that by approximately the beginning of the Christian era, Chinese characters were known in Japan. Although not all people in Japan would know how to interpret them, it is a logical inference that *some* did, even if direct evidence to this effect does not exist.

In A.D. 57, the king of Na (or Nu), probably situated within what is now Fukuoka Prefecture in Kyushu, sent an envoy to the ruling Han emperor, who presented him with an inscribed gold seal for his master. This seal was subsequently lost, but by a stroke of good fortune, in 1784 it was rediscovered near Fukuoka and the Chinese inscription on it supports the theory that Chinese characters were known in Japan by about the beginning of the Christian era. Fifty years later, in A.D. 107, it is recorded that the king of Wa (Japan) sent an embassy to Han China with a gift of 160 slaves, and from that time onward there was increasing, though not unbroken, contact between the two countries, usually through Korea.

In A.D. 239, Himiko, female ruler of Yamatai (the location of which has been a bone of contention among generations of Japanese scholars, some favoring the Yamato plain, others, with more likelihood, Northern Kyushu), sent an embassy to the Chinese kingdom of Wei, one of the three kingdoms that followed the disintegration of the Han dynasty in A.D. 220. In return, she received numerous gifts, including bronze mirrors, some of which must have borne inscriptions.

By about the middle of the fourth century, Japan had emerged as a unified country instead of a collection of small kingdoms of which Yamatai was foremost, and began to become more directly involved with affairs on the mainland. The ideal opportunity was provided when Korea became divided into three warring kingdoms. In about the

15

year 370, the Japanese invaded Korea and established a territory for themselves in the south, which they renamed Mimana and which they successfully held until 562. This close contact with Korea brought a new wave of Chinese art objects into Japan: mirrors, swords, bells, many of which were inscribed with Chinese characters; and it also brought the more lasting cultural import, Buddhism, which arrived probably in the year 538. Books, however, reached Japan from China long before the introduction of Buddhism. The early Japanese historical record, *Nihon shoki* (*Chronicles of Japan*), completed in 720, contains the following entry for the sixteenth year of the reign of Emperor Ōjin (nominally A.D. 285): "Wang-in arrived, and straightway the Heir Apparent, Uji no Waka-iratsuko, took him as teacher, and learnt various books from him. There was none which he did not thoroughly understand. Therefore the man called Wang-in was the first ancestor of the Fumi no Obito [scribes]." (W. G. Aston, *Nihongi*, 1896, Vol. 1, pp. 262–63).

Here, then, is clear evidence of the appearance of books in Japan at an early date. The word used for books in this entry is *fumi* (writings), but it is written with the characters that are now pronounced *tenseki*, which cannot mean anything else but "books," although most certainly they would have been books in scroll form. Wang-in was a Korean and W. G. Aston has convincingly argued that the date of his arrival in Japan was not 285 but 405. (The inaccuracy of the chronology of *Nihon shoki* is now generally recognized, and for some dates an adjustment of 120 years [two 60-year cycles] is desirable.) In the reign of Emperor Richū (nominally 400–5), the *Nihon shoki* states that "recorders were appointed in the provinces in order to note down words and events." This is the first clear indication of a written language being known on anything but a limited scale, and provides proof that by the late fifth or early sixth century, a considerable body of Japanese not only understood but also wrote it. However, more than another century was to elapse before the earliest surviving manuscript of native origin was written.

To sum up, it seems clear that the existence of a written language was known in Japan by 100 B.C. at the latest, but the likelihood that it was understood by more than a handful of people is remote. However, it was probably not until the early fifth century, when the ruling authorities began to use it for official purposes, that the Japanese began to read and write Chinese with any facility.

THE INTRODUCTION OF PAPER

The earliest extant Japanese manuscript of native origin is the subject of some controversy. It is a copy of the fourth *maki* (scroll) of the *Hokke gisho*, a work on the *Lotus Sutra* written by the celebrated statesman and Buddhist scholar Shōtoku Taishi (A.D. 574–622). As well as being a person of considerable historical significance, Shōtoku Taishi is also a "culture hero," accredited with many unlikely feats of learning. Chroniclers tell us that at the age of three he was learning several thousand characters a day—

an impossible feat whatever his genius, since there were simply not that many characters to learn. However, Shōtoku Taishi did study Buddhism and was the author of three commentaries on the *Lotus Sutra*, the *Hokke gisho* being written in either 614 or 615. The surviving manuscript is traditionally supposed to be in his own handwriting, but this has become a matter of considerable debate in the twentieth century. Some argue that although Shōtoku Taishi was probably the author of the *Hokke gisho*, the surviving manuscript was actually written at the end of the seventh century by an unknown person. The counterargument is that since Shōtoku Taishi was revered in his own lifetime, it is not unlikely that the Japanese would have treasured something written by him and taken great pains to preserve it.

What is significant for present purposes, however, is that this early manuscript is written on paper. The existence of the written or printed word does not in itself imply the existence of paper. As has already been mentioned, the earliest Chinese materials to serve as a surface for writing were the bones and shells used for divination by the Shang people, and between the Chou dynasty (c. 1122–256 B.C.) and the Han dynasty (206 B.C.–A.D. 220), a variety of surfaces including metal (principally bronze), clay, stone, jade, wood, bamboo and silk were used for inscriptions. Indeed, long after the

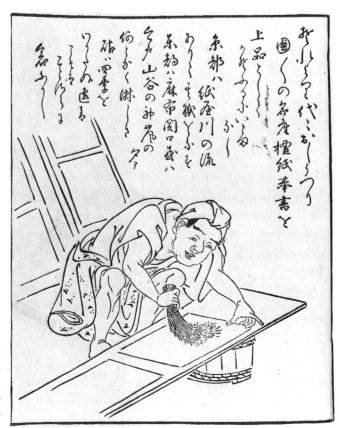

1. Pressing water from sheets of paper before drying them on long wooden boards. This is an illustration by Tachibana Minkō from a black-and-white edition of the *Saiga shokunin burui* (2 vols., 1784), first published in 1770.

17

discovery of paper, silk continued to be used for writing and painting. The Japanese also wrote and even printed on many such materials, but there is no instance of the printed word (in a quantity to make a consecutive text) being produced in Japan on anything but paper, and thus the invention of paper was a key factor in the development of the book in Japan and in the Far East as a whole.

The Chinese records are very precise about the date of the invention of paper as well as the person responsible. The Han dynastic chronicle firmly attributes its invention to one Ts'ai Lun in A.D. 105. Ts'ai Lun was a eunuch who seems to have been charged by the court with the responsibility of collecting information and reporting on various experiments in papermaking that were taking place in China. Unlikely as it is that Ts'ai Lun himself set out to invent paper, which was essentially an evolutionary process, it is more probable that he was credited with the invention in his official capacity as supervisor of the experiments. The word used for paper (*chih* in Chinese, *shi* or *kami* in Japanese) is found in records of events preceding Ts'ai Lun's time, but since no true paper has been discovered predating A.D. 105, it is now generally assumed that what is referred to in earlier times was "quasi-paper," made from silk fibers. The paper "discovered" by Ts'ai Lun was different from this "quasi-paper" in its composition of, according to contemporary records, tree bark (which tree is unspecified), old rags and fish nets. In succeeding centuries the manufacture of paper was refined and spread throughout the Chinese empire, but it was not until about A.D. 400 that paper can be truly said to have supplanted bamboo and silk as the principal writing surface.

During the twentieth century many thousands of manuscripts and printed pieces of paper have been discovered which shed further light on early Chinese papermaking. The earliest known paper to be discovered so far was found in 1942 near Kharakhoto in Mongolia. Made from plant fiber and rather coarse in texture, it is believed to date from around A.D. 109 and is thus contemporary with Ts'ai Lun's discovery. Other manuscript documents, both fragmentary and complete, have been found in various locations in China and Central Asia (Sir Aurel Stein's astounding discoveries at Tunhuang being the most notable), ranging from about A.D. 150 to the end of the tenth century. Examination by botanists of the earlier examples indicate that the first Chinese paper was made from a mixture of raw fibers and rags, the principal fibers being mulberry, laurel and China grass. There has been some controversy over the fact that while rags, bark and fish nets were thought to have been used separately to make different types of paper, examples found indicate that they were pulped together. However, further discoveries may yet be made that reveal a "missing link" in the development of papermaking.

Aside from the question of the ingredients used, on the basis of what is known about traditional methods of papermaking in both China and Japan, it is possible to reconstruct the earliest techniques. Let us assume a paper made from the bark of the mulberry, the material most commonly used in Japan. First, the tree bark (the removal of which was in itself a very complex technique) was cut into pieces and soaked for at

2. Papermaking in Shizuoka with Mt. Fuji in the background, by Hiroshige III, from the *Dainihon bussan-zue*, published in 1877.

least one hundred days in water. The pieces were then pounded in a mortar to separate the inner from the outer bark, which was then removed. The remaining pulp was mixed with either lime or soda ash, heated over a fire to boiling point for at least eight days and nights and then washed repeatedly until the fibers were completely softened. It was strained and pounded into a doughy substance, which was bleached with one of various agents depending on the region. This bleach was then removed by further soaking and the mixture was placed in a large vat (Japanese: *fune*). Some starch was added to prevent the finished sheets from sticking together.

To make the sheets, a frame was dipped into the vat to scoop up a quantity of the mix. This frame had a bamboo mat or screen stretched between its upper and lower parts to retain the fibers of the pulp while allowing the water to drain away. The sheet obtained in this way was pressed to get rid of any remaining water and dried on heated wood or brick walls (Pls. 1, 2).

It is not known when the first paper, presumably made by very similar methods, reached Japan. The *Nihon shoki* contains relevant but inconclusive evidence in the form of an entry for the third month, spring, of the reign of Empress Suiko (A.D. 610), which reads: "The King of Koryö sent tribute of Buddhist priests named Tam-chhi and

Pöp-chöng. Tam-chhi [normally known to the Japanese as Donchō] knew the five (Chinese) classics. He was moreover skilled in preparing painters' colours, paper and ink." (W. G. Aston, *Nihongi*, 1896, Vol. 2, p. 140).

It does not explicitly state that this was the occasion of the introduction of paper to Japan, but many Japanese scholars have taken that to be its implication. Moreover, since the chronology of the *Nihon shoki* becomes progressively more accurate and since it deals here with events of less than a century before its compilation, it is not easy to disregard 610 as the date of Donchō's visit. The 614–15 Shōtoku Taishi manuscript does not necessarily contradict this, but careful examination of it reveals that whoever wrote it had considerable experience of writing on paper, a skill that could not have been acquired so rapidly. There is, too, the previously cited entry in the *Nihon shoki* to the effect that books were imported for the first time in A.D. 285. Assuming W. G. Aston to be correct in placing this event in A.D. 405, it is likely that the books referred to were written on paper, as by that date this material enjoyed much wider use than any other in China. On balance, therefore, it seems most likely that Donchō, although a papermaker, was not the first to bring paper to Japan, and that paper was known to the Japanese at least two centuries earlier.

The topic of paper production in Japan deserves a book to itself and it is not possible here to give anything more than a brief outline of the principal materials used. Four such materials used in pre-modern Japanese papermaking were hemp, paper mulberry (*Broussonetia papyrifera*), *gampi* (from the bark of *Wickstroemia canescens*, which grows wild on the mountains and moors of Japan) and *mitsumata* (*Edgeworthia papyrifera*). Of these hemp was the earliest material used and most likely the paper brought and made by Donchō in 610 was hemp-based. It was certainly this kind of paper that was produced for the practice of sutra-copying during Nara times (710–94). After this, hemp was abandoned in favor of *kōzo* (paper mulberry) and *gampi*, both of which were already in general use during the Nara period because of their abundance and high quality. Paper mulberry fibers are regular and tough, affording both strength and a fine surface, while *gampi* fibers tend to be slender and smooth, giving the paper a lustrous quality. *Mitsumata* fibers, which were probably used in the provinces of Kai and Suruga as early as the fourteenth century but did not enjoy more general use until the seventeenth century, are longer, thinner and somewhat weaker than those of the paper mulberry. However, it was *mitsumata* that proved the most suitable for the mechanized paper industry, and even nowadays it is used for Japanese banknotes. These were the basic materials used for all Japanese handmade paper (generically known as *washi*) before the modern period.

Gampi and paper mulberry papers were more or less equally common during the Heian, Kamakura and Muromachi periods, and many of the finest *Kasuga-ban* editions of the Kamakura period were printed on *gampi* paper, but the majority of Edo-period books were printed on paper mulberry paper. Hemp and *mitsumata* were always of subsidiary importance.

The wide range of individual paper types within these basic categories is beyond the scope of this book, but mention must be made of paper decoration, an important and interesting aspect in the manufacture of paper (Pl. 3). Numerous devices were, of course, used to enhance the appearance of paper, most of which do not concern us here. However, there were three basic methods employed to decorate the paper used for books. First, there was the effect of *ummo*, or mica, sprinkled at random on sheets of paper while still wet after removal from the mat. Second, *gofun*, a powder made from shells, was similarly used, and third, when actual patterns were required as opposed to random scatterings, both *ummo* and *gofun* were applied either by stencil or by wood block, as in the case of the decorative motifs used on the paper in *Saga-bon* books. Another important decorative effect, although seldom used in books, was achieved by tying shapes made from wood or metal to the frame before it was dipped in the mix. These shapes resisted the paper fibers and led to an uneven patterned surface, where the designs have the appearance of water marks. Very often ingredients were actually added to the mix for utilitarian and decorative effects; for example, kaolin added to the mix gave the paper more body.

A word should be inserted here about the making of the *sumi* ink used by block

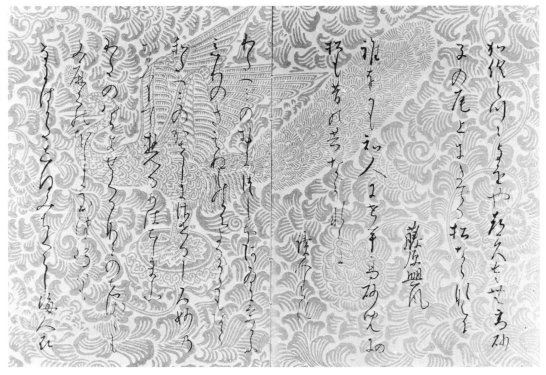

3.   Two pages from the final volume of a copy of the original manuscript *Kokin wakashū* of c. 1118, calligrapher unknown. The peacock and flower designs were produced by the application of *ummo* (mica).

printers. Ink was produced in Japan by one of two traditional methods, both of which involved the erection of "rooms" made from paper *shōji* (sliding screens), with several "windows" in the four walls. In the first method, bundles of lighted pine twigs were thrust through the openings, and as the twigs burned, soot was deposited on the walls and ceilings. When sufficient soot had accumulated, the room was dismantled and the soot scraped from the *shōji*. This was then mixed with resin to make ink. The second method was exactly the same in principle, but involved the burning of wood oil (often of paulownia) in bowls which were set inside the "room." Thereafter, the process was the same.

THE MANUSCRIPT

Before proceding to the introduction of printing in Japan, it is desirable to look briefly at the history of the direct antecedent of the printed book—the manuscript. For despite the early invention of printing, the manuscript remained the principal vehicle for disseminating the written word in Japan until the beginning of the seventeenth century.

It is to the seventh century that we must look to find the earliest surviving Japanese manuscripts. It has already been seen that Chinese books in manuscript form reached Japan much earlier, and we can presume that the inflow of such materials increased enormously following the introduction of Buddhism from Korea, probably in 538. The new doctrines of Buddhism inspired feverish activity in many fields of endeavor in Japan, including the building of temples, the carving of images in wood, stone and other materials, and most importantly for our purposes, the making of books. No manuscripts of native origin survive from the sixth century, the earliest example being the controversial *Hokke gisho* of 614–15. As Buddhism found increasing favor among the Japanese aristocracy, there was a corresponding demand for copies of Buddhist texts. The idea arose that particular merit accrued from copying such texts, and more and more of this work was done as the seventh century progressed. According to the *Nihon shoki*, in 673, copyists were assembled at Kawahara-dera temple in Yamato and work was begun on copying the entire Buddhist canon, known as the *Issai-kyō*. Unfortunately, nothing of this work has survived. In 677, copies were made of the *Konkōmyō-kyō* and the *Ninnō-gyō* sutras and a copy of the *Kongōjō darani-kyō*, believed to date from 686, has been discovered in Kawachi province (present-day Osaka-fu), indicating that at a very early date, Buddhist texts had reached Japan. Unfortunately, however, very little of these early examples of sutra-copying (*shakyō*) has survived to the present, although there are a few examples that date from the end of the seventh and early eighth centuries.

During the Nara period the practice of sutra-copying became institutionalized with the setting up of special *shakyō-sho* (scriptoria) within the precincts of many temples. There were also special *shakyō-sho* at the imperial court and in the homes of members of the aristocracy. The scholar Matsumoto Toshikazu (*see* Bibl.) has recorded the names of twenty-three *shakyō-sho* that existed during the Nara period. The largest of these, the Imperial Scriptorium, employed between two hundred and three hundred copyists, and a huge archival collection relating to its activities is still preserved in the Shōsō-in in Nara.

Naturally, much of the earlier manuscripts produced during this frenzied period of activity has been lost, but Tanaka Kaidō (*see* Bibl.) has recorded well over one hundred titles dating up to the end of the Nara period which still exist. Most of the manuscripts produced during this time are of little interest textually, but one particular manuscript is worthy of comment. This is the *E-inga-kyō*, which was produced in the eighth century, probably at the Imperial Scriptorium. The work is a sutra composed around the life of Buddha, and in the four existing one-*maki* (one-scroll) versions of it, the text is written in the finest T'ang-style calligraphy and accompanied by painted illustrations in crimson, green, yellow-white and other colors. This is the earliest extant example of the Japanese *emaki* or *emakimono* (picture scroll), of which more will be said later. From many general accounts of manuscripts written in the Nara period and just before, it is easy to gain the impression that nothing but Buddhist works were written. This is far from being true, as can be seen by the vast numbers of secular documents (registers, account books, official letters, etc.) still preserved in the Shōsō-in and other places. It was also during the Nara period that some of the earliest works of Japanese literature —the *Man'yōshū* (*Collection of a Myriad Leaves*), the *Nihon shoki*, the *Kojiki* (*Record of Ancient Matters*) and various *fudoki* (gazetteers)—were written, although eighth-century manuscripts of these works do not now survive.

In terms of the importation of Chinese books and works of art, the Heian period (794–1185) is often divided into two periods, with the year 894 serving as the watershed since it was in that year that official embassies to China were discontinued (this did not mean there was no contact at all between the two countries). During the first hundred years of the Heian period there was considerable movement of monks between China and Japan, and two new sects of Buddhism were brought in: the Shingon sect and the Tendai sect, founded in Japan respectively by Kūkai (Kōbō Daishi) and Saichō (Dengyō Daishi). The arrival of these two sects gave a tremendous stimulus to the practice of *shakyō*, and the esoteric doctrines of Shingon Buddhism led to the importation of Sanskrit manuscripts which were faithfully copied by Japanese scribes, thus adding a new dimension to the Japanese manuscript. Indeed, the copying of Buddhist texts continued at a level almost equal to that of the Nara period. As time passed, however, the practice diminished, since there came a point when all the texts had been copied and it was only a question of maintaining sufficient copies for use in the monasteries.

During the period that followed the discontinuation of embassies to China, what had already been adopted was absorbed and a uniquely Japanese culture emerged. The later Heian period, from the mid-tenth century on, was a golden age of Japanese literature, during which classics such as the *Taketori monogatari* (*Tale of the Bamboo-cutter*), the *Ise monogatari* (*Tales of Ise*), the *Genji monogatari* (*Tale of Genji*) and famous anthologies such as the *Kokinshū* (*Ancient and Modern Collection*) were written in Japanese, employing the *kana* syllabary (Pl. 4). Manuscripts became more decorative in appearance, with the use of colored papers, painted illustrations and gold and silver leaf, and in many cases the same care was lavished on Buddhist texts as on works of literature.

It was during the Heian period, too, that the *emakimono* picture scroll came into its own, although none are known to have survived from before the twelfth century. These scrolls generally consisted of pictures either interspersed with the text or placed at the top of the scroll with the text running underneath, as with the *E-inga-kyō*. The most notable surviving *emakimono* belong to the twelfth century, with the *Genji monogatari emaki* (picture scroll of the *Tale of Genji*), the *Shigi-san engi* (*Legends of Shigi-san Temple*) and the *Chōjū giga* (a satirical series of real and mythical animal representations and of human beings at play) considered of outstanding beauty. The technique employed in the *Genji* picture scroll is known as *tsukuri-e*, in which the illustrations were first outlined in black and then filled in with bright colors.

4. *Shin hanatsumi*, the diary of the *haiku* poet Buson, was published in 1784. The text, reproduced from the poet's own graceful calligraphy, incorporates the *kana* syllabary.

There was a fresh wave of copying Buddhist texts during the Kamakura period (1185–1333) owing to the emergence of several new sects—Zen, Jōdo, Jōdo Shinshū and Nichiren-shū—which involved both the importation of works from China and new works written in Japanese. By this time, however, printing had a more substantial influence, and particularly in the case of Zen and Jōdo Shinshū works, printing fulfilled a large part of monastic needs. The Kamakura period was, however, the golden age of *emaki-mono*, with contributions from many talented aristocratic painters, although toward the end of the Kamakura period and during the Muromachi period this art form became increasingly mannered. Okudaira Hideo (*see* Bibl.) lists 119 extant *emakimono* of the highest quality produced during the Kamakura period, compared to 4 for the Nara, 6 for the Heian and 42 for the Muromachi periods.

In the Edo period, despite the fact that printing had to a large extent supplanted the manuscript, more manuscripts were produced than in any other period. This is not due to the increasing importance of the manuscript itself, but to the higher literacy level of the people. Another factor may have been the expense involved, for it was far cheaper to copy a work by hand than to buy the printed book. One genre of Edo manuscripts is especially worthy of mention and that is the *Nara-ehon*, or "books illustrated in the Nara style."

The origins of *Nara-ehon* are not clear, but it is believed that they were produced from the late Muromachi period to the late seventeenth and possibly early eighteenth century by Buddhist monks whose temples had been destroyed during the civil wars. Many of these monks were fine artists and craftsmen and it is thought that they were commissioned by the daimyo to produce extremely lavish versions of *otogi-zōshi* (fairy tale books) and *kōwaka-mai* (historical folk tales). A typical *Nara-ehon* combines the finest paper, frequently decorated with flower and leaf patterns, with excellent calligraphy and vividly painted illustrations, often with gold or silver leaf adorning the top and bottom margins. These manuscripts were given by daimyo as presents at weddings and other auspicious occasions or kept for their own enjoyment.

The earliest examples, produced in the late Muromachi period, were less ornate and presented a vigorous, if somewhat crude, style of painting, but those produced in the second half of the seventeenth century are often color-crowded and clumsy to the point of garishness. Japanese art historians frequently consider *Nara-ehon* to be a primitive stage of the development of ukiyo-e book illustration.

Generally speaking, however, with the exception of *Nara-ehon* and *Nara-emaki* (scroll versions of the former, which were normally produced in three sizes: tall, small or oblong), manuscripts of the Edo period are notable for their quantity and subject matter rather than for their artistic quality. After the introduction of Western printing methods shortly after the Meiji Restoration, the manuscript virtually ceased to exist as a finished work.

BINDING TECHNIQUES

In ancient China it was not until the introduction of silk, and of wood and bamboo tablets as writing surfaces that we find anything resembling a form of binding. It is not clear exactly when wood and bamboo "books" first came into use, for, although no examples have yet been found predating the Warring States period (403–221 B.C.), ancient records indicate that they may have been used long before that time. Most of the tablets discovered so far are not connected in any form, but it is known that cords of silk, hemp or leather were used to hold these tablets together. To some extent "tablets" is a misleading term since documents written on bamboo or wood came in the form of long narrow strips. In the case of longer works, it is believed that a number of such strips were gathered and strapped together with silk or hemp cords to form a "page," and this was placed face to face with a second "page" made in the same way. When sufficient "pages" had been accumulated these were fastened together with other cords, making what is called a *ts'e* in Chinese and a *satsu* in Japanese. It is also believed that the connected strips were occasionally formed into rolls, although this was much less common.

Silk was used as a writing surface from the sixth or seventh century B.C. until the third or fourth century A.D. Books written on silk were produced in the form of rolls or *chüan* in Chinese (*maki* in Japanese), and as this term was also used for paper rolls, it is a reasonable inference that the binding technique was approximately the same in both cases. (Early Chinese manuscript rolls discovered at Tun-huang indicate that the standard size of a sheet of paper was about 24 cm. wide by 41 to 48.5 cm. long, too short for a work of any length, although the standard length of plain silk was 10 meters.) The rolls were assembled by pasting the paper sheets together until the roll reached 10 meters in length, although much longer rolls have also been discovered. This was then attached to a rod made of precious stone, ivory or wood, and occasionally a batch of rolls was enclosed in a silk wrapper.

The books Wang-in brought to Japan in A.D. 405 were most probably rolls of this type, and this binding technique, judging from the earliest extant native manuscripts, was rapidly absorbed by the Japanese. In Japan these books became known as *kansu-bon*, with *kan* written in the same character as *chüan*. This *kansu-bon* format became the dominant form of both printed and manuscript books through the Nara, Heian and Kamakura periods. Yet it had one serious drawback: as it was used, it was unrolled and had to be rolled up again. For this reason several other forms of binding emerged during the Heian period, most of which were derived from China, although none were as popular in the beginning as the *kansu-bon*.

The difficulties of *kansu-bon* binding were to some extent overcome by the use of *orihon* or "concertina binding." Instead of one long continuous roll, the paper was folded up into pages of fixed lengths and paper covers were pasted on the front and back so that it opened and shut rather like a concertina. This Chinese method was used primarily for printed Buddhist texts, particularly of the Shingon sect. When the *kansu-bon* format had virtually ceased to exist by 1600, the *orihon* format continued in limited use until the Meiji Restoration in 1868 and beyond.

Another form of binding introduced in the Heian period was *detchō*, or "butterfly binding." This consisted of individual printed sheets folded in half with paste applied to the outer edge of the fold. This sheet was pasted to the next folded sheet and so on until the whole book had been assembled. Each time the book was opened, the pair of pages stood out like wings of a butterfly, hence its name. Like the *orihon* format, *detchō* seems to have been used almost exclusively for printed texts, but it was never as popular as *orihon* and examples of *detchō* binding are comparatively rare.

Another form of binding which did not rely on the use of paste and one that was uniquely Japanese, was the *Yamato-toji*, which evolved in the late Heian period. This method made use of thread. A number of sheets were placed on top of one another and the whole was folded vertically up the middle to form a gathering, which was then sewn with thread. Several such gatherings were stitched together to make up the complete book. This form of binding, as far as can be deduced, was not used for Chinese or Buddhist texts, but was confined to native works of literature, including *waka* anthologies and *Nara-ehon*. However, it did not survive much beyond the Muromachi period.

The most common form of sewn binding is known as *fukuro-toji*, or "bag-binding," derived from China. Single sheets were printed on one side and folded so that the fold was outside, making double leaves whose loose edges were stitched together at the spine, and the book was then enclosed within paper covers. This form of binding seems to have been adopted on a limited scale during the Kamakura period, but by the early Edo period it had virtually supplanted all other forms of binding described above, and almost all books printed or written between 1600 and 1868, including Buddhist texts, were bound in this style.

Although Japanese binding appears flimsy at first sight, in reality it is just as durable as its Western counterparts. In fact a standard *fukuro-toji* binding has one great advantage over Western cloth, leather and buckram binding (which came into increasing use in Japan after 1868) in that it can easily be repaired without any specialist attention.

Japanese book covers, too, are worthy of mention here, since they are often considered as works of art in their own right. Book covers prove extremely useful in determining the dates of printed or manuscript works since certain styles of covers are confined to certain periods. A bright yellow or orange cover, for example, was only used in the middle and late nineteenth century, and when such a cover appears on an earlier work it can only mean that it has been rebound at a later date or that the text is a late reprint. The covers of printed or written works in the seventeenth century are usually plain and unadorned, and subdued in tone, Prussian and cobalt blues being most common. In the eighteenth and nineteenth centuries, however, covers became much more ornate, with the use of brighter colors, embossed designs and bearing, in certain genres of fiction, representations of the topics concerned. In addition to the cover itself, there was usually a printed slip pasted on, giving the title of the work and sometimes incorporating a pictorial design.

This leaves one major topic concerned with the physical characteristics of the printed book in Japan untouched—that of printing itself. The questions of when printing first reached Japan, where it originated from and the techniques employed in this art are complex and deserve a chapter to themselves.

2 | THE INTRODUCTION OF PRINTING AND PRINTING TECHNIQUES

Most of us were taught at school that the Chinese invented printing. The evidence for this claim is still largely circumstantial, although with the increase of archaeological activity in China at present it seems only a matter of time before any lingering doubts are removed. The strongest argument in favor of this theory is the presence, in China's history, of all the ingredients which would lead to such an invention—the early adoption of a written language, numerous inscriptions on all kinds of material, carved wooden seals (themselves a primitive form of printing) and the early development of paper. However, no actual examples of printing predating those already discovered in Korea and Japan, the only other contenders for the origin of printing, have been found so far. It is certain, nevertheless, that printing was invented in the Far East, and one Japanese authority has put forth an interesting suggestion as to why this was so— because the complexity of written Chinese made handwriting so indecipherable that a more standard and easily recognizable form of writing was absolutely essential.

Although printing was almost certainly invented in China, either during the Sui dynasty (581–618) or early T'ang dynasty (618–907), the earliest example of a printed text (as opposed to carved wooden seals that were used in China long before this) is Korean. In 1966, during excavations at Pulguk-sa temple in Kyŏngju, a single dharani (a Buddhist incantation believed to have magical powers for the preservation of good) was found in Sŏkk-t'ap (the Shakyamuni stupa), which is known to have been sealed up in the year 751, and therefore this dharani must have been printed before then.

Much more information exists concerning the earliest example of Japanese printing, which remains, however, an object of considerable controversy. Two sources throw light on the origin of the earliest Japanese printing: the *Shoku Nihongi* (*History of Japan Continued*), a continuation of the *Nihon shoki* completed in 797, and the *Tōdai-ji yōroku*, the official record of Tōdai-ji in Nara, compiled in 1106. According to the *Shoku Nihongi*, Fujiwara Nakamaro, otherwise known as Minister Emi no Oshikatsu, raised a rebellion against the ruling Empress Shōtoku in 764. Ostensibly, this rebellion was aimed at removing the influence of the Buddhist monk Dōkyō (d. 772), who had for some time been maneuvering to gain the empress's favor and had even persuaded her to name him as heir to the throne. In an age when family rivalries were rife, it is not

5. Part of Hōryū-ji's collection of the million pagodas commissioned by Empress Shōtoku in 764 to contain the *Hyakumantō darani*. A seven-storied pagoda marked each ten-thousandth unit, while one of thirteen stories marked each hundred-thousandth unit.

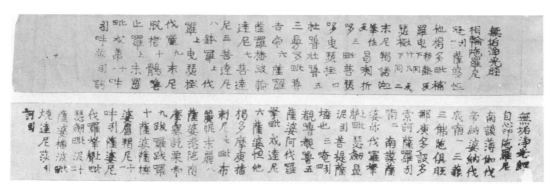

6. The *Sōrin darani* and the *Jishin'in darani*, two of the four charms of the *Hyakumantō darani*, completed in 770 and stored in the pagodas.

necessary to assume that Nakamaro's own motives were entirely altruistic, but whatever the reasons for his revolt, it was speedily crushed and he himself killed.

During the panic of the rebellion, Empress Shōtoku, in fear for her throne and perhaps her life, decided to appease the Buddhist priesthood and seek its protection both during and after the rebellion. To accomplish this, some impressive gesture by the empress was necessary to influence the monks. It was thus that she decided to print one million dharani, each to be placed in a specially made, hollow, three-storied miniature pagoda, surmounted by a five-tiered spire. A larger pagoda of seven stories was made to mark each ten-thousandth unit, while one of thirteen stories was made for each hundred-thousandth unit (Pl. 5). As can be imagined, this placed a severe strain on the resources of the court. In fact, the printing of the dharani and the manufacture of the pagodas, which were lathe-turned from Japanese cypress wood, took six years to complete, the last one being finished in 770.

The finished work was known as the *Hyakumantō darani* (Pl. 6), or the million pagoda dharani, sometimes also called "the million charms of Empress Shōtoku." Ten of the leading temples of the day—Hōryū-ji, Daian-ji, Gangō-ji, Kōfuku-ji, Gufuku-ji, Yakushi-ji, Saidai-ji, Tōdai-ji, Shitennō-ji, and Shūfuku-ji—each received one hundred thousand pagodas and dharani. The collections in all these temples, save Hōryū-ji, perished in fires and natural disasters over the centuries, and even the Hōryū-ji collection has been sadly diminished. Early this century, Hōryū-ji still possessed 1,771 dharani and 43,930 pagodas (mostly broken), but by 1937 only 100 remained, although many of the others can still be found in public and private collections throughout the world. The decrease in the number of the Hōryū-ji dharani is largely accounted for by the temple's custom of giving them as gifts to patrons who contributed toward restoration work, although this practice no longer continues.

If all we had to rely on for information concerning the *Hyakumantō darani* were the two historical records mentioned above, we would probably assume that the dharani were produced by hand-copying, for neither the *Shoku Nihongi* nor the *Tōdai-ji yōroku* specifically mentions the word "printing." Fortunately, however, the surviving exam-

31

ples in Hōryū-ji and other collections have enabled scholars to be certain that they were indeed produced by printing. The controversy arises, nevertheless, over how they were printed, as two contradictory factors exist concerning the venture. On the one hand, the undertaking itself was so massive that it is difficult to imagine anyone embarking on it without previous printing experience. On the other hand, however, the obvious crudity of the printing suggests an almost total lack of such experience.

Four types of dharani are found in the *Hyakumantō* series. All were taken from the *Mukujōkō-kyō*, or the *Vimalanirbhāsa-sūtra*, and consist of the *Kompon darani*, the *Sōrin darani*, the *Jishin'in darani* and the *Rokudo darani*. All were printed on single strips of paper ranging in length from 57 cm. (for the *Kompon*) to 43.9 cm. (for the *Rokudo*), with the width being approximately 5.5 cm. There are two alternative methods by which they could have been printed: either from wood blocks or from metal plates. Both theories have their supporters (the wood-block proponents being in the majority), but the only conclusive solution to the question would be the discovery of the original blocks or plates, and this seems improbable at this late date.

The advantages of using wood blocks for the production of the *Hyakumantō darani* are simple to deduce. Wood blocks are not only much easier and quicker to produce than metal plates, but wood is softer, so that great fineness of detail in the carving of the characters can be achieved. A glance at the copies of the *Hyakumantō darani* in the illustration, however, shows that the reproduction of characters is crude and the lines are thick. Techniques of wood carving in eighth-century Japan were developed enough to preclude simple inexperience as the reason. The other major argument against the use of wood blocks is that wood is not very durable, so the blocks would have worn away with repeated use, resulting in an unevenness of quality in later impressions; but it is a curious feature of the *Hyakumantō darani* that although the quality of the printing is not high, it is consistently even. In our view this suggests that metal plates were used, made either from copper or, more probably, from bronze. That there was certainly sufficient expertise at the time for making such plates is evidenced by the bronze votive bells found in both China and Japan from a much earlier date.

The production of metal plates would also have involved the manufacture of wood blocks in the initial stage, and it might well be argued that once these had been made, it would seem a waste of time and effort to go any further. The answer to this lies in the huge quantity of dharani produced. That one million were actually printed is shown by the survival at the beginning of this century of nearly forty-four thousand in Hōryū-ji alone (of an original quota of one hundred thousand), and to make this number, metal plates were clearly superior to wood blocks on account of their durability. If metal plates had been used, the technique would probably have been as follows: first, a wood block would have been made, but instead of printing from the block, it would have been pressed into a matrix of fine clay or sand. Molten bronze (or copper) would have been poured into the mold and the plate cast. The finished plate would have been durable enough for the purpose required, but there is no question that the finer points in the strokes of the characters would have been coarsened in the process, thus explaining the crudity of the dharani.

Extensive research has been carried out into the paper used, and to date three types have been identified: *kokushi*, made from the paper mulberry; *ōkokushi*, coarser and yellowish in color; and *ōmashi*, or *tsunasogami*, made from a variety of hemp fibers and similar in texture and color to *ōkokushi*.

Thus, in the argument over which country first invented printing, there are three distinct pieces of evidence. In favor of a Chinese origin, there is the overwhelming amount of circumstantial data; in favor of a Korean origin, there is the single dharani (printed either by block or plate) produced prior to 751; in favor of a Japanese origin, there is evidence of a massive printing undertaking carried out between 764 and 770, which might indicate that some printing had been done there even earlier than in Korea. The argument, however, does not stop there. In the case of both Korea and Japan, the production of dharani is simply one isolated instance of the use of printing, with no evidence to suggest that anything else was printed in either country before that or until two or three centuries later. One of the most significant discoveries made by Stein at Tun-huang was a printed copy of the *Diamond Sutra* of Chinese origin, which bears a date equivalent to 868. The technique employed to produce this work was clearly very sophisticated, because it contains as a frontispiece an elaborate and intricate illustration of a type not seen in Japan until the twelfth century. Such sophistication must have developed over a long period, and consequently this is one more piece of circumstantial evidence which leads to the belief that in time the single missing link of an item of Chinese printing predating 751 will be discovered.

THE TECHNIQUE OF BLOCK PRINTING

The developments in the use of printing in Japan after the *Hyakumantō darani* are outlined in the next chapters, but this is perhaps the most convenient point at which to look at the technique itself in Japan. Even if metal plates were used for the *Hyakumantō darani*, it remains true that wood blocks would have served as the initial stage in the process. In China, Korea and Japan, despite periods in which movable type was used, the wood block was the principal vehicle of printing until the modern period. The production and use of wood blocks was a traditional craft that remained substantially the same from the earliest times onward.

Before the Edo period (1603–1868), the wood most often used in Japan for this purpose was that of the *azusa*, or catalpa tree, although on occasion the wood of the *hinoki* (Japanese cypress) was also used. The chief problem, however, with catalpa wood was that it is rather delicate and close-grained, making clear printing difficult to achieve. It was chiefly for this reason that by the Edo period the *yamazakura*, or wild cherry, was used. Once cut, the wood was allowed to dry in the shade, and it was prevented from warping by means of a special wooden clamp known as a *hashibami*.

The text was first written on a sheet of thin paper (Mino or *gampi* paper were the most common, though it varied from period to period). This was in itself an important stage, since although the final quality of the calligraphy rested in the hands of the engraver, the original calligraphic model had to be as good as possible. The sheet was then attached face down to the block by means of a rice-starch paste, and after drying, the upper surface of the paper was rubbed away and hemp seed oil was applied to make the remainder transparent so that the engraver could see the characters more clearly. The characters were not carved into the block, but instead the wood surrounding the outlines of the characters was cut away, so that they stood out in relief in reversed image. Blocks were cut parallel to the grain and not across it as in the West.

A variety of cutting tools were used, generically called *nomi* ("chisel" is the most appropriate translation, although not all of them resembled chisels as we know them). The tools varied in size according to the intricacy of the particular stages in the cutting process, and the *nomi* were used in conjunction with a *saizuchi*, or "mallet." There were two types of mallet: a large, heavy one for cruder work, and a smaller one for driving the smaller *nomi*.

Once the cutting was finished, the block was cleaned with a brush known as a *kushibarai*, and then washed in water to remove all traces of paper. At this point the block, or *mokuhan*, was in its final form and ready for use.

The engraver, or perhaps it would be best to call him the block-cutter, was clearly an important figure in this process. During the age of Buddhist domination of printing, printed texts quite frequently contained endnotes mentioning the name of the block-cutter, usually designated by the term *chō* or *chōkō*. In all cases during this period, the block-cutter was a monk who was usually not high in the temple hierarchy, and this established a pattern for the future when the art of block-cutting was confined to the artisan class.

Once the block was dry, *sumi* (Indian ink) was applied to the block with a brush made from the hair of a horse's tail. Next, the paper to receive the impression, which had been moistened with water for some hours before, was placed on the block with four pieces of wet cotton (known as *yawara*) to keep it in place. Finally, the impression was obtained by rubbing the paper with a *baren*, which consisted of fine cord made of bamboo sheath fiber wrapped around a circular card. Prior to use, the *baren* was rubbed with a small quantity of oil to allow it to move smoothly.

All this was very time-consuming, but it should be remembered that in many cases as few as a dozen or two dozen blocks were sufficient to print a book. Among monks up to the end of the Muromachi period and for the commercial publishers of the Edo period, it was common practice to store used blocks so that they could be brought out again when new impressions of a work were needed.

The technique of making and using wood blocks, once discovered, did not change substantially over a period of twelve hundred years, although the people who did the printing and the purpose of printing itself altered considerably. One major technical innovation, however, was the discovery of color printing, which opened the doors to great advances in the types and scope of book illustrations in the Far East.

THE TECHNIQUE OF COLOR PRINTING

Color printing, altogether a more involved technique, has a much longer tradition than is normally accorded it. There are several instances of color printing in one form or another dating back to the Nara period, but these had no connection with books. In the Shōsō-in, fabrics have been discovered with a single color printed design; some of the celebrated *Sanjū-rokka-sen* scrolls (now in the Nishi Hongan-ji, Kyoto), produced in the late eleventh or early twelfth century, contain block-printed designs in green, blue and brown. Equally celebrated is the suit of Kamakura-period armor at the Kasuga shrine near Nara, with a design printed in red and black on the breast-plate. There are many other similar instances of color printing, but these do not include its use in book illustration, where until the seventeenth century color was always applied by hand. Indeed, illustration in printed books was itself a rare phenomenon until the seventeenth century, and one does not find the regular use of color, even hand-applied, until the *tanroku-bon* editions of the 1630s.

From extant examples it is clear that color printing in book illustration occurred in China before Japan. Several erotic albums which made use of color printing were produced in China between c. 1580 and 1640, and evidence that they were known in Japan is provided by the existence of Japanese monochrome versions of them. These lavishly produced albums were printed privately for a small circle of connoisseurs in Nanking, but they were not as influential as two other Chinese works. These were the *Shih-chu-shu hua-p'u* (*Albums of the Ten Bamboo Studio*), which appeared in print in complete form in 1633 but which was available in partial form some years earlier; and the *Chieh-tzŭ-yüan hua-chuan* (*Mustard Seed Garden Manual*, or *Kaishien gaden*), which appeared over a period of one hundred and fifty years, the first part being published in 1677 and the last part in 1818.

There is evidence that both these works were known to the Japanese quite early on, and while their influence in Japan was considerable, one should beware of assuming that their influence extended very markedly into the field of color printing itself. Both were essentially picture books, a genre which was unknown in Japan in the early seventeenth century and which did not truly evolve until the time of Moronobu. If their influence in the evolution of Japanese color printing had been decisive, one would expect to find similar works produced in Japan at about the same time.

In the introduction to his book *Harunobu and His Age*, D. B. Waterhouse cites various passages from Edo-period writers discussing the origins of color printing in Japan. Although there is some divergence in their opinions, ranging from 1716 to 1765 as the date of origin of Japanese color printing, they are unanimous in placing it in the eighteenth century. In fact, this is very wide of the mark, for color printing was in use in Japan in the early seventeenth century, and just possibly at the end of the sixteenth century. If one discards various dubious references to the astronomical work *Tenmon zue*, published in 1593, as having a color-printed illustration (no one seems to have seen a copy), the earliest authenticated Japanese book to carry color-printed illustrations was the *Jinkō-ki*, a mathematical treatise produced in several editions, some with black-and-white illustrations, others with color. The color editions were made in 1631, 1634 and 1641, although few copies are now extant. The next work to carry color illustrations was the *Semmyō-reki* (Pl. 7), a calendrical volume published in 1644. D. B. Waterhouse also cites a mathematical work, the *Kakuchi sansho* (1657), and a work on military strategy, the *Gumpō goku-hiden sho* (1658–60), as having color printing.

Two things should be noted from these early uses of color printing in Japanese books: first, the small number of examples indicates that it was not in widespread use; and second, all the works mentioned are scientific in nature and to talk about color-printed illustrations is slightly misleading, since the color was used in diagrams rather than in illustrations in the normal sense. The nearest to genuine color-printed illustrations in book form in the seventeenth century was a pattern book by the prolific writer Asai Ryōi called *Shinsen o-hiinagata* (1667), which contained pages of kimono patterns printed in single colors of red, black, blue and olive green.

In the eighteenth century examples of color-printed illustrations became more numerous. Color printing had developed in China with the patronage of wealthy connoisseurs of art, and in Japan, too, patronage played an important part. Thus many of the books with color illustrations produced in the first half of the eighteenth century were private rather than commercial publications. Of particular importance were the *haiku* anthologies printed and distributed privately, such as the *Aki no hina* (1726), the *Chichi no on* (1730), the *Hokku-chō* (1756) and the *Umi no sachi* (1762). Works of the *ōraimono* genre (books for moral instruction, particularly of women) appeared with color illustrations quite early in the eighteenth century in Osaka, and there were several erotic albums such as the *Fūryū Gion zakura* (c. 1720).

The regular use of color printing in prints came later with *beni-e* prints in three colors—pink, blue and yellow—which appeared during the 1740s. Yet the threads of color printing in books and prints were not drawn together until 1764, when a group of connoisseurs had calendars for the following year privately printed. These calendars were printed in many colors and are significant in the development of color in prints rather than in books, but it is noticeable that from that time on color printing in book illustrations was taken up on a large and commercial scale. In China, color printing never became the truly commercial phenomenon it did in Japan. The successful fusion of prints and book illustrations is marked by the way print artists began to work more in the field of book illustration, and artists like Harunobu, while concentrating on prints, did some very fine work in books, such as the famous *Yoshiwara bijin awase*, printed in five volumes in 1770. In fact the golden age, during which many of the finest

7. An illustration from the *Semmyō-reki* (1644), one of the earliest books
in Japan to make use of color printing. The diagram shows the paths of
the sun and moon and is printed in red, black and blue.

examples of book illustration were produced, lasted not more than sixty years, from c. 1770 to c. 1830, after which the quality began to decline.

Technically, color printing was more complicated than black and white and involved the cutting of new blocks for each color required. The most difficult problem was to ensure accurate register with the key block, and thus in the early stages it was usual to use only two colors or three at most. However, a device known as the *kentō* was developed that satisfactorily overcame this problem. This was a right-angled ridge in one lower corner of the color block, with a shorter, straight ridge at the opposite lower corner. By aligning the paper with the *kentō* it was possible to obtain perfect register. According to the writers quoted by D. B. Waterhouse, mentioned above, the *kentō* was devised by one Uemura (Emiya) Kichiemon in 1744. Since it is inherently unlikely that its invention can be so precisely attributed, this probably means no more than that Uemura used the *kentō* in 1744. Possibly he was unaware of previous developments and thought he had invented it, and this view was accepted by his contemporaries, for an examination of earlier books with color illustrations, such as the *Semmyō-reki* (1644), shows that the *kentō* was known at the time of their production.

The fact that color printing was invented is, of course, more important than when it was first used, and the contribution of this technique to the excellence of Japanese book illustration cannot be overemphasized. Later in this book an account of the development of Japanese book illustration, including the use of color, is given, but before that, we must look at the history of printing before the age of the illustrated book.

3 | THE AGE OF BUDDHIST DOMINATION OF PRINTING

It has already been seen that printing was first used in Japan in connection with Buddhism and that the *Hyakumantō darani* established a pattern which continued unaltered until the last decade of the sixteenth century. Up to that time no book was printed outside a temple and very few books not related to Buddhism were produced at all.

After the Heian period the Buddhist monks had a clear motive in using printing to propagate their religion and their particular sects and to provide sufficient copies of texts for use within their monasteries. In addition to this, Buddhist temples had two valuable commodities, time and labor, to make it a practical proposition. There is no doubt that plenty of both was necessary for the printing process, which involved time-consuming procedures, from the felling of trees to the carving of blocks and the manufacture of paper. The court and nobility at that time possessed the wealth to sponsor printing work, which was in all cases carried out within temples, and the works printed were always Buddhist texts. Although many works of literature had been written in the Heian period, none were printed until much later, presumably because the readership, being confined to the Kyoto court, was so limited that manuscript copies fulfilled the demand. It may also be presumed that the Buddhist priesthood would have objected to printing worldly novels within temple precincts. At any rate, neither the nobility nor the provincial officialdom evinced any desire for printed secular works until the end of the sixteenth century, by which time the power and prestige of the Buddhist monasteries had waned considerably.

Broadly speaking, Buddhist printing before the late sixteenth century can be divided into three categories according to the location of the temples: books printed in the Nara temples, known as *Nara-han;* those printed in the Kyoto temples, known as *Kyōraku-han*; and those printed in temples in provincial regions outside these two cities, which were of much less importance.

After the *Hyakumantō darani*, no surviving examples of Japanese printing were produced until the middle of the eleventh century, and this leads to the theory that the art of printing was lost until it was reintroduced from China, probably at the end of the tenth century. This seems most unlikely, since we know that by the middle of the ninth century the Chinese were already printing highly sophisticated books such as the *Diamond Sutra* of 868, and that the Japanese court was in regular contact with T'ang China through embassies until 894. This contact with China would have ensured that the Japanese did not lose the art of printing, even though no examples have survived. A more plausible idea is that a very limited amount of Buddhist printing was undertaken and what was printed was subsequently lost.

Certain factors militated against the use of printing, even among the Buddhist monks themselves. Monks (and laymen by commissioning monks) could acquire religious merit by copying Buddhist sutras by hand (the practice called *shakyō*), and for most of the Heian period such merit did not accrue from the printing of sutras. The Japanese nobles were happy to gain merit for their families and themselves by paying temples to copy texts by hand, but they appear to have been less willing to finance the more expensive printing process. Furthermore, at this early period, the custom of *shakyō* could amply provide the number of texts necessary for the small number of monks there were to use them, and it was when that number increased that printing became a more worthwhile means.

The earliest dated printed book to have survived in Japan after the *Hyakumantō darani* was, however, of Chinese origin. In 983, the first complete printing of the *Daizō-kyō*, or the Buddhist *Tripiṭaka* (the entire Buddhist canon), was finished in China. In that same year a Japanese monk named Chōnen visited China and was granted an audience with the reigning Northern Sung emperor, Tai-tsung. He was presented with a copy of the *Tripiṭaka*, which he brought with him on his return to Japan in 986 and deposited at Tōdai-ji in Nara. There seems little doubt that the receipt of this monumental work stimulated printing activity in Japan, but whether this activity started in Nara or in Kyoto remains uncertain.

Following is an account of printing in both these cities until 1590, when movable type first reached Japan. Although books were also sometimes printed in the provinces, such printing on the whole was confined to Zen temples and the books possess no distinguishing features to mark them from those of Nara and Kyoto.

PRINTING IN NARA

The ancient city of Nara, situated to the west of modern Nara, was established as the first permanent capital of Japan in 710. For almost one hundred years it remained the seat of the imperial court and the government of Japan, acting also as a kind of entrepot for cultural importations from mainland Asia. The chief influence on the development of Nara in all spheres was Buddhism, which had been imported as early as 538 but which only in the Nara period (710–84) evolved the close relationship with the state that was to become one of its main characteristics in the following Heian period (794–1185).

The Buddhism of Nara is typified by the "Six Sects" and the "Six Temples." The

"Six Sects," of which the most important were the Sanron, the Kegon and the Hossō sects, were all of the Hinayana or proto-Mahayana type, propounding doctrines of great religious importance but of little interest for the layman. Later, in the Heian period, the religious importance of the "Six Sects" would diminish before the flexible, all-embracing doctrines of the Tendai and Shingon sects, and in the Kamakura period (1185–1333) too, despite a brief revival, would not be able to compete with the popular teachings of Nichiren, Pure Land and Zen. There is no doubt that the decline of the "Six Sects" reflected the decline in the importance of Nara itself. Nevertheless, until 1590, and particularly in the Kamakura-period revival, those temples acting as head-quarters of the "Six Sects," namely, Kōfuku-ji, Tōdai-ji, Yakushi-ji, Saidai-ji, Hōryū-ji and Tōshōdai-ji, remained influential and were the focus of all printing activities in Nara. (It should be noted that the doctrines of more than one sect were taught and practiced at the same temple and thus no temple can be identified with any particular sect.)

In the Heian period, of the "Six Temples" only Kōfuku-ji is known to have produced any printed books. The first known example of Kōfuku-ji printing that can be dated with accuracy, and hence the first authenticated example of Nara printing, is a ten-*maki* copy of the *Jōyuishiki-ron*, printed in 1088. The last scroll of this work, which was produced in the *kansu-bon* format, bears a printed note to the effect that the blocks were carved by an unknown monk named Kanzō at Kōfuku-ji. In addition to being one of the leading Hossō sect temples, Kōfuku-ji was also the family temple of the ruling Fujiwara, and as a consequence it was probably the wealthiest of all the Nara temples at this time. It also had very close connections with the Fujiwara Shinto shrine at Kasuga, near Nara, where it later became the practice to dedicate books printed at Kōfuku-ji. Because of this practice, books printed at Kōfuku-ji came to be known as *Kasuga-ban*, or "Kasuga editions." Strictly speaking, this term should be used only for books printed at Kōfuku-ji, but since the Meiji Restoration in 1868, it has become customary for Japanese bibliophiles to describe any Buddhist work printed in Nara before the end of the Muromachi period as *Kasuga-ban*. The *Jōyuishiki-ron* of 1088 is the earliest dated surviving example of a *Kasuga-ban* in either sense.

This work, first translated from Sanskrit into Chinese by Hsüan-tsang, is one of the most basic of all Hossō sect texts, and was first printed in Japan at one of the leading Hossō sect temples. This sectarian division in printing was a natural phenomenon, and is useful to historians because if a work printed anywhere in Japan before 1590 can be designated to a particular sect, as the *Jōyuishiki-ron*, then even though there is no direct indication of the temple of origin, an educated guess can usually be made.

The *Jōyuishiki-ron* is the only text produced in Nara with a printed date that can be firmly placed in the Heian period, but there are at least eleven other works printed at Kōfuku-ji which have manuscript notes at the end of the text with dates between 1116 and 1182. Unless these notes are forged in each case, which seems unlikely, these works too must have been printed in the Heian period. No less than eight of these eleven are versions of commentaries on the *Jōyuishiki-ron* (Pl. 8), a sufficient indication of the importance of that text.

Nara printing came into its own, however, in the Kamakura period—an age of political, military, social and religious turmoil that saw the foundation of four popular or semipopular Buddhist sects: Hōnen's Jōdo (Pure Land) sect, Shinran's Jōdo Shinshū (True Pure Land) sect, the Nichiren sect and the Zen sect (imported from China at the end of the twelfth century by Eisai). Despite the fact that all these sects were centered in Kyoto and caused an outburst of printing activity in that area, the Nara temples remained prosperous and wealthy, and due to a revival of Nara's "Six Sects," printing continued to flourish in Nara, so that the Kamakura period was in fact the golden age of Nara printing. Apart from Kōfuku-ji, Tōdai-ji, Saidai-ji, Tōshōdai-ji and Hōryū-ji also produced printed books with the inevitable result, since these temples represented the interests of different sects, that there was a great broadening in the range of Buddhist texts printed.

The dating of printed works during this period continues to be a problem, because it was unusual for a printing date to be provided and often manuscript endnotes bearing dates which are at best approximate have to be relied upon. Since printing styles varied so slightly, where a text has no date at all it is generally impossible to fix its date within one hundred years.

In the early part of the Kamakura period, Kōfuku-ji monks continued to devote most of their attention to Hossō doctrinal works and many copies of the *Jōyuishiki-ron* survive, one of the earliest dated examples being by the monk Yōkō in 1201–2. The leading figure in Kōfuku-ji printing at this time, however, was a monk named Kō-ei who flourished between 1210 and 1230. He was responsible for printed editions of the *Jōyuishiki-ron* (1221), the *Immyō-shōri-mon-ron* (1222), the *Benchūben-ron* (1222), the *Daijō-shōgon-kyō-ron* (1223) and the *Hokke-kyō* (1225), all but the last of which are Hossō doctrinal works. Perhaps his greatest achievement came earlier in 1213, when he was in charge of a one-hundred-*maki* edition of the important *Yugashiji-ron*, the largest printing undertaking in Japan up to that time, apart from the *Hyakumantō darani*. The printed postface to this work records that contributions were received from "the rich and poor of Nara" to finance the printing, the first acknowledged example of what was to become a common practice in later times.

During the latter part of the Kamakura period, the Kōfuku-ji monks expanded their printing activities beyond the narrow confines of the Hossō sect. From Nara times, certain Buddhist sutras had come to be regarded as possessing a special power to protect the country; in other words, it was thought that the copying, and later the printing, of the sutras would protect the state from natural disasters, invasions and similar calamities. Toward the end of the thirteenth century, several such works were printed at Kōfuku-ji, most notably the edition of the *Konkōmyō-saishōō-kyō* produced in 1299.

Perhaps the most famous works printed at Kōfuku-ji during the Kamakura period were the *Shinjō-ban* editions of the *Hokke-kyō*, or *Lotus Sutra*. The 1225 version of this sutra produced by Kō-ei is the earliest known dated copy of the work in printed form (although there are many other undated printed versions that certainly precede it), but sometime afterward the otherwise unknown monk Shinjō acted as a sponsor (*ganshu*, someone who initiates a work of printing in fulfillment of a vow) for another edition based on the 1225 version. This new edition was reissued no less than fifteen times up to 1366, and did much to increase the popularity of the *Lotus Sutra* in printed form, as can be seen from the fact that it served as the model for many other printings of the text outside Kōfuku-ji. The first three printings no longer survive, and the earliest known copy is one of 1263, though two other dated copies (1272 and 1273) survive from the Kamakura period.

Although less famous, the single greatest achievement of Kōfuku-ji printing in the

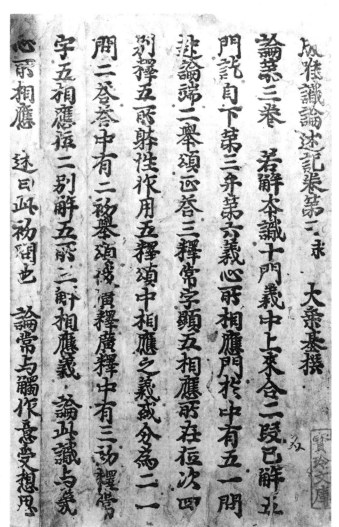

8. An example of Heian-period printing. This third *maki* of the *Jōyui-shiki-ron* was produced between 1170 and 1180, probably at Kōfuku-ji, Nara.

43

Kamakura period, regarded by some as the greatest printing achievement in the whole of the Kamakura period, was the *Daihannya-kyō* (Pl. 9), or *Prajñāpāramitā-sūtra*. This huge text was originally translated from Sanskrit into Chinese by Hsüan-tsang and became one of the basic Buddhist texts in both China and Japan. The exact circumstances surrounding the decision to print this work in six hundred *maki* are not known, but some idea of when it was done can be gauged from the dates printed at the ends of *maki* 34, 35, 46, 53 and 100. These span the years 1223 to 1227, and since four of the five dates fall within the Karoku era (1225–27), this edition of the *Daihannya-kyō* is

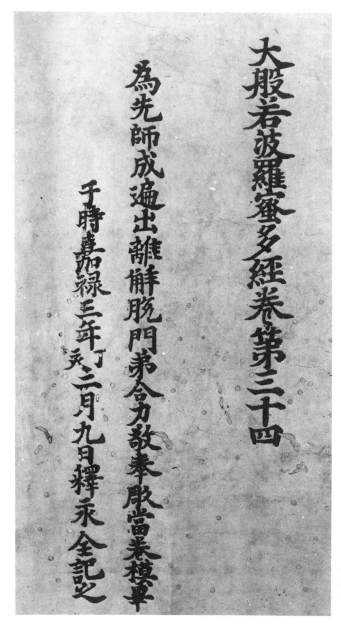

9. The colophon of the 34th *maki* of the *Daihannya-kyō*, printed at Kōfuku-ji, Nara. This *maki* is one of the few to bear a printed date, in this case Karoku 3 (1227).

usually known as the *Karoku-ban Daihannya-kyō*. It is certainly a superb example of the printer's art, with the jet-black *sumi* text printed on paper composed of mulberry and *gampi* fibers and dyed yellow. Like the *Shinjō-ban* editions of the *Hokke-kyō*, this printing of the *Daihannya-kyō* established a standard text, which was used throughout the Kamakura period and beyond. It seems fairly certain that the blocks for the *Karoku-ban* edition were stored for reprinting copies of the work as needed, which has resulted in there being more copies of some *maki* than of others.

Tōdai-ji, though not exclusively devoted to one sect of Buddhism, had a strong interest in the doctrines and practices of the Kegon sect and acted as the center of Kegon Buddhism in Japan. Thus it was natural that when Tōdai-ji monks began to undertake printing, they should concentrate on Kegon doctrinal works.

The earliest known work printed at Tōdai-ji was a one-*maki* edition of a Kegon sect work, the *Daijō-kishin-ron*, produced in 1243. Later, emphasis was placed on the works of the Chinese monk Fa-tsang (643–712), third patriarch of the Kegon sect, and copies of his works were printed in 1283 (the *Kegon-gokyō-shō*), 1297 (the *Daijō-kishin-ron-giki*), 1328–31 (the *Kegon-gyō tangen-ki*) and 1332 (the *Kegon-gyō zuisho-engi-shō*). The first two were printed under the supervision of a monk with strong Zen affiliations named Zen-ni (1253–1325), and the last two under a monk named Rikaku. It is unlikely, however, that either of these monks actually participated in the carving of the blocks. Zen-ni in particular was a comparatively important Buddhist scholar, and his role in the two works that mention his name was probably more in connection with the production of an authoritative text than with the actual printing.

In addition to works of the Kegon sect, the Tōdai-ji monks also devoted considerable time to Zen and Sanron sect works, Zen having strong doctrinal affiliations with Kegon and Sanron being one of the classical studies for monks of any sect. The most notable Zen work was an edition of the *Engaku-kyō* sutra. Although of uncertain date, it is thought to belong to the middle or late Kamakura period and is distinguished by having an illustration of Buddha, which ranks among the earliest of all Japanese printed illustrations used in books. The two leading monks connected with printing works of the Sanron sect were Shoshū (1219–91) and Sokei. In 1251, Shoshū was responsible for editions of the *Sokushin jōbutsu-gi* and the *Urabon-gyō*, which were followed in 1252 by the *Hokke yūi* and in 1256 by the *Sanron gengi*. Probably his most important work, however, was the three-*maki* edition of the *Yuimakitsu-gyō*, printed at Tōdai-ji in 1267. The most important of Sokei's contributions to Tōdai-ji printing was without doubt his edition of the *Hokke gisho* (not Shōtoku Taishi's work, but another commentary in twelve *maki*), printed between 1293 and 1295. Its importance lies not in the text itself, but in the fact that a printed endnote records the names of six monks who were described as *chōkō*, or engravers. This is the first specific reference to engravers, and in our view indicates that where a monk's name appears in a printed endnote without any mention of his role, he was not responsible for the block-cutting, but acted in an organizational capacity. In all, during the Kamakura period, Tōdai-ji produced fewer

45

works in printed editions than Kōfuku-ji, but this is probably only an indication of the greater wealth of the latter.

The Risshū sect, one of the "Six Sects" introduced to Japan in the mid-eighth century, was represented by two major Nara temples—Tōshōdai-ji and Saidai-ji. Naturally, as regards printing, Risshū sect works were concentrated upon, which concerned the Buddhist precepts, discipline and rules of conduct for the monks. Tōshōdai-ji was less prolific than Saidai-ji, and only one fully authenticated example of Tōshōdai-ji printing from the Kamakura period survives. This is the *Hyōmu hyōshiki-shō*, written by Eison, abbot of Saidai-ji, and printed at Tōshōdai-ji in 1292 as part of the ceremonies connected with the death of the Tōshōdai-ji abbot Shōgen. It was intended for distribution to all Risshū sect temples in Japan.

Eison (1201–90) was one of the leading figures in the Kamakura-period revival of the Risshū sect and played a very active role in the development of printing at Saidai-ji. In his capacity as abbot, he seems to have initiated a considerable printing program, from which twelve works have survived, ranging in date from 1256 to 1290. Most of these deal with Risshū doctrine, but Eison was also concerned with "protecting the country" and three of the works he ordered printed belong to that category: the *Ninnō gokoku darani* (1275), the *Konkōmyō-saishōō-kyō kabun* (1288), and the *Konkōmyō-saishōō-kyō daikabun* (1288). An interesting feature of the Saidai-ji works printed on Eison's instructions is that at least half of them are bound in *orihon* style. Although *orihon* binding gained wide acceptance by Kyoto monks as the Kamakura period passed, generally the more conservative monks adhered to the traditional *kansu-bon* format, and Eison's use of *orihon* binding represents a break with Nara tradition. After Eison's death, the Saidai-ji monks continued to print a number of works which, to judge from those produced in Eison's lifetime, conformed to the program he had laid down. This was presumably done as a mark of respect, and Kamakura-period printing continued at Saidai-ji until at least 1318.

The only other Nara temple conclusively proved to have undertaken printing in the Kamakura period was Hōryū-ji, which was a Hossō sect temple, though for some curious reason it does not seem to have been responsible for printing any Hossō works. Shōtoku Taishi, the pious statesman often regarded as the father of Buddhism in Japan, remained an object of reverence through the Kamakura period, particularly in Nara, and a special hall, Shōrei-in, devoted to his "worship" was established at Hōryū-ji. This hall served as the center for a number of Hōryū-ji printings, especially of works concerned with Shōtoku Taishi. Earliest of all works printed at Hōryū-ji was the *Bommō-kyō* produced in 1220, which mentions Shōtoku Taishi specifically in an end-note; this was followed in 1248 by a printing of Shōtoku's commentaries, generically known as the *Sangyō gisho*. Other Shōtoku works printed at Hōryū-ji include a 1285 edition of his famous seventeen-article "Constitution." This could be termed a secular production, but since the Buddhist overtones of this work are so profound, it may be regarded as "Buddhist" in a printing context. Other works may have been printed at Hōryū-ji after 1285, but nothing else survives from the Kamakura period.

The Nambokuchō period (1333–92) and the Muromachi period (1392–1603) saw the decline and eventual collapse of Nara printing, almost certainly occasioned by the lessening importance of Nara itself and of the Buddhist sects with headquarters there. There is considerable evidence of printing activity during both periods, but surviving items are comparatively few in relation to the amount of work probably carried out, and some temples active in the Kamakura period seem to have been less so in successive periods.

However, Kōfuku-ji still continued to be the leading printing temple in the Nambokuchō and Muromachi periods. In 1894, a collection of 2,760 wood blocks stored in Kōfuku-ji's Hokuen-dō, many of which were in good condition, was examined by two leading authorities on Japanese printing. Most of the blocks were undated and many even untitled, which posed great problems in their identification and categorization. However, it was generally concluded that half the collection belonged to the Kamakura period and half to the Nambokuchō period, suggesting that printing activity at Kōfuku-ji did not decline until the Muromachi period at least. Despite the large number of extant blocks, very few Kōfuku-ji printed works survive from the Nambokuchō period, the most noteworthy example being the fourteenth issue of the *Shinjō-ban Hokke-kyō*, dated 1355.

It was during the Nambokuchō period that the first recorded extant example of the printing of another of the "Six Temples," Yakushi-ji, was produced. This was a single scroll edition of the *Yakushi-hongan kudoku-kyō*, printed in 1344. However, as far as can be determined, not a single item was printed at Saidai-ji, which had been comparatively prolific in the previous period. This said, it must be admitted that what survives from all the productions of the Nara temples in the Nambokuchō period represents only the tip of the iceberg, as the number of blocks found at Kōfuku-ji tends to confirm. Throughout most of the fourteenth century Japan was politically divided and wracked by civil war, not the best conditions for printing to flourish in, and undoubtedly many books were destroyed in fires.

By the beginning of the Muromachi period in 1392, Nara printing was in a state of decline. The collection in the Hokuen-dō revealed a certain number of blocks datable to the Muromachi period, but these were mostly blocks for printings of the *Daihannya-kyō*, dating from the fifteenth century. There is also evidence of new blocks being carved at Kōfuku-ji to replace those which had been used earlier in the Kamakura period, but which had been subsequently lost or damaged. The presence of so many blocks for the *Daihannya-kyō* is not surprising since the increased formalization of Buddhism made it common practice to acquire merit through *tendoku*. This involved special ceremonies at which passages of a text were selected and read at random, the belief being that this was as efficacious a method of acquiring merit as reading the whole text. The *Daihannya-kyō* was a particularly long text and thus was most often used for this purpose.

To judge from surviving examples of Kōfuku-ji printing in the Muromachi period, there was a marked decline in the quality of paper used, due to the sharp increases in cost resulting from the civil war. The Kōfuku-ji blocks are evidence that at least some printing was done at that temple during the Muromachi period. Examples of printed texts produced at Tōshōdai-ji and Yakushi-ji also survive, but in such limited numbers as to suggest that no large-scale printing was undertaken. By the time movable type was introduced in 1590, Nara printing was, to all intents and purposes, dead.

This is a convenient point at which to attempt a brief summary of the characteristic features of Nara printing and to assess its importance. To begin with, there is no question that the Kamakura period marks the golden age of Nara printing, for the doctrinal revival of Nara Buddhism during that time was accompanied by the best and most prolific period of Nara printing.

The typical *Nara-han* work was printed on the highest-quality paper (almost invariably made from *gampi* or mulberry fibers), distinctive for its thickness, with the characters reproduced in bold, black *sumi* ink. Decoration with gold and silver leaf either on the printing frames or in the margins surrounding the text is not uncommon but seems to have been reserved for important or prestigious productions, which are, incidentally, the ones most likely to have been preserved to the present. Illustrations, while not unknown, are very rare, and their presence, usually as a frontispiece printed separately and pasted to the beginning of the scroll, seems to indicate that a Chinese exemplar was used. Styles of binding were similar to those used by Kyoto temples, but the *orihon* format was much less popular than it was in Kyoto.

The identification of a *Nara-han* at first sight is not an easy matter, because there is no objective difference between a *Nara-han* and a *Kyōraku-han* as far as printing and production methods are concerned. Even calligraphic styles, cited by Japanese authorities as a means of differentiation, are not conclusive. The distinction of the Japanese style of calligraphy (*Wayō*, generally more common in Kyoto printed texts) as compared to the Chinese style (*Tōyō*) often rests on whether a Japanese or a Chinese exemplar was used.

The most obvious method of identifying a *Nara-han* is by looking at the endnote, whether printed or in manuscript form, specifying the connection of a Nara temple with the edition. Though absent in the majority of cases, these endnotes generally furbish reliable information regarding the origin and date of a given printed text. Quite often when the notes are printed, additional information, such as the name of the engraver (denoted by the terms *chōkō*, *chōshi* and *chōshu*) is given as well as the monk who sponsored the work (*ganshu*). When the endnote mentions the name of a monk without specifying his role, the situation is not so clear-cut, but it may be thought that in such cases the monk was responsible for some kind of textual collation or for ordering the printing work, though not in the specific sense of *ganshu* (Pl. 10).

The second method of identifying a *Nara-han* is by the type of Buddhist work printed. With non-sectarian scriptures, such as the *Hokke-kyō* and the *Daihannya-kyō*, and in the absence of any endnote, it is impossible to determine the place of origin, but when a text can be closely related to a specific sect (i.e., one of the "Six Sects" in the case of Nara), one can be certain at least of the city, if not the actual temple.

The importance of Nara printing lies mainly in the context of religion and art. Its religious importance is seen in the fact that through printing, most of the important texts of Nara Buddhism reached those interested. Also, as fine, authoritative versions of non-sectarian texts were printed in Nara, this had a broadening effect on the development of Buddhism in Japan as a whole. In artistic terms, there is no question that the finest examples of *Nara-han*, printed boldly on thick paper with gold and silver leaf decoration, represent a considerable achievement that can be enjoyed today, seven hundred years after they were produced.

PRINTING IN KYOTO

The city of Kyoto, modeled on the T'ang Chinese capital of Ch'ang-an, was established as capital of Japan in 794 A.D. It is likely that books were printed in or near Kyoto from quite early in its history, and it continued as a center of printing and publishing right through the Edo period. Even today it is only second in importance to Tokyo as a publishing city.

Kyoto owed its status as a printing center in the first instance to two major factors: first, as capital of Japan it was the home of the imperial court and the nobility; second, the first two Mahayana sects of Buddhism established temples in and near Kyoto, thus developing and strengthening their links with the aristocracy and the court. These two sects were Tendai, introduced from China by Saichō (Dengyō Daishi) in 805, and Shingon, introduced by Kūkai (Kōbō Daishi) in 806. The Tendai sect established its headquarters on Mt. Hiei (or Hiei-zan), which is quite close to Kyoto, and the Shingon sect on Mt. Kōya (or Kōya-san), which is situated some distance from Kyoto, though its printed productions are always classified by Japanese scholars as *Kyōraku-han*. This is because the relations between the Kōya-san temples and the Kyoto court were always close, though not always amicable, and the monks there often played a prominent role in Kyoto's Buddhist ceremonies and in "the protection of the country." It is to these two sects that one must look to find the origins of Kyoto printing.

There is a persistent tradition that copies of the *Hokke-kyō*, the basic scripture of Tendai Buddhism, were printed on Hiei-zan during the lifetime of Saichō (767–822), and indeed, at his express order. If there is any truth to this, then these *Dengyō-ban*, as they are known, must have been block-printed and would constitute the earliest example of a Japanese block-printed text, postdating the *Hyakumantō darani* by some forty years or so. Unfortunately, however, as no *Dengyō-ban* have survived, it is impossible to be certain that they ever existed.

As with Nara, a certain amount of printing work was probably undertaken in or near

Kyoto in the ninth and tenth centuries, though there are no extant examples. Similarly, it was not until the Kamakura period that Kyoto printing came into its own, though printing activity during the course of the eleventh century is indicated by contemporary diaries and manuscript records referring to a number of important printed texts dated between 1009 and 1096. All of these belong to the type known as *suri-kuyō*, or printed texts (*suri* being the earliest word used for printing, derived for its original meaning of "rubbing" the paper against the block), commemorating the death of some notable or celebrating his recovery from illness. While there is no clear indication in the records whether such texts were printed in Nara or Kyoto, two factors argue strongly in favor of the latter: first, where the person responsible for commissioning the printing is known, he invariably proves to be a member of the Kyoto aristocracy; second, the idea that souls could be helped in the afterlife by such acts of devotion is associated more with Mahayana than with Hinayana Buddhism. This does not mean that no examples of *suri-kuyō* printing were produced in Nara (handwritten copies of sutras were certainly produced for similar purposes) and so the case for Kyoto is by no means overwhelming; nevertheless, cultural evidence favors Kyoto.

A typical example of *suri-kuyō* printing (no longer extant) is the production of sixty copies each of the *Hokke-kyō*, the *Muryōgi-kyō* and the *Kanfugen-kyō*, commissioned in 1043 by Fujiwara Sanenari (975–1044) on the death of the head of his family. These three sutras came to be particularly associated with this kind of memorial for the dead, while others, such as the *Yakushi-kyō*, were specifically associated with recovery from illness.

Between these lost examples of Japanese printing and the 1088 copy of the *Jōyuishiki-ron* which is firmly connected with Nara and is the earliest completely authenticated example of Japanese block-printing, two other dated books exist, which cannot be conclusively attributed to either Nara or Kyoto. These are the one-*maki* version of the *Bussetsu rokuji jinshuō-gyō*, bearing a manuscript date of 1053 and a copy of the second *maki* of the *Hokke-kyō*, with a manuscript date of 1080. Ōya Tokujō (*see* Bibl.) implies that both were printed in Nara, but there is no convincing evidence to support this view and they could equally well have been printed in Kyoto. Neither has sufficiently strong affiliations with any one sect or group of sects for this to be a factor in locating the place of printing. It must be said in general terms that the argument over whether Nara or Kyoto was the birthplace of Japanese block-printing is liable never to be satisfactorily resolved. The discovery of new printed works firmly linked with Kyoto and predating any other known work would in itself prove nothing, because there is always the possibility that something else remains to be discovered or that a book printed earlier has been lost. It is certainly true, however, that new discoveries are likely to be made in the future, for the 1053 copy of the *Bussetsu rokuji jinshuō-gyō* was not found until this century.

When Kyoto printing flourished in the Kamakura period (1185–1333), the major difference was that whereas in Nara printing was confined to a few temples, in Kyoto many more temples were involved and many more works were printed covering a wider range. One factor, however, is common to both, and that is until the introduction of movable type in 1590 and with the exception of a number of books published at Zen temples from the thirteenth to the fifteenth centuries, printing activity in Nara and Kyoto was confined to Buddhist works and was never regarded as a commercial undertaking.

The story of printing in Kyoto from the beginning of the Kamakura period to 1590 is confusing due to the involvement of so many different temples and so many types of Buddhist works. Although many works cannot be identified with any one sect, in general works can be divided among four main sects: Tendai, Shingon, Jōdo and Zen. Tendai works were printed either at the Mt. Hiei headquarters or at various Tendai temples in Kyoto and later in the provinces; Shingon works were printed mainly at its Mt. Kōya

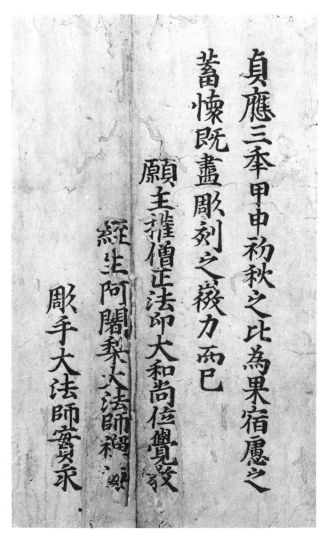

10. This *Butsumo daikujaku myōō-gyō*, a Shingon text, is the earliest known extant example of Tō-ji printing. Shown here is the colophon of the third *maki*, giving the date of printing (1224), the names of the sponsor (*ganshu*), copyist and block-cutter.

51

headquarters but also at other locations; Jōdo sect works were printed mainly within Kyoto; and Zen sect works were printed at various places, but principally at the Gozan (Five Monasteries) complexes near Kyoto.

From as early as 1148 in the Heian period there is an extant copy of the *Hokke-gengi-shakusen*, printed by a monk named Ryōkan. Although this work is specifically associated with Tendai, there is no clear indication whether it was printed at Mt. Hiei or at one of the Tendai temples in Kyoto itself, and this reflects one of the major problems of locating the place of printing of a Tendai work. The doctrines of Tendai were so all-embracing that with the exception of Shingon and Zen, all the Buddhist sects of the Kamakura period find their origin in Tendai, and consequently many works of Tendai origin are equally associated with other sects. This is particularly true with many Jōdo works.

Perhaps due to this, Japanese printing historians generally avoid making a specific category of Tendai publications, with the exception of works printed at Mt. Hiei, known as *Hiei-zan-ban*. For the Kamakura period, this seems a slightly false category in as much as despite the immense religious activity, very little in fact was printed there. Indeed, only one *Hiei-zan-ban* is known, the one-hundred-and-fifty-*maki* version of the *Hokke sandaibu* with attendant commentaries. In all, this consisted of three of the principal works of Tendai Buddhism, the *Hokke-gengi* (twenty *maki*), the *Hokke mongu* (twenty *maki*) and the *Makashikan* (twenty *maki*), with three important commentaries on these works, the *Hokke-gengi-shakusen* (twenty *maki*), the *Hokke mongu-ki* (thirty *maki*) and the *Makashikan bugyō kōketsu* (forty *maki*). This vast printing enterprise took eighteen years to complete, from 1278 to 1296. Unfortunately, very few complete copies survive. Apart from the sheer magnitude, the work is remarkable in that it contains the calligraphy of some of the most distinguished monks of the day, who were especially invited to contribute. The finished work, therefore, has a bewildering variety of calligraphic styles, but the total effect is pleasing.

It seems almost certain that no works were printed at Mt. Kōya during the Heian period, though *Kōya-ban* were to prove the most lasting of all genres of Buddhist printing. Numerous examples survive from as late as the eighteenth century, and in his epic study, Mizuhara Gyōei (*see* Bibl.) lists an example printed at Mt. Kōya in 1865. Since the doctrines of Shingon are esoteric, the lack of Heian-period examples may well be because printing seemed alien to Shingon's interests. However, the early Kamakura period saw the rise of a group of reforming Shingon monks, such as Dōhan (1184–1252), who took the opposite view. The earliest known Shingon work printed was the *Butsumo daikujaku myōō-gyō* (Pl. 10), produced in 1224, but since this was almost certainly printed at Tō-ji in Kyoto, it is not strictly a *Kōya-ban*. The earliest known genuine *Kōya-ban* is the one-*maki* version of Kūkai's famous *Sokushin jōbutsu-gi* (or *Sokushin-gi*), which was printed in 1251. This was still in existence in 1743, but seems subsequently to have been lost, leaving the 1253 printing of the *Sangyō shiki* as the earliest extant *Kōya-ban*.

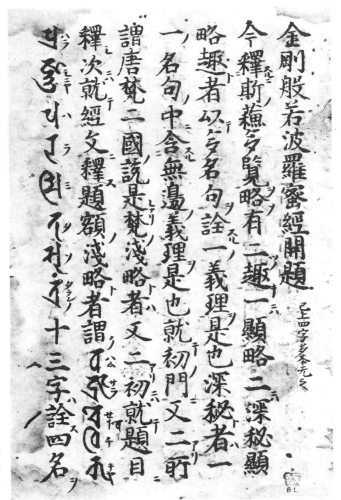

11. The first page of the *Kongō-kyō kaidai*, by Kūkai, printed at Mt. Kōya in 1280. The book is bound in one volume in *detchō* style.

At least seven *Kōya-ban*, including the missing *Sokushin jōbutsu-gi*, were printed on Mt. Kōya between 1251 and 1258, and all were the work of one man, an otherwise obscure monk named Kaiken. No details of his life are known, another instance where someone who can be regarded as a pioneer of printing was of no particular importance in his own temple, otherwise more facts would be known of his life. Clearly printing was an artisan's craft, and the printer in question simply acted on instructions received from higher authorities. Even well into the Edo period, when printing became more sophisticated, the man who engraved the wood blocks received scant credit for what, after all, was the most important stage of the printing process.

No examples of Kaiken's work survive from a date later than 1258, and his role seems to have been taken over by two other monks, Keiken and Taisei. Keiken's name appears on six works printed between 1277 and 1302, and Taisei's on seven works dating from 1277 to 1280, the largest and most important of which was the *Dainichi-kyō-sho*,

53

a commentary on the *Mahāvairocana-sūtra*, one of the basic works of Shingon. This was produced in twenty volumes between 1277 and 1279, constituting the largest of early *Kōya-ban* works. Both Keiken and Taisei were connected with the Kongō Sammai-in, or Hall of Diamond Meditation, which appears to have been the center of early *Kōya-ban* printing.

In their printing style, early *Kōya-ban* bear strong similarities to Nara *Kasuga-ban* at the beginning of the Kamakura period, suggesting that the printing of Nara temples, particularly of Kōfuku-ji, had a stimulating effect on *Kōya-ban* (Pl. 11), and even that monks were brought from Nara to assist in carving the wood blocks. In the earliest examples of *Kōya-ban* works, high-quality *torinoko* paper seems to have been most widely used, but in later years the monks manufactured their own or had it made in the nearby villages. This paper, commonly used in the Muromachi and Edo periods for *Kōya-ban*, is known as *Kōya-gami*, or more popularly *kasa-gami*, and is regarded as inferior in quality. The skill of the calligraphy and the engraving, on the other hand, is much better, particularly in the Kamakura period, but by and large the Mt. Kōya monks did not favor the elaborate use of gold and silver leaf typical of many of the finest examples of *Kasuga-ban* printing. One has the impression that in Shingon Buddhism printing was regarded as more utilitarian than in Nara Buddhism. Interestingly, *Kōya-ban* printing seems to have departed from Nara traditions in that the majority of early examples were bound in *detchō* or *orihon* styles rather than in the *kansu-bon* format typical of Nara printing. Both styles were, of course, used, but for *Kōya-ban* the *kansu-bon* style of binding was less popular.

Shingon printing was not confined to Mt. Kōya but spread to various other temples of the sect in and around Kyoto, notably to Tō-ji. After the Kamakura period, *Kōya-ban* printing went into steady, rather than spectacular, decline, and although examples are found from the fourteenth to the nineteenth centuries, the primary interest of these works after the thirteenth century is in terms of the history of Buddhism.

The doctrines of Jōdo, or Pure Land Buddhism, were developed in Japan by the monk Genkū, who is normally known as Hōnen Shōnin (1133–1212) and did not reach any level of popularity until the end of the twelfth century. Some of the basic texts of Jōdo, such as the *Amida-kyō*, did exist in printed form before the advent of the sect itself, but such works could not be termed Jōdo printing. The earliest extant example of *Jōdo-kyō-ban* is a copy of the *Muryōgi-kyō*, one of the three basic Jōdo sutras, printed at an unknown location in 1204 (thus predating the earliest known *Kōya-ban*). That the place of printing is unknown is in itself significant.

During the Kamakura period, instead of a temple of any sect printing a work in large quantities, it was customary to print a limited number of copies and store the blocks until more were needed. The customary printed endnote or colophon denoted the temple responsible for the original printing, but in the case of the Kamakura-period *Jōdo-kyō-ban* this was absent, and consequently we have no notion of where they were printed, except that it was in or near Kyoto. In fact, wherever they did their work,

Jōdo monks were extremely active in printing during the Kamakura period, certainly more so than any of the other Kyoto monks. At least forty works were printed, from the *Muryōgi-kyō* of 1204 to the *Anraku-shū* of 1325. Unlike the Nara and Tendai and Shingon sects which were financially backed by the court and the aristocracy, the Jōdo sect preached the invocation of the name of Amida Buddha as a means of salvation as well as rebirth into the Western Paradise, and thus it attracted the poorer classes of medieval Japan. Much of the early support of Jōdo came from these classes, and the sect itself was not in any sense wealthy. It seems possible, therefore, that the absence of a fixed location for its Kamakura-period printing is due to the fact that the Jōdo sect did not possess any temples.

The forty items printed by the Jōdo monks during the Kamakura period do not comprise a large number of works, for the *Muryōgi-kyō*, the *Amida-kyō* and the *Ōjōyō-shū* were each printed six times. The most interesting of these works, and the first indication of a development of popular printing in Japan, was the *Kurodani shōnin gotōroku*, produced in 1321. Hitherto, it had been the custom to produce the text in Chinese characters only, sometimes with reading marks added for native use. The monks of the Tendai, Shingon and Nara sects read Chinese as easily as Japanese and certainly read more in Chinese than in Japanese, which was confined to literary works in manuscript form. *Kurodani shōnin gotōroku*, however, is a collection of the sayings of Hōnen written in *hiragana-majiri*, a mixture of Chinese characters and the Japanese *hiragana* syllabary. This meant that someone who read only Japanese could, for the first time, read a Buddhist text. This innovation undoubtedly owed much to the humble origins of the sect, but would probably not have extended readership of the text to the peasantry, who were largely illiterate. It did mean, however, that when the work was read to an audience, its meaning was understood. The monks responsible for printing the early *Jōdo-kyō-ban* were disciples of Hōnen—Myōshin, Nyūshin and Ōsei being among the most common names found at the end of the texts.

As with *Kōya-ban*, the *detchō* and *orihon* styles of binding were preferred to the *kansu-bon* for early *Jōdo-kyō-ban*, although all three styles were employed. One unusual piece of work printed in 1315, was the *Hōnen shōnin-zō* (Pl. 12), consisting of a single-sheet portrait of Hōnen with a brief religious text. This seems to be a unique development in early Buddhist printing, where illustration was not regarded as important. Occasionally, early Buddhist works of all sects were illustrated, but the idea of printing a single-sheet illustration is certainly unique to Jōdo. Pictures are obviously useful when preaching to an illiterate audience.

In the Nambokuchō period (1333–92), characterized by social unrest and civil strife, only twelve *Jōdo-kyō-ban* were printed (Pl. 13), but these works have points of considerable interest. In 1365, another of Hōnen's works, the *Ichimai-kishō-mon*, was printed in *hiragana-majiri*, as was the *Kurodani shōnin gohōgo* of the same year. The original blocks of both these works survive and show how much more complicated it was for the engraver to reproduce the cursive script (*sōsho*) of Japanese handwriting.

It was during this time that mica (*ummo*) was used increasingly on paper, a decorative phenomenon common to *Kōya-ban* of the same period.

Another thirty-seven *Jōdo-kyō-ban* were printed in the Muromachi period until the introduction of movable type. Illustrations were not uncommon in these, the most notable examples of which are the *Amida-kyō* (1426), the *Hōnen shōnin-zō* (1440), technically more advanced than the 1315 portrait of the same title, and the *Zendō daishi-zō* (c. 1450–60).

So far no mention has been made of the Chinese influence on Japanese printing. Technologically this was very limited, because with block-printing little progress is possible and is confined to the field of illustration, which will be discussed later. Throughout the Kamakura, Nambokuchō, Muromachi and Edo periods, books were brought to Japan from China, mostly by monks who visited Chinese monasteries, and the intro-

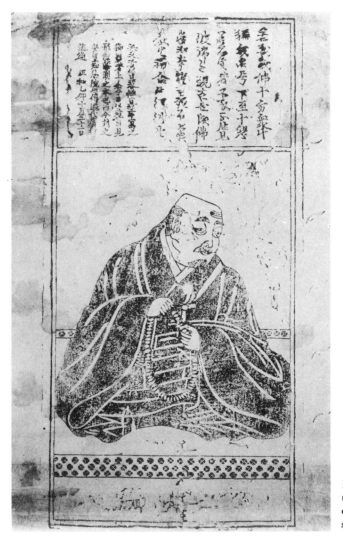

12. An early portrait of Hōnen (1133–1212), founder of the Jōdo sect of Buddhism in Japan. This printed sheet is dated Shōwa 4 (1315).

duction of such books served as a stimulus to Japanese printing activity, particularly when the doctrines of a new sect were imported. Chinese influence in the actual production of books, however, was confined to calligraphy and format and illustration. Techniques of binding have been discussed in the first chapter, but it is worth noting that all Japanese forms of binding, with the exception of *Yamato-toji*, which had limited use and was restricted to native literary works in manuscript form, were adopted from Chinese exemplars brought by monks.

Nowhere was Chinese influence more profoundly felt than in the publications of the Zen sect. Zen doctrines of the Rinzai branch were introduced to Japan by Eisai (1141–1215) and those of the Sōtō branch by his pupil Dōgen (1200–53). Their books were printed at various locations in Japan, including the temples of Nara, but the chief source of Zen printed books was the Gozan complexes of Kamakura and Kyoto.

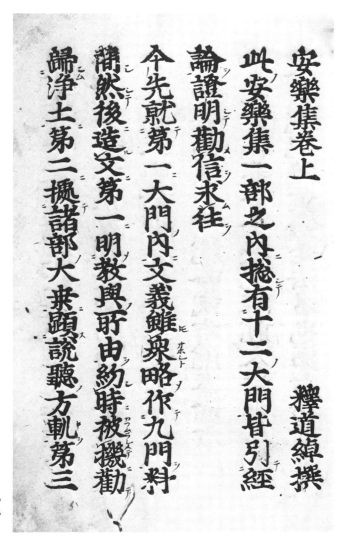

13. The opening page of the Jōdo sect edition *Anraku-shū*, printed at an unknown location in 1386.

It is difficult to achieve a satisfactory definition of these works, called *Gozan-ban*, because Japanese historians use the term in different ways. The literal meaning of the word is "Five Mountains," a name taken from a group of Zen temples in China and applied to two separate groups of temples in Kamakura and Kyoto. The Kamakura temples, built at different times, were Kenchō-ji, Engaku-ji, Jufuku-ji, Jōchi-ji and Jōmyō-ji; and the Kyoto temples, similarly built at various dates, were Nanzen-ji, Tenryū-ji, Kennin-ji, Tōfuku-ji and Manju-ji. Nominally, only books published at these temples should be called *Gozan-ban*, but Japanese historians of printing usually include other Kyoto temples in this category, notably Rinsen-ji, founded by Musō Kokushi in the fourteenth century. Since Rinsen-ji was in fact built before Tenryū-ji, it is easy to see how the confusion arises. The interesting aspect of *Gozan-ban* is that not only were the majority based on Chinese exemplars and bear a close resemblance to Sung- and Yüan-dynasty Chinese printing, but also that a large collection of non-Buddhist works are included among them, the first and only ones of their kind before the age of movable type.

Reprints of Sung-dynasty editions began quite early on in the Kamakura period, the first known being the copy of the *Shuryōgon-gyō* printed in 1239 at Chōraku-ji in Ueno province. Several more were printed at the Shingon sect Senyū-ji in Kyoto by the disciples of the monk Shunjō (1166–1227), who studied Zen and Ritsu doctrines in China between 1199 and 1211. These works are not necessarily connected with Zen, and certainly not with the Gozan temples, but they are noted for their faithful representation of Chinese printing and calligraphic styles. (The *Shuryōgon-gyō* has a frontispiece copied from the Chinese exemplar.) Shunjō, it seems, brought a number of works back to Japan for use as models.

The doctrines of Zen Buddhism appealed to members of the warrior class who ruled Japan at the time, and since the *de facto* capital of Japan during the Kamakura period was Kamakura itself, it is not surprising that the first dated *Gozan-ban* was produced at one of the Kamakura temples (though which is unknown) in 1283, printed through the patronage of the warrior Hōjō Akitoki (d. 1300), who was celebrated for his great love of books and also expanded the Kanazawa Bunko library founded by his grandfather, which exists to this day. The next *Gozan-ban*, the *Zenmon hōkun*, was also printed in Kamakura at Kenchō-ji in 1287, and in the following year no less than five works were printed at Tōfuku-ji in Kyoto. However, between 1288 and 1333, only twelve other dated titles are recorded as having been printed, although others may have been lost. It should be noted that at this time no non-Buddhist works were printed at all.

In the Nambokuchō period, social turmoil stemmed from the refusal of the ruling emperor, Go-Daigo, to recognize the usurper, Shogun Ashikaga Takauji. Go-Daigo fled from Kyoto and set up his court in Yoshino, while Emperor Kōmyō, the nominee of Takauji, ruled in Kyoto. There was less printing done during this period in every printing temple in Japan except the Zen temples, particularly of Kyoto, which were supported by both Takauji and Go-Daigo with the result that the Nambokuchō period proved to be extremely prolific for *Gozan-ban* works. One of the most notable pioneers of the period was the monk Soseki, better known as Musō Kokushi (1275–1351), who supported Go-Daigo but remained on good terms with Takauji and sought to bring about a reconciliation. As a reward, Go-Daigo conferred on Musō Kokushi the position of abbot of Rinsen-ji, which for a time became one of the chief centers of Gozan printing.

In his detailed study of *Gozan-ban*, Kawase Kazuma (*see* Bibl.) lists a total of 272 works printed—195 works of Zen Buddhism and 77 *Kanseki* works (i.e., those written by Chinese authors of either Buddhist or non-Buddhist type, but not commentaries on Buddhist texts). Of these, approximately 120 Zen works and 60 *Kanseki* works were printed in the Nambokuchō period. These figures themselves speak for the enormous volume of printing undertaken in a very short period; naturally, not all these works are dated, but their attribution to the period is firm. Thus Nambokuchō-period dated works comprise just under half the total, and of them approximately ten percent are ascribed to one man—the monk Shun'oku Myōha (1311–88). This man studied Zen under Musō Kokushi and became abbot of four different temples: Tōji-ji, Nanzen-ji, Tenryū-ji and Shōkoku-ji. If Musō Kokushi was the architect of Gozan printing in the Nambokuchō period, then Shun'oku Myōha was certainly the builder.

As has been noted, *Gozan-ban* as a rule bear a close similarity to Sung and Yüan printing and differ markedly in appearance from that of pre-1590 native printed works. Though a question of personal taste, *Gozan-ban* pages always seem crowded and less aesthetically satisfying than some of the finer examples of, say, *Kasuga-ban*. Questions of format and aesthetics aside, there is no doubting the historical importance of *Gozan-ban*, which lies not so much in the number of fine Zen works printed, of which the *Kei-toku-dentō-roku* and the *Jūgyū-zu* ("Ten Ox-herding Pictures") are typical and outstanding examples respectively, but in the works of Chinese philosophy and poetry, which had never been previously printed in Japan.

Seen in retrospect, the key psychological breakthrough in the printing of non-Buddhist Chinese works was the publication in 1364 of the *Rongo shūkai* in ten *maki* (five volumes). This is a Japanese Gozan edition of Ho Yen's collected commentaries on the *Analects* (*Rongo*) of Confucius, and because it was published in the Shōhei era (1346–69), it is always known as the *Shōhei-ban Rongo*. One or two anthologies may have been printed before the *Rongo shūkai*, but since they are undated this cannot be confirmed, and the *Rongo shūkai* is normally termed the earliest non-Buddhist work printed in Japan. It had taken almost six hundred years for such a work to be produced, and the fact that it was printed stems from the involvement of Japanese Zen monks not merely with the narrow area of sectarian doctrines but with the Chinese world where those doctrines originated. Fittingly perhaps, the man responsible for the printing of the *Rongo shūkai* was not a well-known figure but an obscure monk called Dōyū. Since we are not absolutely sure that this work was the first example of the printing of a non-Buddhist work in Japan, it would be misleading to suggest that it initiated the steady stream of similar productions that followed. However, it is true that a number of important non-Buddhist works were printed at the Gozan temples in Kyoto after this, ranging from literary miscellanea, such as the *Reisai yawa* (c. 1390), to the *Isho taizen* (1528), the first printed medical work in Japan, and the 1590 edition of the *Setsuyōshū*, a dictionary, which is the last known *Gozan-ban*.

The Gozan temples continued to produce books in the Muromachi period on only a slightly lesser scale than in the Nambokuchō period, but after about 1450, production began to decrease. This was almost certainly due to the lengthy period of civil war which began in the second half of the fifteenth century and was not resolved until Tokugawa Ieyasu's triumph at Sekigahara in 1600. In fact, in this period, book production in all sects was very limited.

The printing of Buddhist books did not end with the sixteenth century, for the Jōdo sect played an important role in the history of movable type printing. The major difference between the pre-1590 period and the post-1650 period was that in the former, all Buddhist printing was carried out within temples, whereas in the latter, the same kind of books were produced by commercial publishers, the intervening years being the embryonic period of a full-scale publishing industry.

In this sense, 1590 marks the end of Buddhist domination of printing. In view of the variety of works produced by Gozan temples in the later Muromachi period, it might be said that *Gozan-ban* acted as a bridge between Buddhist printing in the strictest sense and the printing of Japanese classics and other types of work in the Edo period. However, *Gozan-ban* suffered the fate common to Buddhist printing in general, and its death blow was delivered by a combination of historical and social circumstances and by the advent of movable type. Buddhist achievement in printing terms was not minimal: some of the finest examples of the printer's art throughout its history are Buddhist, but, that said, it must be admitted that the overall effect of its domination was stifling. It is not possible to estimate the total number of works produced by the Buddhist temples, but considering the length of time, their output was not high, and with some exceptions, was confined to a narrow field of interest. By 1590 the groundwork of printing technique had been laid and it was time to move on.

4 | THE MOVABLE TYPE BOOM

The period of movable type supremacy lasted only from 1600 to 1640, although it was introduced earlier and continued in diminishing use until about 1650. Yet these forty years were sufficient to transform Japanese printing beyond recognition. In fact, the advent of movable type was probably the most significant single occurrence in the development of printing in Japan up until then. The significance lay not so much in the technology of movable type, which ultimately proved less advantageous to the Japanese than the traditional wood-block method, but in the variety of uses to which it was put. In 1590, the only examples of non-Buddhist printing in existence were a few copies of Chinese works produced by the Gozan temples. By 1650, there was a considerable corpus of works printed by movable type—almost all the major classics of Japanese literature were in print for the first time. By 1650, too, the art of book illustration for its own sake had evolved, and printing had become a commercial process, bringing the role of the Buddhist monasteries in printing to a gradual end.

Movable type reached Japan from two independent sources almost simultaneously, and because of this followed two separate developments within Japan. One origin was Portugal and the other Korea, the former introduction representing something quite new, while the latter conformed to the traditions of East Asian cultural development. In the long term the Korean introduction was much more significant, but the books produced by the Portuguese and their Japanese assistants at what has come to be known as the Jesuit Mission Press are not without interest.

THE JESUIT MISSION PRESS

In 1542 or 1543, a Portuguese ship was wrecked off the Kyushu coast on an island called Tanegashima. The surviving mariners were entertained most hospitably by the Japanese, not least, one suspects, on account of the firearms they possessed, which had never been seen in Japan before. This event proved to be the first encounter between Europe and Japan, the fabled goal of many European explorers since the days of Marco Polo. In keeping with other Western voyages of discovery, the finding of Japan was an accident, but that it was the Portuguese, however, who made the discovery was no accident at all. As early as 1493, a Papal Bull issued by Alexander VI had divided the world into two hemispheres, allocating the Western hemisphere to the Spanish throne and the Eastern hemisphere to the Portuguese, and authorizing these two nations to explore and conquer all the non-Christian territories they might find. Just as it was the prerogative of the Portuguese throne to trade and conquer without restriction in the Eastern hemisphere, so it was the responsibility of the Society of Jesus to carry the Christian faith to those regions. By the mid-sixteenth century, Portugal had established numerous, if often tenuous, footholds in Asia, and although these were to vanish in time in the face of competition from the Northern European maritime powers, England and Holland, there is no question that when Japan was first discovered, Portugal was the leading European nation in Asia.

In 1544, the first official entreaty was made by the Portuguese for the establishment of trade relations between the two countries. And five years later, a few Jesuits, led by the redoubtable Francis Xavier, landed in Japan to begin their missionary work. As a result of the religious zeal and ability of men like Xavier, there were 130,000 converts in the country by 1579 and an estimated 300,000 converts when missionary success was at its peak before Christianity was actively proscribed. The figures themselves are misleading, for if a single daimyo was converted, his entire retinue automatically followed his example. Furthermore, political undercurrents lay behind many conversions, especially those in Kyushu where the new faith was most successful, for many daimyo were persuaded by the possibility of Portuguese arms and assistance in the civil wars that prevailed at this period in Japan. Nevertheless, these figures do reveal a considerable achievement, and if Christianity had not been proscribed, no doubt further progress would have been made.

The Jesuits naturally also encountered much opposition in Japan, both openly in the hostility shown by some sectors of the Buddhist faith and by implication in the alien social customs of the people not conducive to the acceptance of the new religion. However, the biggest difficulty in the early years was language. None of the missionaries knew any Japanese, of course, a language that Xavier himself referred to as "the language of the devil." With the few missionaries on hand in Japan, preaching the new doctrine had to be done in an easily understandable fashion. And furthermore, some system of teaching Japanese to the newly arrived missionaries from Portugal and the colony of Goa had to be devised. For these reasons books were a necessity for the missionaries, an idea that would certainly have been much in the mind of the Visitor-General Alessandro Valignano, when he arrived on a tour of inspection of the country in 1579. At the direct instigation of Valignano, the Kyushu daimyo of Ōtomo, Arima and Ōmura sent a mission to Europe in 1582, which was warmly received by various rulers including Pope Gregory XIII himself. When the mission returned to Japan in 1590, it brought with it a printing press and a number of European printers to embark on the publications sorely needed by the Jesuits. Whether the press was obtained in Lisbon or in Rome in 1586 is not clear, but with its arrival the Jesuit Mission Press was established and its publications, known as *Kirishitan-ban* (Christian printings), began to appear (Pls. 14, 15, 16).

The Jesuit Mission Press was rather short-lived: the first book being printed in 1591 and the last in 1611, when persecution of the Christians in Japan intensified and the press was transferred to Macao. Due to these persecutions a great many of the books printed by the Jesuits were lost or found their way out of the country. However, four fragmentary and thirty complete works — a total of seventy-three copies — are known to have survived. The latest research shows that Japan possesses sixteen *Kirishitan-ban*, the United Kingdom fourteen, Italy ten, China six, France five, Portugal five, Spain four, Holland three, the Philippines three, United States three, Germany two and the Vatican two. A complete list of the known works of the Jesuit Mission Press, excluding fragmentary works, is given below. The Portuguese, Latin or quasi-Japanese titles are preferred to pure Japanese titles, and in cases where the work is untitled, a brief English title is supplied in parentheses.

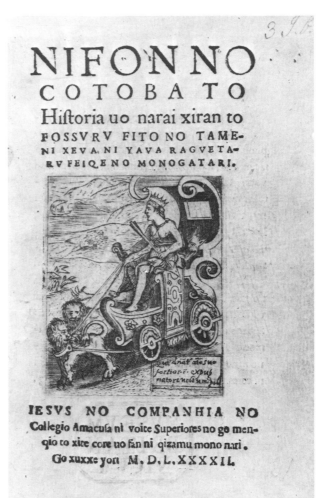

14. The title page of the *Kirishitan-ban* edition of the *Heike monogatari*, printed at Amakusa in 1592. This was also the first Japanese novel ever to be printed.

Title	Language	Location	Date
1. (*A prayer leaf*)	Japanese	Unknown	Unknown
2. *Sanctos no gosagveo no vchi nvqigaqi*	Romanized Japanese	Kazusa	1591
3. (*Christian Doctrine*)	Japanese	Unknown	Unknown
4. *Doctrina Christan*	Japanese	Amakusa	1592
5. *Fides no Dŏxi*	Romanized Japanese	Amakusa	1592
6. (*On Baptism and Preparation for Death*)	Japanese	Unknown	Unknown
7. *Feiqe no monogatari*	Romanized Japanese	Amakusa	1592
8. *Esopo no fabvlas*	Romanized Japanese	Amakusa	1593
9. *Qincvxv*	Romanized Japanese	Amakusa	1593
10. *De Institvtione Grammatica*	Latin-Portuguese-Romanized Japanese	Amakusa	1594
11. *Dictionarivm Latino Lvsitanicvm ac Iaponicvm*	Latin-Portuguese-Romanized Japanese	Amakusa	1595
12. *Exercitia Spiritvalia*	Latin	Amakusa	1596
13. *Compendivm Spiritvalis Doctrinae*	Latin	Unknown	1596
14. *Contemptvs Mvndi jenbv*	Romanized Japanese	Unknown	1596
15. *Racvyoxv*	Japanese	Nagasaki	1598
16. *Salvator Mvndi*	Japanese	Unknown	1598
17. *Gvia do Pecador*	Japanese	Unknown	1599
18. *Doctrina Christan*	Romanized Japanese	Unknown	1600
19. *Royei. Zafit.*	Japanese	Unknown	1600
20. *Doctrinae Christianae*	Japanese	Nagasaki	1600
21. *Doctrina Christam*	Japanese	Nagasaki	1600
22. *Aphorismi Confessariorvm*	Latin	Unknown	1603
23. *Vocabvlario da Lingoa de Iapam*	Portuguese-Romanized Japanese	Nagasaki	1603–4
24. *Arte da Lingoa de Iapam*	Portuguese-Romanized Japanese	Nagasaki	1604–8
25. *Manvale ad Sacramenta*	Latin	Nagasaki	1605

26. *Spiritval Xvgvio*	Romanized Japanese	Nagasaki	1607
27. *Floscvli*	Latin	Nagasaki	1610
28. *Contemptvs Mvndi*	Japanese	Kyoto	1610
29. *Fides no Qvio*	Japanese	Nagasaki	1611
30. *Taiheiki nukigaki*	Japanese	Unknown	Unknown

15. The title page of the *Kirishitan-ban* edition of *Aesop's Fables*, published by the Jesuit Mission Press in 1593 at Amakusa.

16. The last page of the *Kirishitan-ban* edition of the *Qincvxv* (*Kinkushū*), a collection of Chinese maxims, printed at Amakusa in 1593.

It is interesting to note that no attempt was made by the early missionaries to produce a Japanese-language edition of the Bible, a task which none of them was competent enough to undertake. Although the majority of these titles were standard texts on Christian doctrine which are interesting only in a technical sense, the remaining works command attention from the viewpoint of content. Several dictionaries and grammars are among these, compiled for the missionaries themselves, such as the *Vocabvlario da Lingoa de Iapam* and the *Arte da Lingoa de Iapam*. These two noteworthy examples are the work of the scholar João Rodrigues (1561–1633), who was also responsible for the *Arte Breve da Lingoa Iapoa*, published in Macao in 1620, when the Jesuits still hoped for an early end to the persecutions in Japan. The Jesuits even thought it worthwhile to publish a Chinese-Japanese dictionary, the *Racvyoxv*, better known today as the *Rakuyōshū*.

The works of most interest published by the Jesuit Mission Press are related neither to Christianity, nor, save in an indirect way, to language. There is a total of five such works: the *Feiqe no monogatari* (*Heike monogatari*); the *Esopo no fabvlas* (*Isoho monogatari*); the *Qincvxv* (*Kinkushū*); the *Royei. Zafit.* (*Wakan rōeishū*); and an abridged version of the *Taiheiki* (*Taiheiki nukigaki*). The purpose of such production was probably twofold. In the first instance, the Jesuits felt it necessary to provide light reading material for the converts as well as some stimulating reading practice for the missionaries themselves. Secondly, the Jesuits in Japan, as in other parts of Asia, must have realized that there were cultural barriers which had to be broken if their mission were to be successful, and one of the best methods of achieving this would be to display interest in the local culture. In many cases, especially where doctrinal problems were not concerned, this interest was entirely genuine, for the Jesuits were men of intelligence and wide interests. Certainly it is noteworthy that none of the five works mentioned above existed in popular printed form before their arrival.

The *Feiqe no monogatari*, the *Esopo no fabvlas* and the *Qincvxv* (despite separate publication dates, these are known only in a single volume with continuous pagination, now in the British Library) are particularly interesting because they represent the product of three distinct cultures. The historical *Feiqe no monogatari* is the first printed version of a Japanese novel. The *Esopo no fabvlas* is *Aesop's Fables*, a product of Western culture calculated to stimulate the interest of the Japanese. In this it certainly succeeded, for long after the Christians had left Japan, we find printed editions of the work under its Japanese title, *Isoho no monogatari*. Lastly, the *Qincvxv* is the *Kinkushū*, a collection of Chinese maxims. The juxtaposition of three such works can hardly have been accidental, but the supreme irony lies in the fact that each text was produced in romanized Japanese, so the number of people able to read them must have been extremely limited.

The original press, acquired in Lisbon or Rome, reached Japan via Lisbon, Goa and Macao, and was first set up at Kazusa, one of the earliest centers of Christianity in Kyushu. Shortly afterward it was moved to the island of Amakusa off the coast of

Kyushu, and finally it was taken to Nagasaki. The dates of these moves are somewhat conjectural, but they can clearly be linked to the dates and locations printed on the *Kirishitan-ban* themselves. It was clearly at Amakusa in 1592 and seems to have been moved to Nagasaki between 1598 and 1600. The position is complicated, however, by the fact that there were at least two other presses of uncertain origin, one of which was certainly being used in Nagasaki by 1600 and the other in Kyoto produced a 1610 edition of the *Contemptvs Mvndi*. The fate of these two presses is not known, but they probably passed out of use by 1614. It is more than likely that both were constructed in Japan by the Japanese under Jesuit supervision. Although the earliest printing work was carried out under the supervision of Europeans such as Constantino Dourado (1567–1620) and João Baptista Pesze (1560–1626), there is ample evidence of Japanese involvement, as such names as Pedro de Hizen and Antonio Harada figure prominently in the history of *Kirishitan-ban*.

The original press was large enough to cope with both Japanese and European type, and typefaces designed by the eminent François Guyot, Claude Garamond and Robert Granjon have been identified. Japanese typefaces were used in thirteen out of the thirty *Kirishitan-ban* listed, and they include Chinese characters (*kanji*) as well as the *hiragana* and *katakana* syllabaries in two sizes. In the earlier *Kirishitan-ban*, matrices for Japanese type were made in both Japan and other Asian countries, but eventually they were all made in Japan itself. The types were exclusively of metal at first, but after the turn of the seventeenth century wood type came into use, as in the case of the *Contemptvs Mvndi*, printed in Kyoto in 1610.

There is nothing particularly beautiful about *Kirishitan-ban*, which were produced for a primarily utilitarian purpose, and it cannot be said that the Jesuit Mission Press heavily influenced the history of printing in Japan since their activities were mainly confined to the island of Kyushu. It was for the printing presses introduced from Korea and operated with official sanction to activate the "movable type boom."

THE INTRODUCTION OF MOVABLE TYPE FROM KOREA

The *de facto* ruler of Japan in 1590, when the printing press was brought over from Europe, was Toyotomi Hideyoshi (1536–98). Although he issued various edicts against Christianity in the last decade of the sixteenth century, it was his successors Tokugawa Ieyasu (1542–1616) and, more particularly, his son Hidetada (1579–1632) and his grandson Iemitsu (1604–51) who virtually wiped out Christianity in Japan. Hideyoshi had other matters on his mind in 1590, when the country was at last emerging from a long period of civil war.

Hideyoshi looked for a means of building an overseas Japanese empire. Korea, the traditional target of Japanese overseas expansion, was selected as the first stage of Hideyoshi's plan and in 1592 he launched an invasion. This campaign was militarily an unmitigated disaster. Despite initial successes, the Japanese forces were decisively

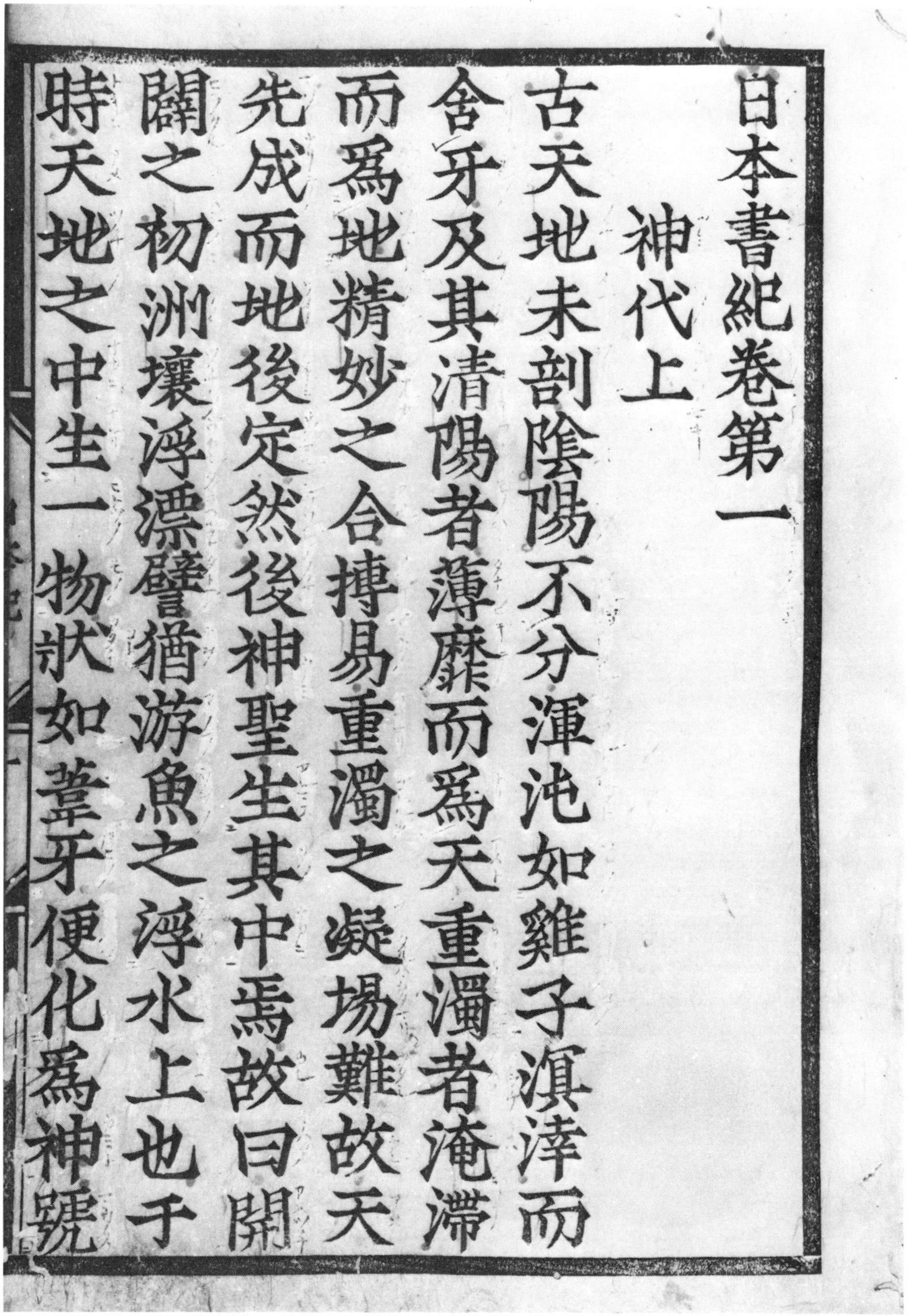

日本書紀卷第一

神代上

古天地未剖陰陽不分渾沌如雞子溟涬而

含牙及其清陽者薄靡而爲天重濁者淹滯

而爲地精妙之合搏易重濁之凝竭難故天

先成而地後定然後神聖生其中焉故曰開

闢之初洲壤浮漂譬猶游魚之浮水上也于

時天地之中生一物狀如葦牙便化爲神號

17. The first page of the movable type edition of the *Nihon shoki jindai no maki*, printed at the command of Emperor Go-Yōzei in 1599.

beaten on land and sea, and when Hideyoshi died in 1598, all Japanese soldiers in Korea were recalled.

Although the invasion was a military failure, it has great significance in the history of Japanese printing, for one of the items brought back by the soldiers was a number of printing presses complete with type. It should be mentioned that the technique of movable type printing was invented in Sung China (960–1279), where it was never used much, and brought to Korea, where it functioned alongside traditional wood-block printing, employing bronze type as well as type made from pottery. It is a curious fact that movable type did not reach Japan before the end of the sixteenth century, as there was certainly frequent contact between the two countries before then.

Hideyoshi made a present of the captured presses and types to Emperor Go-Yōzei, who nominally ruled Japan from 1586 to 1611 and who made use of the gift by having the Chinese classic *Kobun kōkyō* printed. No copy of this work has survived, but there is evidence to suggest that it was printed as early as 1593, two years after the first *Kirishitan-ban*, and it seems not unlikely that some new pieces of type were made in Japan to supplement those brought from Korea. Thereafter development was rapid, and in order to understand this it is helpful to categorize movable type works, for different sections of society used the new invention for different reasons and in different ways.

Emperor Go-Yōzei displayed great enthusiasm for the new process, and not content with the original type brought back from Korea, ordered a new set of wooden type to be made. This was engraved between 1597 and 1602, and the books printed from this new type are generically known as *choku-han*, or "imperial printings." Indeed "imperial" is a fitting description of these works, for they are among the finest unillustrated books ever produced in Japan. Not only was the typeface larger, but the best-quality paper and the finest ink were used to achieve this effect. Very few *choku-han* works were actually printed between 1597 and 1603, and if we exclude the 1593 edition of *Kobun kōkyō*, almost all the titles were copies of Chinese philosophical classics. The complete list of known *choku-han* for which Go-Yōzei was responsible is as follows: the *Kangaku-bun* (1597); the *Kinshūdan* (1597); the *Nihon shoki jindai no maki* (1599); the *Kobun kōkyō* (1599); the *Daigaku, Chūyō, Rongo* and *Mōshi* (1599, and known collectively as the *Shisho*, although only one complete combined edition is known, which is in the British Library and illustrated on p. 70); the *Shokugenshō* (1599); and the *Chōgonka biwakō* (c. 1603). Of all these works, only the *Nihon shoki jindai no maki* is of Japanese origin. One other *choku-han* is known to have been printed by order of Emperor Go-Mino-o in 1621, and that is the *Hōruien*, although one or two other titles were printed and have been lost. All these works are considerable examples of the printer's art and show how quickly the Japanese were able to make full and aesthetic use of movable type (Pls. 17, 18).

These *choku-han* editions are one arm of what might be described as "official" movable type printing in Japan, that is, printing sponsored by the authorities. Tokugawa Ieyasu, shogun and effective ruler of the country from 1603, also displayed interest in the new process. Under the auspices of Sanyō (1548–1612), ninth head of the famous Ashikaga Gakkō center of learning, Ieyasu established a printing works at Fushimi in Kyoto. Eight books were printed there between 1599 and 1606 under Sanyō's supervision, and are known generically as *Fushimi-ban*. At Ieyasu's command, thousands of new pieces of wooden type were made for this somewhat abortive undertaking. How direct an interest Ieyasu himself took in the project is revealed by the types of works produced, which included books on history, military strategy and the Chinese classics. However, as with the *choku-han* editions, only one work of native origin, the historical chronicle *Azuma kagami*, was selected for inclusion in the program. Ieyasu, like so many eminent men of his day, particularly in government and administration, had the profoundest respect for Chinese learning. In chronological order the eight *Fushimi-ban* are: the *Kōshi kego* (1599); the *Sanryaku* (1599); the *Rikutō* (1599); the *Jōgan seiyō* (1600); another edition of the *Sanryaku* (1600); the *Azuma kagami* (1605); the *Shūeki* (1605); and the *Shichisho* (1606). Each of these bears a printed endnote identifying the origin

18. A page of the *Rongo* (*Analects*) section of the 1599 *choku-han* movable type edition of the *Shisho*, which bears the printed date *Keichō tsuchinoto-i* (Keichō 4).

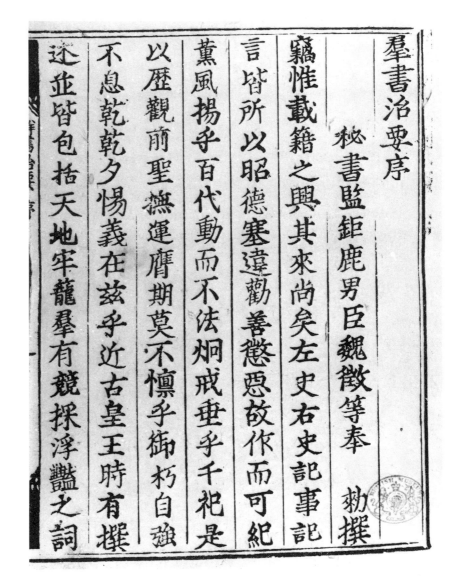

19. The *Gunsho chiyō* (1616), one of two *Suruga-ban* works produced by Dōshun at the order of Tokugawa Ieyasu.

and purpose of the printing by Sanyō in five of them, and by Saishō Shōda (1548–1607) in the remaining three. These *Fushimi-ban* are also considerable works of art, but because of the smaller typeface used in them, they do not have quite the same opulent effect as the *choku-han*.

After 1606, Ieyasu abandoned these activities until his retirement at Suruga (now part of Shizuoka Prefecture), when he ordered a large quantity of new bronze type and commanded the talented official Hayashi Razan (1583–1657), also known as Dōshun, to commence a new program of printing. Unfortunately, only two works were ever produced: *Daizō ichiranshū* (1615) and *Gunsho chiyō* (1616). The reason for the untimely

71

discontinuation of these *Suruga-ban* (Pl. 19), as they are called, was the death of Ieyasu in 1616, who must also have financed the project. He died before seeing the completion of the latter work, and according to one contemporary work (*Honkō kokushi nikki*), without making use of the 89,814 pieces of bronze type he ordered.

Aside from official printing, there were three other categories that relied on movable type: private printing carried out in Buddhist temples at the expense of a wealthy sponsor; Buddhist texts printed in temples as in the first instance, but using movable type instead of, or alongside, traditional methods; and private printing carried out on a commercial basis. The very fact that movable type was introduced from Korea naturally gave official circles first use of it, although the temples followed closely behind. And for a brief period Buddhist printing enjoyed some resurgence before its final eclipse by the commercial printing houses.

There were no sectarian barriers to the use of movable type in Buddhist temples, and books were printed by temples of the Tendai, Shingon, Jōdo, Nichiren, and to a lesser extent, Zen sects. The temples of Kyoto were the initiators, and curiously enough (since the Nichiren sect appears to have printed no books previously), two temples of the Nichiren sect in Kyoto, Honkoku-ji and Yōhō-ji, were first in the field. In 1595, the *Tendai shikyōgi shūkai* and the *Hokke gengi no jo* (Pl. 20) were printed at Honkoku-ji, and a series of important works were printed at Yōhō-ji between 1600 and 1614. The leading figure in Yōhō-ji printing was a learned monk named Nichishō (d. 1614), also known as Enchi, who not only supervised the temple's printing but also wrote and edited most of the works himself. Among the works that he did not write was one of the earliest editions of the *Taiheiki* (1605) and the celebrated *Monzen* (1607).

The *Monzen* is an interesting yet typical example of the joint roles of the Buddhist temples and the feudal nobility in the promotion of movable type. The book was printed at Yōhō-ji at the specific request of Naoe Kanetsugu (1560–1619), an influential retainer of the Uesugi family, from a specially commissioned set of bronze type. The production of this *Naoe-ban* edition, as it is known, not only highlights the long-established tradition of temple patronage by the nobility but also reveals the interest of the nobility in the use of movable type for cultural purposes. Ieyasu, no doubt, set an example in this, but while he could easily afford it, others had to make use of temple facilities.

Many other temples produced books from movable type throughout the Keichō (1596–1615), Genna (1615–24) and Kan'ei (1624–44) eras, but it is superfluous to detail these publications since comments made about the material produced by Buddhist temples up to 1590 apply equally to the period 1590–1650. The principal temples involved during this period were Honnō-ji, Kitano Kyōō-dō, Kōdai-ji, Ichijō Seiwa-in, Shinren-in, Nishi Hongan-ji, Myōshin-ji, Hōju-in and several others within Kyoto and in the provinces. However, the activities of the temples on Mt. Hiei and Mt. Kōya deserve special mention.

Movable type printing on Mt. Hiei is believed to have begun with the publication of two works, the *Makashikan ryōkai* and the *Ryōchū tendai shikyō-gi*, in 1603, but the golden age of Hiei-zan movable type printing (the Hiei monks were the most active of any temple) lasted from 1616 to 1634, when some fifty separate works were produced. Although large typefaces were used in these works, probably influenced by the *choku-han* editions, the faces became smaller as time passed and this is generally true of all early Edo-period movable type printing. On Mt. Kōya, movable type was first used in the printing of the *Kōmei shingon shoshin yōshō* in 1604, but as there is some doubt about the date, the *Himitsu mandara jūjū shinron* of 1609 is normally regarded as the earliest proven example. Between 1609 and 1642, the publication date of the last known Kōya-san *kokatsuji-ban* (old movable type editions), several works were printed, but production never achieved the same scale as that of Mt. Hiei. However, the temples of both Mt. Hiei and Mt. Kōya were responsible for a large proportion of the Buddhist output of *kokatsuji-ban* up to the early 1640s.

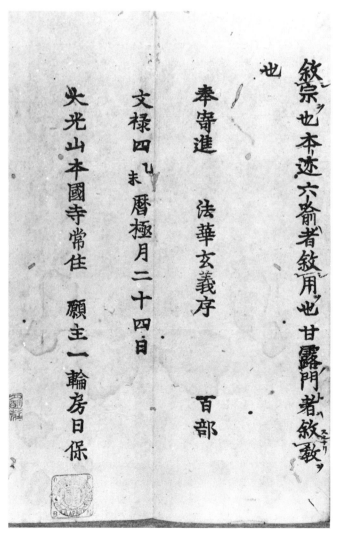

20. The colophon of the 1595 edition of the *Hokke gengi no jo*, stating that only one hundred copies of this work were printed.

The clear significance of all this printing activity in so many Japanese temples is that the usefulness of movable type was recognized very early on, and within twenty years of its introduction from Korea, a considerable number of presses were in use, especially in Kyoto, all of which, including the typefaces, were manufactured in Japan itself. As the new process gained favor in official circles in Kyoto, its use spread to the temples and from these to other temples in outlying regions. By the late 1630s, it had reached the new capital of Edo, where it was put to use for the first time in the printing of a complete set of the *Daizō-kyō*. This ambitious project, the first recorded example of Edo printing with wooden type, was launched by the Tendai monk Tenkai (1536–1643) of the Kan'ei temple in 1637 and completed in 1648.

The *Naoe-ban* edition of *Monzen* has already been cited as an example of private printing carried out by arrangement with a temple, and there are many similar instances of books being produced in the same way. It is in these private editions (*bōkoku-bon*) that popular printing in the Edo period had its origins. While some printing was undertaken purely for commercial motives, books like *Monzen* did not fall into this category, although it is often difficult to distinguish between commercial and non-commercial projects. Printing operations begun out of personal interest sometimes proved so profitable that they were continued as commercial ventures. As literacy spread and the demand for books increased, temples which served as convenient printing centers became the focal points of this industry, indicated by the fact that a number of commercial publishers in the later Edo period had their premises within temples or outside their gates.

Many of the individuals who embarked on private printing operations were physicians, a not unnatural situation since doctors formed a special class in Japan, were often wealthy and had more contact with the feudal nobility. Three eminent physicians who turned to printing were Ose Hoan (1564–1640), once the personal physician of Toyotomi Hidetsugu, Isokawa Ryōan (1579–1666) and Manase Gensaku (1549–1631), all of whom produced both medical texts and other types of works. Whether these men turned to printing for profit or printing for personal interest can best be gauged by the books they produced. Between 1596 and 1597, Ose printed five or six medical works, although he is best remembered for his printing of the *Hochū mōgyū* in 1596, a revised version of the Chinese classic. Isokawa Ryōan printed an edition of the *Taiheiki* in or about 1603 and participated in the 1605 *Fushimi-ban* edition of the *Azuma kagami*, both non-medical works, while Manase produced virtually only medical books in the first decade of the seventeenth century. On the whole, these works, important as they are, cannot be considered commercial ventures, for too few were printed in too short a period of time to suggest any kind of commercial undertaking. They were most probably undertaken as an extension of the personal interests of the men involved.

Perhaps more in line with commercial trends were the activities of an obscure figure named Baijuken (virtually all the publishers of the later Edo period were obscure). Between 1608 and 1630, Baijuken produced about thirty books with movable type, almost all of which were reprints of Ming Chinese medical texts. As Baijuken devoted at least twenty-two years of his life to printing and publishing, he must, therefore, have earned a living from it and treated it as a commercial venture.

The best-known and most influential genre of movable type books in the early Edo period are those designated as *Saga-bon* (*see* Pls. 34, 35). This term is applied to a collection of at least thirteen Japanese classics in various editions, printed by Hon'ami Kōetsu and Suminokura Soan at what has become known as the Saga Press (Saga, near Kyoto, being the village in which Soan lived). The precise roles played by these two men is unclear, but Kōetsu (1558–1637) was one of the most famous painters and calligraphers of his day and he seems to have been the moving spirit behind the beautiful design of the *Saga-bon* editions, whereas Soan (1571–1632) worked on the actual printing of them. The *Saga-bon* editions occupy a special place in the history of Japanese literature as well as printing, for they form the first concerted attempt to produce a collection of Japanese literary works in printed form, and some examples provide the first instances of printed, illustrated literary classics (Pl. 21). The illustrations, which will be discussed in more detail later, are not especially distinguished in any way, but were influential in the development of Japanese book illustration. Aside from the illustrations, the *Saga-bon* are works of great beauty. Kōetsu personally

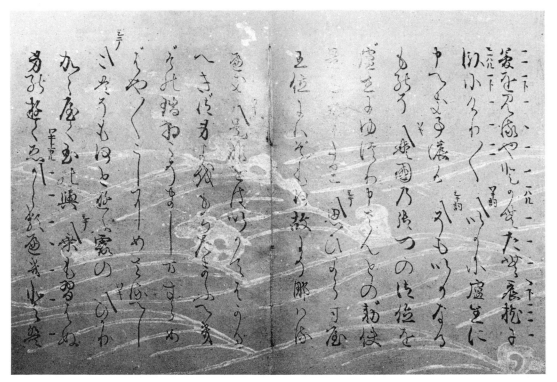

21.   The text of a *Kōetsu-bon* edition of the *nō* play *Kantan*. The calligraphy was printed directly onto the background pattern, which was block-printed with mica.

designed the typefaces used in some of them so that in effect they represent his own handwriting in printed form. Some authorities even categorize these books separately as *Kōetsu-bon*. As far as can be deduced, the *Saga-bon* editions were not meant for sale but were designed as gifts for the friends of Kōetsu and Soan and a lot of thought went into their production. In addition to the typefaces, Kōetsu created special paper of the *gampi* variety with different colors so that the first page might be pink, the next white, the next green, and so on. To complete this pleasing effect, Kōetsu used stenciled mica patterns in thirty-six designs, ranging from bamboo, cherry blossoms and wistaria, to birds, insects and animals.

Of the thirteen *Saga-bon* (some authorities have expanded the number to as many as twenty), easily the most important was the first, the *Ise monogatari*. This was printed in 1608, and by 1610 it had been reprinted eight times, some later printings being almost identical to the first (suggesting that the same typeface was used with very minor alterations), while others differed quite considerably. The *Ise monogatari* was an important literary work and in considerable demand, but this cannot be the only reason for so many printings of it, and no other *Saga-bon* went through so many editions. One reason may be that with the very first *Saga-bon*, Kōetsu and Soan were both striving for perfection and were not entirely satisfied until they felt no further improvement could be made. As most of the *Saga-bon* went through more than one edition and as very few of them have dates printed on them, their chronology is rather difficult to establish. Most of the work was done in the latter part of the Keichō era during the years 1608 and 1615, but some productions were certainly completed in the Genna era (1615–24). Apart from the *Ise monogatari*, the complete list of *Saga-bon* includes: *Ise monogatari ketsugishō* (1609); *Genji kokagami* (1610); *Hōjōki* (1610); *Senjūshō*; *Tsurezure-gusa*; *Kanzeryū utaiban*; *Kusemai sanjū kyokuhon*; *Kusemai sanjūroku kyokuhon*; *Shin kokin wakashū* (part only); *Hyakunin isshu*; *Sanjū-rokka-sen*; and *Nijūshi-kō*.

Apart from these various categorized forms of movable type printing, many literary works began to appear in print, both in movable type and in block form, after 1624. Unfortunately, as there is seldom any evidence to suggest exactly when and where such works were printed, it is possible only to mention some of their characteristics. Literary works such as the *Taiheiki* and the *Ise monogatari* were written long before they were printed and thus there existed several manuscript versions of them (this applies to all the Japanese literary classics). Therefore, there was a tendency on the part of the emerging commercial publishers to print each variant manuscript, which is why so many different printings of the same work are recorded. Eventually, one came to be accepted as the principal version and this was reprinted in much greater numbers. This is equally true of movable type and block-printed editions, and the term usually applied to these "standard" texts is *rufu-bon*. Every Japanese classic, as time went by, acquired its own *rufu-bon* edition which served as a model for subsequent editions.

All early *kokatsuji-ban* were printed versions of texts, both Chinese and Japanese, which had been in existence for a long time, but by 1624, with the era of the commercial publishers dawning, it became common for works to be written specially for publication, though it is rare to find an identifying publisher's mark or name. Naturally between 1596 and 1644, there was also a considerable development in typefaces. The earliest works, such as the *choku-han* editions, were Chinese texts which did not incorporate either *hiragana* or *katakana*, and thus it was possible to use the large and pleasing *kaisho* (the "printed" or square form of a character) faces embodying the finest Chinese calligraphic styles. However, with the increasing production of works written with the *kana* systems, it was essential to originate a completely different typeface that reflected the calligraphy of the original manuscript. This resulted in a typeface representing *sōsho* (a cursive form of writing where characters and *kana* were linked together), which led to the use of "linked type," where one piece of type represented two or more connected *kana* symbols— a technique used in virtually all movable type printing of native works in the early Edo period.

So much progress was made with movable type that it comes as a surprise to find that its use almost disappears after 1650 and there is a complete return to traditional block printing. The basic reason for this was economic: new type was considerably more expensive to produce than blocks. It is true that once a type has been founded it can be used again for reprinting the same work or for an entirely new work, an advantage not possessed by block printing, but too heavy a demand for a particular work

22. A portrait of the emperor of Han China, Wen-ti (r. 179–157 B.C.), from the first Japanese movable type edition of the Chinese work *Kunshin zuzō* (c. 1605–10), one of the earliest movable type books to contain illustrations.

meant that all the available type had to be used. This meant that if more than one work was required at the same time, more type had to be manufactured, a costly and time-consuming process in an age where there was no mechanized means of manufacturing type. This situation arose so frequently that commercial publishers were forced to return to the more economical block-printing techniques. It is hard to believe, but true, that movable type was a victim of its own success. (The few movable type editions printed in the eighteenth and nineteenth centuries were all produced under direct control of the central feudal government or the provincial daimyo and consisted only of Chinese Confucian texts.)

The chief significance of the short-lived movable type boom is that it stimulated the growth of a publishing industry, if that is not too positive a word for a process with three centuries of development to undergo before achieving its present status. It is not possible to guess the number of publishers in existence by 1650, but they were certainly one- or two-man concerns with a limited output. Block printing was still in use during the period when movable type gained ascendency and very soon it triumphed over the latter, since block printing in commercial hands became vastly different from what it had previously been. Under the rule of the Tokugawa, society was slowly changing as cities developed and a new way of life was being ushered in. During the next two centuries, while Japan remained closed to the outside world, printing was to play an important role in the changing society as a means of disseminating information and providing entertainment. By the time movable type had ceased to be used, it had given a new direction to printing, but the wheel was to come full circle at the end of the nineteenth century when movable type completely supplanted block printing. The intervening two hundred years was a golden age of Japanese printing, and it was between 1650 and 1850 that most of the books so much admired today as masterpieces of the printer's art were produced.

5 | PUBLISHING IN THE EDO PERIOD

If one had to sum up printing in Japan up to 1590, it might well be said that printing was an activity undertaken by Buddhist monks for Buddhist monks, with the main research problems lying in what was printed and when and where it was printed. In the Edo period (1603–1868), the situation is much more complex, for printing and publishing became almost totally commercial in nature. In addition to the obvious questions of what was published, when and where, it is necessary to inquire who did the printing as well as who it was meant for. In other words, Edo-period printing and publishing has to be seen against the social and economic background of the times. (Incidentally, it was during this epoch that publishers came into close and often unfavorable contact with the law for the first time.) Of the thousands of books produced then, the most important illustrated ones will be discussed in the next chapters, while the present chapter will examine the background of the publishing industry at that time.

Even allowing for the growth of commercial publishing, it is surprising that Buddhist printing underwent such rapid decline after 1650. The probable reasons for this were threefold: under Tokugawa rule Buddhism became doctrinally stagnant; Buddhist temples were severely impoverished during the civil wars of the sixteenth and seventeenth centuries; and Tokugawa propagation of Confucianism did not encourage a Buddhist revival.

Tokugawa Ieyasu (1542–1616), founder of the Tokugawa family which ruled Japan from 1603, came to power as a result of his victory at the battle of Sekigahara in 1600. In the preceding three centuries, the Japanese had been involved in a series of intermittent but often protracted civil wars, and so when Ieyasu took over the reins of government, he devoted much of his effort to ensure peace and to allow internal commerce to develop. To accomplish this end, firm administrative control was necessary, and successions of shoguns produced a multitude of laws regulating the lives of the Japanese, thus giving Tokugawa rule an essentially legalistic flavor. Society was rigidly divided into four classes, with the samurai warrior class at the top, excluding the emperor and those in power, followed by the peasant on whose produce rested the wealth of the country, then the artisan who worked with his own hands and lastly the merchant and tradesman, who were regarded as unproductive. Three of these classes were involved in the process of book production: the samurai, usually as author or illustrator; the artisan who served as block cutter; and the merchant who was the publisher.

AUTHORS AND ILLUSTRATORS

In general before 1600, the only people who wrote books that were ever printed were the Buddhist monks. Works of literature were written by both monks and laymen, but, as we have already seen, these were not printed and remained for centuries in manuscript form. In the seventeenth century, however, although monks still wrote books both of a religious and literary nature, which often continued to be printed in temples if the work was religious, non-Buddhist books were being printed for the first time by commercial publishers. They brought out editions of nearly all the classical novels and poetry anthologies which had been written during the Nara, Heian, Kamakura and Muromachi periods. Also, for the first time, works of a non-Buddhist nature were printed almost immediately after they were written, thus giving rise to a new literary class. Just as authorship of Buddhist texts before the Edo period had been the monopoly of the monks, so authorship of literary works became the virtual monopoly of the court nobility (although here monks were also prominent, being often related to the nobility). After the Kamakura period, members of the emerging samurai class also wrote books, but more often they acted as patrons rather than authors.

In the Edo period, however, the authors of literary works came predominately from the samurai class. The nobility continued to engage in writing, particularly *waka* poetry, always an aristocratic domain, but it is hard to think of a single great name in seventeenth-century literature who was not of samurai origin. The notable exception was Ihara Saikaku, who was not a member of the nobility but came from a rich Osaka merchant family. Other *chōnin* (since merchants and artisans tended to live in the larger cities, they were collectively known as "townsmen") authors emerged in the eighteenth and nineteenth centuries, but authorship remained very much the preserve of the samurai.

When one talks of literature in the Edo period, it is fiction which demands the most immediate consideration. The different genres of fiction—*kana-zōshi, ukiyo-zōshi, kokkei-bon, yomi-hon, aka-hon, ao-hon, kuro-hon, kibyōshi, gōkan-mono,* etc.—were numerous, although less varied in nature that the number of categories suggests. *Ukiyo-zōshi* and *yomi-hon* usually contained a great deal of text and were meant for the literate class, while *kuro-hon* and *kibyōshi,* catering to the semiliterate and to children, consisted mainly of pictures. The leading authors, such as Kyokutei Bakin (1767–1848), Jippensha Ikku (1765–1831) and Ryūtei Tanehiko (1783–1842) in the fields of *yomi-hon, kokkei-bon* and *gōkan-mono* respectively, were of samurai origins, although there was also a leavening of *chōnin* authors. In poetry and drama the situation was largely the same. The Edo period also gave rise to three new genres of poetry—*haiku, senryū* and *kyōka*—and to two new forms of drama—*jōruri* and *kabuki.* Matsuo Bashō (1644–94),

23.   This anonymous illustration of rice harvesting is an example of Edo-period printing, from the first volume of Miyazaki
Yasusada's encyclopedia of agriculture, *Nōgyō zensho* (1697).

the most famous *haiku* poet of the Edo period, and Chikamatsu Monzaemon (1653–
1724), the famous dramatist, both came from samurai stock.

Edo-period authors were active in all fields of writing aside from the purely literary.
Books were being produced on all kinds of subjects, from Chinese philosophy, military
strategy and weaponry, to science, particularly botany and medicine, and agriculture
(Pl. 23), and in these the predominance of the samurai was even more complete.

This range of works naturally gave artists more scope in illustration than ever before,
and it is to this very diversity that Japanese illustration in Edo times owes much of
its excellence. By and large, the social background of artists corresponds closely to
that of the authors, although many also came from aristocratic and *chōnin* origins,
according to the school of painting they belonged to. This topic, however, is related to
the development of ukiyo-e, and its treatment will be left to a later chapter.

THE PUBLISHER

In a discussion of publishers in the Edo period, it seems best to begin with some statistics. The most complete list of Japanese publishers in the Edo period, although it contains no more than 75 percent of the whole, is still Inoue Kazuo's *Keichō irai shoka shūran* (*see* Bibl.) published in Kyoto in 1916. Inoue lists some 1,181 individual publishers active between the Keichō era (1596–1615) and the Meiji Restoration (1868), of whom 506 were located in Kyoto, 375 in Edo (present-day Tokyo), 248 in Osaka and 52 in locations unknown or outside these cities. The other publishing cities were Nagoya, Nagasaki, Hiroshima and Ise, although their total contribution was minimal apart from the Nagoya publisher Eirakuya Tōshirō, whose books include several of Hokusai's sketchbooks. A few books were also published in Wakayama and Kanazawa, but not sufficient to justify considering them as publishing centers.

In view of the fact that Edo was the *de facto* capital of Japan throughout this period, it is surprising to find more publishers in Kyoto, but it must be remembered that Edo did not become a publishing city until the late seventeenth century (nothing at all was printed in Edo until the *Daizō-kyō* of 1637–48) and did not begin to rival Kyoto until the mid-eighteenth century. A more accurate guide to the periodization of publishing activity can be gained by analyzing the contents of Suga Chikuho's *Kyōka shomoku shūsei* (*see* Bibl.), published in 1936. This work chronologically lists all *kyōka* (comic poetry) books published in the Edo period, and although *kyōka* is a relatively minor genre associated principally with pleasure-quarter society in Edo, the number of such works printed reflects the rapid development of publishing in the city.

Between 1624 and 1700, 29 *kyōka* books were published in all (Suga's work is also not more than 75 percent complete): 6 in Kyoto, 3 in Edo, 4 Osaka and 16 in cities unknown but probably mostly in Kyoto. Between 1700 and 1750, 40 *kyōka* books were published: 7 in Kyoto, 5 in Edo, 23 in Osaka, 1 in Nagoya, 1 in Ise and 3 unknown. Between 1750 and 1850, however, 960 *kyōka* books were published: 77 in Kyoto, 569 in Edo, 181 in Osaka, with the remaining 133 in cities unknown. One obvious deduction from these figures is that *kyōka* was a great deal more popular in Edo, and to a lesser extent, Osaka, than it was in Kyoto, and it would be difficult to find another publishing field which Edo so dominated. Up to about 1720, Kyoto was unquestionably the leading publishing city in Japan; between 1720 and 1770, Kyoto shared the honor with Osaka; and from 1770 until the present day, Edo took over as the first publishing city in Japan. Kyoto's earlier dominance in the field is easily explained, since Edo and Osaka were only developing towns in 1603, whereas Kyoto was still the home of the emperor and the nobility, with the most influential and wealthy temples situated in or near it. Moreover, it had been the historical center of printing in Japan since the end of the Kamakura period in 1333.

The whole atmosphere of Kyoto printing in the seventeenth century was colored by a tradition which one would expect from this combination of circumstances. It was in

Kyoto that almost all the classical works of literature were printed for the first time. As one might also expect, the seventeenth century was certainly the most prolific age for this kind of printing and publishing, which in a sense was akin to clearing up a backlog of several centuries. Curiously, famous literary works were generally only printed in full during the seventeenth century, and in the subsequent two hundred years many of them were produced in abridged forms, allowing illustrators of the day to display their art. Whenever they were printed in full the publishers almost invariably can be traced to Kyoto. In contrast, Osaka and Edo were much less traditional and entirely different in character. Both developed into bustling commercial centers, with Edo possessing additional importance as the capital. Both these cities were the home of ukiyo-e and they provided audiences with a parallel taste in reading matter, largely different from that of Kyoto audiences.

Little is known about publishers of the Edo period as individuals. More information exists, however, on their methods of doing business and their relation to each other in a commercial sense, as well as their standing with the law. From this fragmentary knowledge it is possible to piece together some information about them, and to make deductions about how books got into print and who their audiences were.

Socially, the publisher belonged to the merchant class, and because of this, was barred by the authorities from any role in government. However, since he was usually wealthy and was connected with books, a prized commodity among all classes, the publisher's role in society, though technically similar to a fishmonger's, was not quite so lowly as this might suggest. Generally, publishers left little information about themselves, and neither were they sufficiently important in the Edo-period hierarchy to be written about, although occasional mention of them is made by authors, such as Takizawa Bakin, in their memoirs.

One significant source of information concerning publishers of the Edo period comes from their books, especially from the colophons, *okugaki*, which literally means "written at the back," since the last page was the usual place for the colophon. Colophons were used fairly regularly in the seventeenth century, and became customary in the eighteenth and nineteenth centuries. The first colophons that appeared were rather simple, stating no more than the date of publication and the publisher's location, occasionally giving just the city and sometimes a precise address. As the publishing organization became more complex, colophons, too, began to carry more information, but more of this will be said later.

From the colophons, the following deductions can be made about Edo-period publishers. Firstly, publishing was clearly a hazardous business, for it was unusual for a publisher set up in, say, 1660 to be still operating in 1860. The usual lifespan of publishing houses was frequently less than fifty years. Death or unwise gambles or specializing in books that relied too much on vogue (Edo-period consumers could be exceedingly fickle) accounted for a great proportion of failures. Secondly, publishing houses were almost always small family concerns passed on from father to son, either real or adopted. Outstanding examples of this practice are the Izumiya publishing firm of Edo and Osaka (with a branch in Kyoto), and the Kawachiya firm, mainly of Osaka. Thirdly, publishing businesses were generally conveniently located within a city, for instance near a temple or shrine, where a large number of pilgrims might pass by. There were itinerant book peddlers who journeyed through the country selling books, and primitive traveling libraries, but by and large the publisher was responsible both for producing and selling his own wares. Thus, it was also common to find publishers established in the Yoshiwara district, where once again there was plenty of guaranteed custom. Such areas, incidentally, were also common meeting places for authors and artists.

As a businessman, the publisher's prime decision about what books to print was dictated by commercial considerations. In earlier periods this had never been a question of importance, but now the publisher had to know his clients and to cater to their tastes. Naturally, an increasing population created a wider market, and there is no doubt that improved education and literacy in the Edo period also led to a demand for more books.

24. A glimpse of the business boom in Edo. Townsmen throng to a papermaking shop selling fans, lanterns and color prints (*nishiki*), from the *Dainihon bussan-zue* (1877), illustrated by Hiroshige III.

Basically the boom in the publishing industry stemmed from the new kind of society which emerged under Tokugawa rule. The merchant class prospered, and denied of any participation in government by the authorities, tended to spend its money on amusements of one kind or another. At the same time, prolonged peace meant that many samurai were out of work and turned to the various arts, both as contributors and as readers and spectators. Publishing was also encouraged by the immense popularity of *kabuki*, which created a demand for portraits and books of favorite actors. Interests such as these, once kindled, only increased, and enormous demand arose for all types of written works designed to entertain rather than to inform. Even those who could not read wanted books with pictures in them, such as *kuro-hon* and *kibyōshi* and other such genres that were initiated then. (These were equivalent to comic books and dime novels, designed as ephemera, although many possessed more enduring qualities.)

The audience for books, however, was not only confined to *chōnin* in search of cheap entertainment, for books covering most fields of human endeavor were also being produced. Since an audience existed for any kind of reading matter from Chinese philosophy to cheap fiction, publishers were equally flexible in their approach. Some chose to publish books on a variety of subjects while others preferred to concentrate on specific fields such as *kyōka* poetry. Almost invariably, publishers in the latter category had a shorter lifespan than publishers such as the Kashiwaraya house of Osaka, which produced books on all sorts of subjects, including cartography, and which prospered and endured.

How publishers came by their material is not so clear. Most likely such matters were arranged on the basis of personal acquaintance and letters of recommendation in accordance with traditional social behavior. The publishing circle was demonstrably limited and everyone in the business knew everyone else. The late eighteenth-century publisher of *kyōka* books Tsutaya Jūsaburō even kept authors such as Santō Kyōden and artists such as Utamaro as members of his own household. In return for their keep they were expected to help with the printing, done at the publisher's own premises, and thus it is not surprising that Tsutaya (Pl. 25) published many of their books. This arrangement was not an isolated phenomenon, but, for all that, writers of Edo-period Japan were not particularly loyal to one publisher.

The relationship between the government and the publisher was virtually non-existent before the Edo period, and the only interest in publishing taken by the authorities was from the viewpoint of patronage. Prominent members of the feudal authorities would finance the printing of some particular work either out of interest or, in the Buddhist context, to gain merit for themselves and their families. However, when the Tokugawa family came to power, they sought to keep potential enemies powerless, and and a very elaborate system of legal controls was imposed on the people, particularly on the feudal nobility, who were forced to spend parts of every year in Edo. Publishing was also regarded as a vehicle for potential sedition, and before long the shogunate began to look for means to control the publishers' activities, even though there was

85

little to suggest that they were engaged in anything remotely seditious. (In fact, authors, artists and publishers catered to the *chōnin*, who were distinguished by their lack of interest in political affairs, although it is impossible to say whether this would still have been true had the Tokugawa regime pursued a different policy.) At the same time as the publishers developed their businesses, they became more anxious to protect their interests against competitors, and sought ways of controlling their own industry.

The first move of the authorities had no direct bearing on publishing, except inasmuch as it was a portent of things to come. Concerned about the potential undermining influence of Christian doctrine on the security of the state, the Bakufu, as the govern-

25.   Kōshodō, the publishing house of Tsutaya Jūsaburō, from the *Ehon azuma asobi* (1799), illustrated by Hokusai. The figure on the extreme left is believed by some to be Tsutaya himself.

ment was known, issued a ban on the import of all books in 1630. The intention was to eliminate Christian material, but the ban also extended to books printed in China, regardless of the contents. Non-Christian material continued to reach Japan, however, though the ban on Christian books seems to have been effective. At this time there was no commercial publishing in the country on any scale, so it is doubtful that the ban caused much disquiet to the publishers, but the next step taken by the authorities made a stronger impression.

This law, enforced in 1673, required any work to be published to be examined for seditious content. By further decrees and amendments in 1682, 1688 and 1711, the Bakufu strengthened its control on the publishing industry. In 1694, it went even further by permitting only certain, specified publishers to produce books. Hitherto, anyone with an appropriate license from the authorities could publish (although groups of publishers formed into guilds known as *honya nakama* in the late seventeenth century for the mutual protection of interests), but on investigation, of the 28 people engaged in publishing in Edo then, only 7 were actually operating under license. This is a clear indication that existing regulations were not being rigidly enforced, and the number of books actually banned by the Bakufu was very small at this time.

All the regulations imposed on publishing up to 1720 only skirted the problem, and it was left to Shogun Tokugawa Yoshimune (1684–1751) to issue a code of practices which took in previous measures and laid down the basis of a law on publishing for the remainder of the Edo period. Between 1720 and 1722, he repealed the 1630 ban on imported books, although Christian literature was still prohibited; he banned all books proffering political opinions that diverged from establishment views; he banned all pornography; and finally he demanded that all printed books should bear a clear statement of the author and publisher responsible. These regulations varied in the degree to which they were enforced, and after the 1840s, the disintegration of the Bakufu itself was accompanied by an almost total collapse of these controls. In general, the ban on politically seditious works and those concerning the Tokugawa family were the most rigorously enforced. For example, in the early nineteenth century, the famous *yomi-hon* novel *Ehon taikōki* (a pictorial biography of Toyotomi Hideyoshi) was suppressed because it dealt with the period leading up to Tokugawa Ieyasu's seizure of power. The ban on pornography was not rigidly enforced, since, as in modern society, the definition of what was "pornographic" was so vague that only the grossest examples were censored. The demand for a clear statement of author and publisher on all printed books was designed so that the Tokugawa could "know their enemies," but by the time the regulation came into force it was common practice for books to carry either the name of the author or that of the publisher (and, more often than not, both). To all intents, this rule was not strictly enforced in cases where the contents of a book were not objectionable, and even after 1720, quite a number of books appeared in print without the name of the publisher and particularly without the name of the author. At any rate after 1722, the publisher must have had a good idea where he stood in relation to the government, and experience subsequently taught him what was safe to publish.

The publisher's relationship with his fellow publishers was similarly complicated, especially in view of the Bakufu's interest in what went on. As licenses were necessary for publishers to stay in business, there was, from quite early on, some cooperation among license holders to keep out competitors. Consequently, by the end of the seventeenth century, there were publishers' associations (known also as *shorin nakama* and *jihondoiya no nakama*) loosely equivalent to guilds, in the three major publishing cities. These associations sought to protect members' interests and to cooperate with one another, despite repeated government interference—in 1840–41 the Bakufu abolished the *nakama* only to reestablish them in 1851, with the proviso that they were compelled to take any new publisher into their ranks.

One of the earliest problems with which the *nakama* had to deal was that of copyright. In 1698, an Osaka *nakama* complained to the authorities that their most successful publications were being pirated by outside publishers and asked for a law of copyright. The Osaka publishers were granted their request, and henceforth, it became, in theory at least, illegal for works to be reprinted without receiving permission from the original publisher. This ruling, however, applied only to Osaka and it was not until 1721 that it was applied to Edo. From the first half of the eighteenth century, one begins to see books with words equivalent to "not to be reprinted without permission," on the title page, but such examples are rare. This primitive copyright law served only to protect the publisher and there was nothing resembling a copyright for authors until 1844, which was also ineffective.

Cooperation in publishing is a different and less clear situation. Until about 1680, in general, only a single publisher's name appeared on the colophon, suggesting that publishers worked alone. Occasionally, when two names appeared, they were invariably from the same city of origin, suggesting some effort at cooperation, such as sharing the expenses of production. This state of affairs continued through the first half of the eighteenth century, but just before 1750, and reflecting some of the effects of the Yoshimune decrees, colophons began to become more complex. From the late eighteenth century until 1868 and shortly after, a colophon often mentioned as many as a dozen publishers grouped according to their city of origin. To take a hypothetical colophon, the right side of the page might give the names of four Edo publishers, followed by the names of four Osaka publishers in the center and those of four Kyoto publishers on the left. Invariably, when this occurs, the book is a "best seller" and not a first edition.

What appears to have happened was this. The original publisher from Edo had the blocks carved for the work, and he would then enter into arrangements with fellow publishers in the same city or members of the same *nakama* to produce the book under joint imprint, sharing the costs of production and the ensuing profits. If the book proved successful, a similar arrangement was entered into with groups of publishers in Kyoto and Osaka so they could bring the book out under their imprint. New blocks were not carved each time this situation arose, nor were the original blocks transported to the publishing group in Kyoto or Osaka, but an order was placed with the first Edo publisher for a specific number of copies. Thus, in the case of the hypothetical colophon, of the four Edo publishers whose names appear on the right, the one on the extreme right is the original publisher and the other three are associate publishers. Of the four publishers' names from Kyoto on the left, the one on the extreme left is the one who placed the order for copies with the original Edo publisher and the other three are his associates. In other words, the book was printed in Edo but sold in Kyoto. In a book where the colophon is identical except with the Osaka publishers on the extreme left and the Kyoto publishers in the center, then that copy was printed in Edo but sold in Osaka. Therefore, the position of the publisher whose name appears on the extreme left is that of distributor, never producer, although this only applies to books with colophons giving the names of publishing groups from three or four cities (occasionally two). In the case of a colophon giving only two publishers' names from the same city, then the one on the left is the original publisher, except where the word *gōkan* or its equivalent appears beneath, indicating joint responsibility.

There is some reason to believe that on occasion in the nineteenth century this process occurred simultaneously, and a book was brought out in three cities at the same time under the names of various publishers, no doubt when they were sure the book was going to be a success. It was also common practice, as in the past, for publishers to store the blocks and use them again when more copies of the book were needed. Sometimes, blocks were stored away for as long as a century, with the result that later impressions are extremely poor in quality. For this reason it is possible to have a book published in 1750, according to the colophon, but actually printed in 1850. This explains why there have been so many inaccurate datings of Japanese books by Westerners.

Not all publishing in the Edo period was operated commercially. In 1799, following the government's reorganization and standardization of the educational system, the Bakufu began to have copies of Chinese texts printed for use as textbooks in the Shōheizaka Gakumonjo (Bakufu schools) throughout Japan. Between 1799, when editions of the *Shisho* and *Shōgaku* were published, and 1867, more than two hundred titles were printed, all of them Chinese works. These are known as *kanpan* or "government editions," but they are more important to historians of society and education than to the historian of the printed book.

ENGRAVING, PRINTING AND BINDING

So far in this chapter the terms "printing" and "publishing" have been used interchangeably, as if their meanings were identical. Early in the Meiji period (1868–1912), colophons invariably indicate publisher and printer as separate entities when Western movable type was reintroduced and editions were larger to satisfy a wider public. All this demanded the establishment of separate printing firms. However, before 1868, the situation was very different, and only occasionally would a book printed in the Edo period (usually a work of quality illustration produced for connoisseurs) specifically mention an individual responsible for "printing" as opposed to engraving. In general, the production of a book, from the organization of the manuscript to the engraving, printing, binding and retailing was the sole responsibility of the publisher and was carried out on his premises. The exact relationship to the publisher of those individuals who did this work, however, remains uncertain.

Of these people, the one who played the most important role in publishing was undoubtedly the engraver, a frequent subject of eighteenth- and nineteenth-century illustrators depicting crafts in Japan. However, in Edo-period publications, it is the exception rather than the rule for the engraver's name to be specifically mentioned, indicating that the engraver, like the other employees of the publisher, was not considered important enough to be given special mention. Engravers occasionally worked on a freelance basis, being hired by a publisher for a specific job, but more normally were part of the publisher's work force. However, it is not clear why the engraver's name was mentioned in the colophon on some occasions. We can assume that the artisans involved in such cases were the masters of their craft and received not only payment but also credit for their work. Examples of well-known engravers of the Edo period are the Egawa of Edo, Fujimura Zen'emon of Osaka, Inoue Jihei of Kyoto and the Higuchi house of Kyoto. It is interesting to note that some publishers, such as Nishimuraya Yohachi and Yamadaya Sanshirō, were engravers themselves.

The printing and the binding were carried out by members of the publisher's staff, and on occasion the binding was "subcontracted" to women living in the neighborhood. The usual number of copies printed of a typical *yomi-hon* work with text and illustration would run around three hundred, either because this number was usually sufficient or because the blocks became too worn after this. In works of pure illustration, such wear was probably noticeable after fewer impressions, although the number of works in existence printed on worn-out blocks indicates that the publisher was not unduly concerned about such matters.

This, very briefly, gives an outline of publishing as it developed throughout the Edo period. From this basis it is possible to proceed to a more detailed discussion of some of the most outstanding examples of book illustration in this period, which are masterpieces in the history of the printed book in Japan.

PART TWO

THE HISTORY OF
PRINTED BOOK ILLUSTRATION

6 | EARLY BUDDHIST ILLUSTRATION

Considering the overwhelming contribution of Buddhism to Japanese art and civilization as a whole, the manifestation of that contribution in the field of printed book illustration is surprisingly small. It is true that in the seventeenth, eighteenth and nineteenth centuries many fine books with Buddhist illustrations were produced, but in all these cases the artists responsible were secular, without any connection with the temples. During the period from 764 to 1590, when printing and printed illustration were entirely in the hands of the monks, very few printed book illustrations were published. In the few published examples, the works were almost always copied from Chinese printed illustrations. If one ignores what might have been printed but has since been lost and the fact that the same illustration was reproduced in different books, it is probable that in almost nine hundred years of Buddhist domination of printing in Japan, less than one hundred books with printed illustrations were produced.

The idea of illustrating Buddhist texts originated in the T'ang dynasty (618–906), when both hand-painted and printed illustrated texts are known to have been attempted in China. This is borne out by the fine printed illustration which is the frontispiece of the 868 edition of the *Diamond Sutra* discovered at Tun-huang. It is a fair assumption that this illustration was by no means unique in its quality and complexity, and in itself attests to a sophistication of technique that must have developed over a long period. It is also fair to assume that Japanese monks, such as Kūkai and Saichō, who spent long periods of study in China at the beginning of the ninth century, must have seen some similar examples and might even have brought some back, although none have survived. The existence of the Nara-period manuscript of the *E-inga-kyō*, already cited, is additional evidence that from early on the Japanese were aware of the possibility of illustrating Buddhist texts. A considerable number of printed works, both religious and secular, were also produced by the Chinese during the Sung dynasty (960–1279), and many of these found their way to Japan during the course of the Kamakura (1185–1333) and the Muromachi (1336–1573) periods. Nevertheless, there is little evidence that Japanese monks wanted to illustrate their texts themselves, and where this was done, the illustrations were copies of Chinese exemplars.

There are three main reasons for this. First, even after printing became fairly widespread during the Kamakura period, the conviction that more merit could be acquired from copying texts by hand still persisted. Often a great deal of time was spent on beautifying the manuscript by careful calligraphy, the application of gold and silver leaf and occasionally painting the illustrations for it. Printed texts, on the other hand, were regarded as more utilitarian, and thus illustrations were considered unnecessary adornments. Second, there was the question of expense. The *Diamond Sutra* with its complex printed frontispiece was produced as a result of private patronage and devotion, for in China as in Japan, examples of printed Buddhist texts with illustrations are the exception rather than the rule. Works for general monastic use were usually unaccompanied by illustrations. Third, illustrations were provided in the text for the following reasons: functional, where they served to illustrate the text more clearly; devotional, where a religious object was depicted for venerative purposes; and very occasionally, purely decorative, although this was a very minor aim of Buddhist monks. In Japan, the earliest sects were not concerned with spreading doctrine to the masses. They needed texts, written and printed, for their own use and illustration was superfluous as the monks were capable of reading the texts themselves. Later, with the rise of other, more popular sects concerned with reaching the people, illustration came to play a functional role in the work, although of the pre-1590 printed illustrated books that have survived, more were intended for devotional purposes than for functional purposes.

The earliest form of printed illustration used in books was the *imbutsu* or "stamped Buddha." These were impressions, usually not more than three or four inches high, of various Buddhas and bodhisattvas on paper or cloth, made with a seal or stamp (Pl. 26). Similar images were obtained through the use of a wood block and ink, over which paper was applied with a *baren*. The result was known as *suributsu* or "printed Buddha." Amida, Yakushi and Kannon were among the most common deities represented in this way. Images similar to this were discovered by Stein at Tun-huang, some believed to date from the beginning of the eighth century, leaving no doubt that *imbutsu* were of Chinese origin.

The primary purpose for making *imbutsu*, as in the case of the *Hyakumantō darani* and the practice of *shakyō*, was to gain merit. Consequently, they were usually stamped in large numbers on sheets or rolls of paper, with the implication that the more *imbutsu* produced, the greater the merit acquired. The production of *imbutsu* was also a source of revenue for the temples, especially during the Kamakura period when laymen were willing to pay monks to undertake this work for them. Frequently, these impressions on rolls of paper were stored in the hollow cavities of statues of the Buddha or bodhisattva represented, and thus many examples have survived in a comparatively good state. The dating of *imbutsu*, however, creates a problem, since the production technique remained unchanged and images were very similar to one another in style. On occasion, the engraver wrote down the date he finished a particular group or the purpose they were printed for, again accompanied by a date. References in Japanese

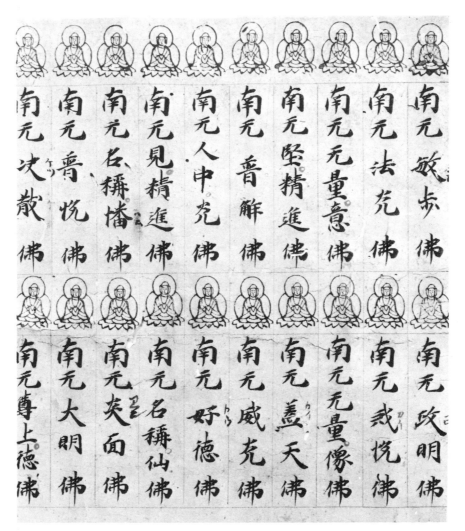

26. *Imbutsu* stamped above each appellation of the Buddha, from the *Three Thousand Names of the Buddha Sutra*, printed at Tōshōdai-ji, Nara, in the late Kamakura or early Muromachi period.

literary works and other sources indicate the possibility that *imbutsu* were produced in the Nara period, and the certainty that they were produced in the Heian period.

The earliest dated example to have survived is a collection of Bishamon-ten images made in 1162. Ishida Mosaku (*see* Bibl.) records additional dated examples of *imbutsu* and *intō* (impressions of pagodas made in the same way but much rarer) from the following years: 1170 (Kannon); 1175 (Bishamon-ten); 1194 (Amida); 1207 (Yakushi); 1212 (1,000 Buddhas); 1223 (Bishamon-ten); 1224 (Kannon); 1228 (Amida); 1232 (Dainichi); 1232 (Taizō-kai Mandara); 1239 (Jizō); 1239 (Amida); 1240 (Amida and Kannon); 1255 (pagodas); 1256 (Amida, Kannon and Jizō); 1275 (Amida); 1278 (Five Forces); 1278 (3,000 Buddhas); 1300 (Jizō); 1302 (Monju); 1319 (Kannon); 1336

(Jizō); 1338 (Kannon); 1372 (Monju); 1378 (Jizō); 1379 (Amida); 1386 (Aizen Myōō); 1387 (Jizō); and 1392 (Jizō). This list refers only to dated examples and extends to the end of the Nambokuchō period (1333–92), after which both *imbutsu* and *intō* became extremely rare.

If *imbutsu* and *intō* were only designed as decorations on paper and cloth, or if they had been printed on rolls of paper without text, they would have little significance in terms of printed book illustration. However, on rare occasions they were used in printed texts, both as illustrations and as integral parts of the text. Such usages were not only confined to Buddhist printed texts since they were also used in manuscripts. Of the two types of impressions, *intō* were used as integral parts of the text, for pagodas were stamped over the sheet of paper and a single character, printed or handwritten, was enclosed in each, as in the case of a fine undated manuscript of the *Hannya-shin-gyō* of the late Heian period, now in a private collection, where the characters were written in gold on blue paper, and each character was enclosed in a stamped pagoda of the *gorintō* (five-tiered) variety. Larger pagodas were sometimes stamped to enclose groups of four characters.

The use of *imbutsu* in printed texts is usually associated with works generically known as *Butsumyō-kyō*, or "Name of the Buddha Sutras," although such works were not sutras but collections of various appellations of the Buddha, which when recited in a spirit of penitence were believed to erase sin. Seven such texts are known, each bearing stamped Buddhas, with one usually situated at the top of each appellation. There were two types of *Butsumyō-kyō*, the "Thousand Name of the Buddha Sutra," and the "Three Thousand Name of the Buddha Sutra"; the former involved stamping one thousand Buddhas, and the latter three thousand. The most celebrated example of this is found in a manuscript *Butsumyō-kyō* of 1187, which contains one thousand images of Maitreya Buddha, but similar use of *imbutsu* in both printed and manuscript texts are known from the Kamakura period and later.

The use of *imbutsu* and *intō*, even when applied in the margins of texts, was intended for devotional, never artistic, purposes. The position of more orthodox illustrations, i.e., those designed to illustrate the text, remains less clear, however. From the beginning of the Kamakura period and perhaps before that, illustrations were certainly produced to accompany printed texts, usually as frontispieces and portraying a central incident from the work. Such illustrations were almost invariably copied from Chinese exemplars and contain no evidence of native artistic inspiration. However, they do have a certain interest. The remainder of this chapter is devoted to a chronological list with descriptions of such illustrations until the end of the sixteenth century. They are comparatively few in number and the selection is based on three main sources, supplemented by Japanese library catalogs and the author's own observations. The sources used are Kawase Kazuma's *Gozan-ban no kenkyū*, Ishida Mosaku's *Kodai hanga* and Louise Norton Brown's *Block Printing and Book Illustration in Japan* (less reliable than the former two).

THE HEIAN PERIOD (794–1160)

No printed illustrations specifically designed to accompany printed texts are known to have been produced in the Heian period, although this does not mean to say that there were none. However, L. N. Brown records that Kōshō-ji in Kyoto possesses a number of manuscripts each of which has, as a printed frontispiece, a representation of nine Buddhist statues. These were part of the prized collection of Sairaku-ji, and when this temple was destroyed by fire, the manuscripts survived and found their way to Kōshō-ji. It is quite clear from Brown's description that the illustrations were produced entirely separately from the books they accompany, had no relation to the text and were pasted on later. (This was quite normal, for frontispiece illustrations were always printed separately and then attached to the main text, but this does not affect the probability that such illustrations were specifically designed for a text.) The statement that no printed illustrations were specifically designed to accompany printed texts should be qualified by the fact that illustration blocks of the period have been found, which were possibly intended for this very purpose.

THE KAMAKURA PERIOD (1185–1333)

Shuryōgon-gyō (Daibutchō shuryōgon-gyō) (1239)
A printed version of this, the *Śūraṃgama-sūtra*, produced in ten *maki* at Chōraku-ji in Ueno province, contains the earliest known, fully authenticated example of a printed illustration specifically designed for a printed text. It is a frontispiece with Shakyamuni (the Historical Buddha) seated on a lotus throne with his disciple Ananda at his feet, accompanied by a woman of the lowest caste, a Mātaṅgi who, through her love for Ananda, came to revere the Buddha's teachings. This story is told in the sutra. The central figures are surrounded by various deities from the Buddhist pantheon, with one of the Four Guardian Kings in each corner. This illustration was taken from a T'ang or Sung Chinese exemplar.

Bussei biku rokumotsu-zu (1246)
This was first printed in Japan in one *detchō* volume at Senyū-ji in Kyoto, and is the first known Senyū-ji edition. It contains six illustrations all related to the text, which deals with the six possessions of a monk—the patched robe, the seven-piece stole, the five-piece inner garment, the begging bowl, the stool and the water-strainer. The representations of these objects are copied from a Sung exemplar.

Bommō-kyō (Bommō-kyō bosatsu kaihon) (1248)
Printed at Senyū-ji, a one-*maki* version of this, the *Brahmajāla-sūtra*, concerns Buddhist precepts and codes of conduct for bodhisattvas. There is a printed frontispiece of Shakyamuni on a lotus throne, expounding these rules to various bodhisattvas, and it is thought to have been copied from a Sung exemplar.

Bommō-kyō (*Bommō-kyō bosatsu kaihon*) (1267)
An illustration identical to the one in the 1248 edition was used in this two-*maki* version of the same text printed at Kennin-ji in Kyoto. Either there was some collaboration between the two temples, or this was the only appropriate illustration in Japan.

Daihannya-haramitta-kyō (*Daihannya-kyō*) (1279)
In six hundred *maki*, this, the *Mahāprajñāpāramitā-sūtra*, is one of the longest Buddhist scriptures, but despite its length was widely printed, often accompanied by a frontispiece. Its first appearance in Japan in printed form was in the famous *Karoku-ban* edition produced at Kōfuku-ji, Nara, between 1223 and 1227, which was not illustrated. There is a *Kasuga-ban* edition probably printed at Saidai-ji in 1279, of which only the 274th *maki* survives. This has a frontispiece showing Monju riding a lion, with which he is usually associated both in Chinese and Japanese representations. This illustration is of interest because it departs from the usual type of printed frontispiece, and is thought to have come from the suggestion of Abbot Eison, indicating that it might have been drawn by a Japanese monk. However, in view of the obvious Chinese style of the illustration, it was probably copied from a T'ang or Sung exemplar.

Dembō shōjūki (1287)
This Zen work was first produced at Ryōzan-ji in twelve *maki*. Unfortunately, although this work is believed to have carried illustrations, it only survives in one incomplete copy from which the illustrated section is missing. However, there is a Gozan edition of 1384, described below, which does have illustrations, almost certainly the same ones.

Engaku-kyō (Late 13th century)
A printed edition of this sutra produced at Tōdai-ji probably between 1278 and 1288 contains a single printed illustration of Ida-ten, or Skanda in Sanskrit, one of the eight generals under Virūḍhaka. He is a protector of the Buddhist faith, and this perhaps explains why his image always comes at the end of a printed book in both China and Japan, as if he were "watching over" the text.

Zengyō hōryō gimon (Late Kamakura period)
Kawase Kazuma in his work *Gozan-ban no kenkyū*, Volume 1, pp. 85 and 403, states that a one-*maki* edition of this Zen work produced in the late Kamakura period is notable for "an image of the Buddha" located in the middle section of the work, but he has been unable to examine this in detail.

Sanken itchi sho (1317)
L. N. Brown states on p. 15 of her work that a printed edition of this book on Buddhist, Confucian and Taoist teachings was produced in 1317 containing primitive illustrations of religious emblems and temple service utensils. Her view, however, is based on seeing a 1649 edition of the same work and we have been unable to find any evidence that the 1317 edition still exists.

THE NAMBOKUCHŌ PERIOD (1333–92)

Hokke-kyō (*Myōhō-renge-kyō*) (1365)

The edition of the *Lotus Sutra* printed in eight *maki* at Rinsen-ji in Kyoto contains a frontispiece at the beginning of each *maki* and other illustrations at the end of each *maki*. We have been unable to examine a copy of this work, but written descriptions indicate that the frontispieces are very similar to those contained in the edition of 1412 (*see* below). According to the description of the copy of the 1365 edition in the Ryūmon Bunko (the library of the late Sakamoto Yū), the end illustrations include depictions of the demonesses mentioned in the *Lotus Sutra*, together with other Buddhas and bodhisattvas. The illustrations are of Chinese origin.

Daihannya-haramitta-kyō (*Daihannya-kyō*) (1383)

An edition of this was produced at Kōfuku-ji, Nara, in 600 *maki*, each one bearing a handwritten date of 1383 (Eitoku 3), indicating that the work was printed either then or shortly before. Each *maki* has a large printed frontispiece depicting Hsüan-tsang, the most famous and prolific of Chinese monks who engaged in the translation of the Buddhist scriptures from Sanskrit, meeting the Buddha in order to receive the *Tripiṭaka*, or Buddhist canon. The Buddha, seated on a lotus throne is surrounded by various deities whom he commands to protect Hsüan-tsang on his journey back to China. This illustration was copied from a Sung Chinese exemplar (Pl. 27).

Bussetsu-daihō-bumo-onju-gyō (1383)

This is one of the most copiously illustrated of all early printed Buddhist works, and was produced at one of the Gozan temples in a one-volume *orihon* edition. It contains twenty illustrations, twelve full-page ones and eight of two-thirds page size. The sutra

27. The frontispiece of the 1383 edition of the *Daihannya-haramitta-kyō*, depicting the Chinese monk Hsüan-tsang receiving the *Tripiṭaka*. Printed at Kōfuku-ji, Nara.

is non-canonical, dealing with the obligations of children to their parents. The illustrations are divided into two categories, the first ten depicting the obligations and the final ten showing the punishments awaiting those who fail in their filial duties. The final illustration is a particularly graphic depiction of the Buddhist Hell, and it is believed that the illustrations were copied from a Korean exemplar (Pl. 28).

Dembō shōjūki (1384)

This work, first printed in twelve *maki* at Ryōzan-ji in 1287 (*see* above), was produced in a new *Gozan-ban* edition in 1384. It contains a large number of small illustrations interspersed with the text, depicting the thirty-three patriarchs of Zen. Once again it appears that these were copied from Sung exemplars.

Hokke-kyō onkun (1386)

This one-volume work related to the *Lotus Sutra* was probably printed as a result of samurai patronage and contains a half-page frontispiece showing a figure holding up a banner with the words "Myō hokke-kyō" on it. Ishida says that this figure, surrounded by Buddhist emblems, has no relation to the text, which was written by the monk Shinkū, and was included simply for decoration.

Daihannya-haramitta-kyō (Daihannya-kyō) (1391)

This edition of the sutra bears the same frontispiece illustration as does the 1383 edition cited above, and there are at least two undated editions of the Muromachi period with the same frontispiece. However, a difference of size each time the illustration was used indicates that new blocks were cut each time. Not surprisingly, therefore, there are differences in detail, particularly of headdresses, although the design in each case is the same.

Daihōkō Engaku shudara ryōgi-kyō (Engaku ryōgi-kyō) (c. 1390)

There is an edition of this work, probably printed at Tōdai-ji in the late Nambokuchō period (some authorities place it in the first decade of the Muromachi period), which contains a frontispiece with the Historical Buddha on a lotus throne under a canopy surrounded by eighteen bodhisattvas and other deities. Right at the end of the two-*maki* work is a depiction of Ida-ten.

Kunshin-koji (Bunrui gappeki zuzō kukai kunshin-koji) (late Nambokuchō period)

This interesting work is known in two *Gozan-ban* editions, one of two *maki* in two volumes and one of two *maki* in one volume. Kawase places both in the Nambokuchō period, although neither is dated, while other authorities, notably Ishida, place both editions in the early Muromachi period. This is a non-Buddhist Chinese work dealing with moral education and the illustrations are taken from Chinese history and legend. Two-thirds of each page is occupied by text, but at the top of each page is an illustration related to the text below. These illustrations, mostly figures, are simple in style and are believed to have been taken from Yüan models (Pl. 29).

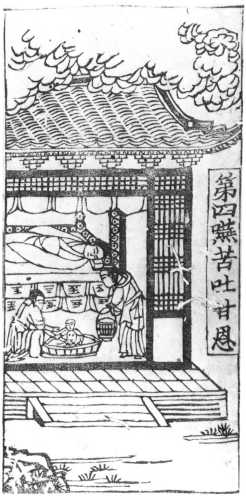

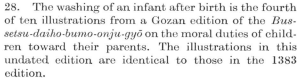

28.   The washing of an infant after birth is the fourth of ten illustrations from a Gozan edition of the *Bussetsu-daiho-bumo-onju-gyō* on the moral duties of children toward their parents. The illustrations in this undated edition are identical to those in the 1383 edition.

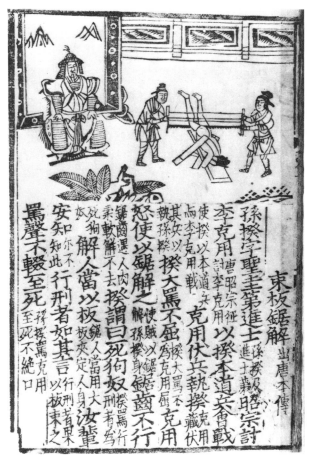

29.   A representative illustration by an unknown artist from a one-volume Gozan edition of the Chinese moral work *Kunshin-koji*, printed in the late fourteenth or early fifteenth century.

Kaihon taisō shigon zatsuji (late Nambokuchō period)

The surviving copy of this one-volume Gozan edition was destroyed in the Great Earthquake of 1923, but a facsimile edition produced shortly before shows it was designed as a textbook for children. It contains groups of four related objects (e.g., the sun, moon, stars, constellation), each accompanied by small illustrations which imitated a Chinese exemplar.

Ryōga-kyō (Late Nambokuchō period)

L. N. Brown records on p. 15 a ten-*maki* edition of this, the *Laṅkāvatāra-sūtra*, printed at Tenryū-ji in the *orihon* format. This has a frontispiece showing Buddha seated on a lotus throne, surrounded by various figures from the Buddhist pantheon. Brown, however, describes this as the *Ryōgon-gyō*, a confusion on her part since this is the name of the *Śuraṃgama-samādhi-sūtra*, although she clearly means the *Ryōga-kyō*.

THE MUROMACHI PERIOD (1392–1603)

By most reckonings the Muromachi period lasted until 1573, when it was followed by the Momoyama or Azuchi-Momoyama period until 1603, but for convenience the term Muromachi period is used to cover both.

Hokke-kyō (*Myōhō-renge-kyō*) (1412)

This edition of the *Lotus Sutra* was printed in eight *maki* at an unknown temple (at present it is in Tōshōdai-ji, Nara) at an unknown date. It does, however, bear a manuscript date of 1412, with an indication that it was sponsored by an unknown monk named Kenkaku. At the beginning of each *maki* is an illustration of a scene from the work, all of which have been reproduced both in *Kodai hanga* (*see* Bibl.) and Kabutogi Shōkō's studies of old printed editions of the *Hokke-kyō* in *Hokke hangyō no kenkyū* (*see* Bibl.). The illustrations were taken from Southern Sung exemplars.

Yakushi-hongan-kyō (*Yakushi-hongan kudoku-kyō*) (1412)

Ninna-ji, a temple of the Shingon sect in Kyoto, possesses a one-*maki* edition of this work which is prolifically illustrated and contains two frontispieces, one of Buddha expounding the Law and the other of scenes from the sutra, with numerous smaller illustrations. These include depictions of ten bodhisattvas and the twelve guardian spirits of Yakushi-nyorai.

Shusshō-amida-kyō (1426)

A monk of the Jōdo sect named Na-a was responsible for the printing of a one-*maki* edition of this work, which contains a standard frontispiece, probably borrowed from a Sung exemplar, and illustrations at the top of the text, all representing scenes from the sutra.

Bussei biku rokumotsu-zu (Early Muromachi period)

This one-volume work, first printed in 1246 at Senyū-ji in Kyoto, described above, was reprinted in a *Gozan-ban* edition at Nanzen-ji in the early Muromachi period. It contained the same illustrations as the 1246 edition.

Hokke-kyō (*Myōhō-renge-kyō*) (1433)

According to Kawase, a *Gozan-ban* edition of this sutra was printed in 1433, of which only one incomplete copy, in the Ryūmon Bunko (the library of the late Sakamoto Yū), survives. The illustrations in this are identical to those in the 1365 Rinsen-ji edition.

Hokke-kyō (Myōhō-renge-kyō) (1504)

L. N. Brown records on p. 20 a one-scroll edition of the *Fumon-bon* section of the *Lotus Sutra* printed in 1504. (This section is also known as the *Kannon-gyō*, or *Avalokiteśvara-sūtra*, and was frequently printed separately from the rest of the *Lotus Sutra*.) This scroll, now housed in the British Library, has rather crudely drawn illustrations depicting the "Mercies of Kannon."

Hachijūichi-nan-kyō (Hachijūichi-nan) (1536)

This work, despite its title, is not a sutra but a Chinese medical work, known sometimes as the "Classic of Eighty-one Ailments." This six-*maki*, three-volume *Gozan-ban* edition of 1536 marks the first printing of it in Japan, and it contains several illustrations, including a portrait of the author, and diagrams showing the points for moxa and acupuncture treatment, the organs and skeletal structure of the body. These illustrations are believed to have been taken from Korean exemplars.

Yakushi-hongan-kyō (Yakushi-hongan kudoku-kyō) (1538)

A one-volume, *orihon*-format edition of this work (not a reprint of the better-known 1412 *Gozan-ban* edition, described above) contains a frontispiece showing Yakushi-nyorai surrounded by the twelve guardian spirits. The colophon states that this new edition was printed to replace one destroyed by fire and no longer extant, and Ishida suggests that the earlier edition had the same frontispiece.

Hokke-kyō (Myōhō-renge-kyō) (1557)

The Spencer Collection of the New York Public Library possesses a printed edition of the *Fumon-bon* section of the *Lotus Sutra*, which was produced at Ampuku-ji in Iga province (present-day Mie Prefecture). No other copy is known. Its frontispiece is rather similar to that of the 1412 edition of the *Yakushi-hongan-kyō*, and the 41 other illustrations depict in rather crude style subjects such as the "Mercies of Kannon."

Jizō-kyō (c. 1558–70)

L. N. Brown states on p. 20 that this edition of the *Jizō-kyō* contains "a primitive but interesting engraving representing the Buddhist Hell." It is interesting to note that the 1666 edition of a commentary on this work, the *Jizō-bosatsu-hongan-gyō te-kagami* contains a frontispiece showing the bodhisattva Kṣitigarbha (Jizō) being received by Shakyamuni seated on a throne and surrounded by Chinese sages and figures from the Buddhist pantheon. This illustration, judging by its style, must have also been used in a pre-1600 edition of the *Jizō-kyō*.

Kongō-hannya-kyō (Late Muromachi period)

A one-volume edition of this, the *Diamond Sutra*, printed at an unknown location (probably a Shingon sect temple) in the late Muromachi period has a frontispiece, half of which is damaged, depicting the Buddha's disciple Subhūti being received by the Buddha.

It should not be thought that this list includes every single printed book illustration produced before 1600. L. N. Brown's work contains a few other works which have been omitted here owing to unsatisfactory identification. Moreover, several works with single illustrations have also been left out, such as the late Kamakura period *Gozan-ban* edition of *Reisai yawa*, which in one copy only has an intaglio illustration of a crane and fish, and the 1494 *Gozan-ban* edition of *Santaishi*, which has a printed map. There is also much to be learnt from examining Edo-period editions of Buddhist texts, particularly sutras, which continued to make use of illustrations in the pre-1600 style. Often these may be copies of illustrations used before 1600 which no longer survive in pre-1600 editions, but nevertheless they do not add much to the overall picture and the illustrations in them are all rather similar.

Four works have been deliberately omitted from the list above on the grounds that they deserve more detailed description. They are the *Bussetsu-jūō-kyō*, the *Jūgyū-zu*, the *Yūzū-nembutsu-engi* and the *Kōya daishi gyōjō zuga*.

The *Bussetsu Jizō bosatsu hosshin innen jūō-kyō* (Pl. 30), to give it its full name, is a non-canonical work written in the Sung dynasty by the Chinese monk Tsang Ch'uan. It

30. A judgment scene from the *Bussetsu jūō-kyō* (*Sutra of the Ten Kings of Hell*), written by the Chinese monk Tsang Ch'uan and printed probably in 1594.

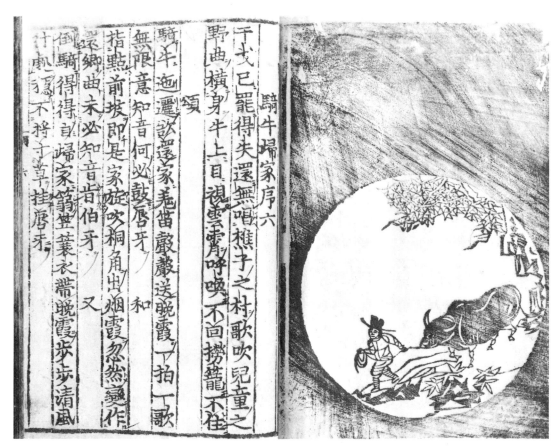

31. A Gozan edition of the popular Buddhist parable *Jūgyū-zu*, printed around 1419. The fifth of ten illustrations, here the man leads the ox.

is sometimes known in English as the *Sutra of the Ten Kings of Hell*. The Buddhist Hell was regarded as being ruled by the Ten Kings, or Regents, who controlled a host of demons responsible for inflicting untold tortures on those committed to Hell. Depictions of such scenes were a favorite theme with Chinese and Japanese artists, both religious and secular. Only one Japanese edition of this work is known, and all the surviving copies have a manuscript date of 1594 (Bunroku 3), and a note saying that an unknown priest by the name of Tokusen was responsible for the printing as well as the illustration. It is not known, however, where the book was printed. Certain Japanese authorities have cast doubt on the 1594 manuscript date, believing a date around 1650 to be more accurate, but in our view the illustrations and other aspects of the book are perfectly compatible with a 1594 printing.

In all, this work contains 23 illustrations of graphic simplicity of scenes of torture in Hell. The illustrations are Chinese in style and were probably taken from Yüan exemplars. Some bear a close resemblance to the much smaller illustrations contained in the late Nambokuchō-period Gozan edition of the *Kunshin-koji*, described above. It is not thought that this edition was printed in a Gozan temple, however.

The *Jūgyū-zu* is a group of ten illustrations usually known in the West as the "Ten Ox-herding Pictures," which was printed on several occasions in Japan. The ten illustrations form a series and have their origin in Zen, with each picture printed in a roundel, three inches in diameter, on a black background (Pl. 31). The symbolism of the illustrations is self-explanatory and the series might be a subtle and abbreviated Zen pictorial equivalent to *The Pilgrim's Progress*. The ox is the symbol of man's true self and the series depicts the struggle for self-knowledge and enlightenment.

In the first illustration, a man with a rope is running along a path by the river in search of the ox; in the second, he finds ox dung on the path, a sign of progress; the third one shows the ox disappearing into the trees with the man hurrying after it; in the fourth the man has a rope over the ox's horns and is being dragged uphill by the ox. The fifth illustration shows the man leading the ox; in the sixth he is astride its back playing the flute (this became a recurring favorite in Japanese illustration); while the seventh shows the man meditating in front of a hut by the river with the moon rising behind the mountains. The eighth illustration shows simply a white roundel on a black background, symbolizing the effect of meditation; the ninth shows a pretty landscape with flowers; and the last one shows the man at the end of his quest meeting with the Buddha.

This work is known in eight different *Gozan-ban* editions ranging in date between the late Kamakura period to 1419. As far as can be deduced, the *Jūgyū-zu* was never published in Japan by itself but always in conjunction with either three or four other works. It appears either as part of the four-work volume entitled *Shiburoku* (which also contains the *Sansō daishi shinjimmei*, the *Shōdōka* and the *Zazengi*) or the five-work volume entitled *Gomizen* (with the additional *Nyūshū nichiyō*). Editions of the *Shiburoku* seem confined to the Nambokuchō and Muromachi periods, while editions of the *Gomizen* appeared in the late Kamakura, the Nambokuchō and the Muromachi periods. Each edition of these works carries the same illustrations, although occasionally there are slight differences in detail. Certainly, no single illustration or series of illustrations was printed more frequently before the Edo period than these. The illustrations of the *Jūgyū-zu* are of Chinese origin and date from the Sung period, although no Sung printed editions appear to have survived.

The next work, the *Yūzū-nembutsu-engi* (Pl. 32), is even more interesting because it is the earliest known example of native illustration in a printed book. It had its origin in a scroll painting by late fourteenth-century artists of the Tosa school—Kasuga Yukihide, Tosa Mitsukuni, Awataguchi Takamitsu, Rokkaku Jakusai and Tayū Hōgen Eishun. This scroll told in words and pictures the life of the monk Ryōnin (1072–1132), the founder of the Yūzū-nembutsu sect, one of the forerunners of Jōdo. The printing of this scroll was begun in 1389 and the textual section was completed in 1390, but the illustration blocks were not started until 1391 and only completed in 1414 or 1417, according to different authorities. This indicates that enormous care was taken over what was obviously a prestigious undertaking. The finished work was printed in two

32. An illustration from the *Yūzū-nembutsu-engi* scroll, depicting the
"Invitation to Paradise" scene. The printing was completed in either
1414 or 1417 at Seiryō-ji, Kyoto.

scrolls, each of which measured approximately eleven inches wide and seventy-six feet
long. Altogether there were twenty illustrations, some several feet in length, which
after printing were then carefully hand-painted, possibly by the original artists. This
edition of the *Yūzū-nembutsu-engi*, which was reprinted several times in the Edo period,
is known as the *Meitoku-ban* edition (i.e., printed in the Meitoku era [1390-93]). Toda
Kenji's statement in the catalog of the Ryerson Collection that the only copy was
destroyed in the 1923 earthquake is not accurate, since the headquarters temple of
the Yūzū-nembutsu sect, Dainembutsu-ji of Osaka, still holds a copy. (The school of
art represented by this scroll, the Tosa school, will be discussed in the next chapter.)

The last of the four works, the *Kōya daishi gyōjō zuga*, also known as the *Kōbō daishi
gyōjō zuga*, is an illustrated biography of Kūkai, or Kōbō Daishi, founder of the Shingon
sect, and in intent, at least, has basic similarities to the *Yūzū-nembutsu-engi*. It was
printed in ten *maki* under the direction of the priest Kōzan on Mt. Kōya in 1593, and
contains 105 illustrations, some five feet in length; at least one of these was hand-
painted. The model for these printed scrolls was a scroll painting, now in Jizō-in on
Mt. Kōya, which is thought to be by the fourteenth-century artist Tosa Yukimitsu.
The author of the text was one Konoe Michitsugu. Like the *Yūzū-nembutsu-engi*, this
work was reprinted several times in the Edo period, notably in a codex edition produced
in the Kan'ei era (1624–44).

Both of these works have been described in considerable detail by more than one
Western authority. What is so significant about them is not that they are fine works
of art but that they are pioneering works. They provide the only examples of pre-1600
native Japanese printed book illustration and the earliest examples, in printed book

illustration, of Japanese secular artists working in Buddhist fields. It is true that both works were originally executed as scroll paintings rather than books, but here we find Buddhist monks for the first time making use of secular artists in their publications. The influence of both works should not be underestimated—they were reprinted many times, and they also served as forerunners of a series of printed illustrated books produced in the Edo period that gave secular treatment to Buddhist themes. The fine Edo-period collection of illustrated biographies of Kūkai, Saichō, Nichiren and Hōnen, to name but a few "saints" to be so treated, did not occur spontaneously but can be traced to well before 1600. It is unfortunate is some ways that Japanese monks, with the resources at their disposal, displayed such reticence in illustrating their printed works before 1600. Yet, on the other hand, the secular artists of the Edo period more than made up for this deficiency.

7 | BOOK ILLUSTRATION AND THE TOSA SCHOOL

In the Edo period, many thousands of books with printed illustrations were produced in Japan representing the work of a legion of artists and a variety of styles of illustration. When confronted with such a wealth of material in both quantity and quality, it is difficult to know how best to present the subject. The usual method adopted by the handful of Westerners who have written on Japanese illustrated books has been the school-by-school and artist-by-artist survey of the best works. On the whole, the merits of such a method outweigh the defects and a similar system is used here. However, disadvantages do exist and can be described as follows. First, illustrations to books were not produced in isolation, but were designed as integral parts of the book. Thus they are closely related to the textual matter and must be considered in their context. Second, although Japanese artists did often see themselves as belonging to a school of painting, most of them studied a variety of different styles and would not necessarily attach themselves to schools in which art historians of Japan and the West have placed them. Third, there is the obvious danger of allocating illustrations to schools when they do not clearly belong to any; similarly, some artists, demonstrably belonging to one school, sometimes also produced work which cannot really be identified with that school.

Within these limitations, Japanese book illustration of the Edo period can be broadly divided among five schools—the Tosa school, the ukiyo-e school, the Kanō school, the Nanga school and the Maruyama-Shijō and related schools—bearing in mind that the actual divisions between the schools themselves are not always clear-cut.

Of these, it was the Tosa school that dominated book illustration in the seventeenth century until 1680. In common with all schools of book illustration, the Tosa style derived from a school of painting. (It should be noted here that all illustrators were primarily painters, often forced into book illustration to earn a living, and as a result the development of book illustration also embraces the development of painting, although this fact is often neglected.) However, the Tosa school differed from other schools in that whereas the latter represented flourishing schools of painting, the Tosa school, during the time that it dominated book illustration, was already in a state of rapid decline.

THE DEVELOPMENT OF THE TOSA SCHOOL OF PAINTING

The earliest Japanese paintings date back to the Asuka period (552–645). During the Asuka, Nara and early Heian periods, a large number of paintings on Buddhist themes were produced, which directly copied Chinese styles and techniques. However, after the discontinuation of the embassies to T'ang China in 894, the Japanese gradually developed an indigenous culture, combining what had been learnt from China with concepts of their own. A distinct style of painting soon emerged in Japan, which at first took the same themes but treated them in a Japanese style, introducing, for example, Japanese landscape backgrounds instead of Chinese in the traditional Buddhist paintings. This new style of painting was given the name Yamato-e, literally "Japanese pictures" (it was apparently first used by Fujiwara Yukinari in a manuscript diary dated 999), to distinguish it from Kara-e, or "Chinese pictures."

Yamato-e painting was always closely related to literature, since its themes were borrowed from Japanese classics. However, although such novels concentrated entirely on the lives of the Kyoto aristocracy, Yamato-e not only featured aristocratic subjects but also depicted the lives of ordinary folk. By the fourteenth century, this tradition was beginning to decline, but was revived, to some extent, by the emergence of the Tosa school.

According to Japanese tradition, the founder of the Tosa school was the eleventh-century artist Fujiwara Motomitsu, but the Tosa name was not employed until the time of Tosa Tsunetaka, who was active in the middle of the thirteenth century. The view of Japanese art historians seems to be that the Tosa school derived from the Yamato-e tradition and later came to embody and preserve that tradition. It is certainly a fact that the school concentrated on "Japanese" subjects, but Tosa artists also enjoyed the patronage of the Kyoto nobility and thus tended toward aristocratic subjects such as portraits or scenes taken from the classics, and to a large extent ignored the more popular aspect of Yamato-e. The school's firm social and artistic standing in society is shown by its long period of domination of the post of head of the E-dokoro, or the Imperial Painting Bureau. By the early fifteenth century, the Tosa school was already in decline but was briefly revived in the Muromachi period by Tosa Mitsunobu (1434–1525), who ranks in Japanese tradition, along with Tosa Mitsunaga and Tosa Mitsuoki, as one of the three Tosa grandmasters. However, the Tosa school suffered another decline when Mitsunobu's daughter married Kanō Masanobu, founder of the Kanō school, and the headship of the E-dokoro passed to him. By the early seventeenth century, the Tosa style had become both mannered and repetitious, but the tradition in book form continued through the rather inferior *Nara-ehon* and *Nara-emaki* genres until it was revived again by Tosa Mitsuoki (1617–91).

The Tosa school at its best was responsible for some remarkable works of art, for the school is noted for its sumptuous use of vivid colors in the portrayals of court life and of aristocratic scenes from literature (Pl. 33). It was precisely this tradition that made the Tosa style the most appropriate for similar scenes in book illustration. Unfortunately, since the key factor of Tosa painting was its use of color, and since the early seventeenth-century printers could not reproduce that color in printed form, Tosa book illustration was deprived of most of its effectiveness. This is the major reason why Japanese illustrations of the first half of the seventeenth century seem so flat and monotonous to the modern eye.

It was not far into the Edo period before the Tosa style made its appearance in printed books. A brief account of the *Saga-bon* of Hon'ami Kōetsu and Suminokura Soan has been given in Chapter Four, although the Saga Press was only one of Kōetsu's many activities. In 1615, he was given a tract of land by Tokugawa Ieyasu in the village of Takagamine, north of Kyoto, together with an annual grant of rice, and he used this to establish a flourishing art and craft community. Three of the outstanding artists and craftsmen who joined him in this enterprise were Soan, Sōshi the paper-maker and Tawaraya (Nonomura) Sōtatsu the painter. Kōetsu and Sōtatsu developed an original painting style, which was never sufficiently systematized and formalized to be given a name, but had a great influence on successive generations of artists. Kōetsu's striving for the refined elegance of Heian court life manifests itself in the *Saga-bon*, in which

33. A typical Tosa-style work by an unknown artist from the 1646 edition of the *Taketori monogatari*, showing the stylized pine and cloud formations.

111

34. This illustration from the 1608 edition of the *Ise monogatari* (*see also* Pl. 35) is in Tosa style, which was to prove so influential in subsequent seventeenth-century illustrated editions of poetry and novels.

35. The famous first edition of the *Ise monogatari* (1608), the *Saga-bon* produced by Kōetsu and Soan, who through the use of quality paper and a graceful calligraphy sought to recapture Heian court life.

112

high-quality colored sheets are used, often decorated with motifs, together with a graceful calligraphy and a distinctive style of illustration (Pls. 34, 35).

Of the thirteen official *Saga-bon*, only the *Ise monogatari*, the *Hyakunin isshu*, the *Sanjū-rokka-sen* and the *Nijūshi-kō* are illustrated (as opposed to being decorated), although the block-printed *Ōgi no sōshi*, often regarded as a *Saga-bon*, also deserves mention. The most famous illustrated *Saga-bon* is the *Ise monogatari*, first printed in 1608, and reprinted nine times in both movable type and block editions within a short period. The two volumes of the 1608 edition contain 48 illustrations in *sumizuri* (black-and-white line drawings), depicting various episodes of the tales, which closely resemble Tosa handscrolls of the same work painted in the Kamakura and Muromachi periods. (Tosa-style interiors, usually viewed from the outside and from above, are prominent in these illustrations, as are the schematized cloud formations and pines, features that dominated Tosa-inspired book illustration in the first half of the seventeenth century.) Japanese authorities have long argued as to who the artist was, and while Kōetsu and Soan are both prime candidates, Sōtatsu is another possibility. Since all these illustrations are demonstrably in the Tosa style, and since none of the artists belonged to that school, it is most likely that they were copied from Tosa originals, with minor adaptations here and there.

The *Nijūshi-kō*, of uncertain date but probably produced in the Keichō era (1596–1615), differs markedly from the *Ise monogatari*. It is a collection of stories on outstanding examples of filial piety in the Chinese tradition, and contains small illustrations at the top of each page, probably copied from a Chinese original. The *Hyakunin isshu* and the *Sanjū-rokka-sen* are both famous *waka* anthologies, the compilation of the former normally attributed to Fujiwara Teika (1162–1241) and the latter to Fujiwara Kintō (966–1041), although there are doubts about both. The *Hyakunin isshu* is a collection of the hundred best poets up to the time it was compiled, and *Sanjū-rokka-sen* contains one poem each by thirty-six poets whom Fujiwara Kintō considered to be the best up to his time. There is naturally some overlapping of poets. The portraits of the poets in the two *Saga-bon* editions (undated, but of the Keichō era) are clearly by two different artists. In style, they conform to classical Tosa portraiture, but the figures in the *Sanjū-rokka-sen* are fuller and rounder than those in the *Hyakunin isshu*. It seems likely here, too, that the portraits were copied, with alterations, from earlier originals.

The *Ōgi no sōshi* is one of those works that belong to the *Den Saga-bon* category, that is, a work traditionally attributed to the Saga Press but not of the official thirteen. It was block-printed some time between 1596 and 1624, and consists of eighty fan-shaped *sumizuri* illustrations, thought to be by Kōetsu, done in Tosa style and accompanied by poems. Another work that falls into the same category is the *jōruri-bon* novel *Jūnidan sōshi* (known by a dozen other titles including *Jōruri monogatari*). This is block printed in three volumes, produced probably in the Keichō era, with illustrations very similar to those in the *Ise monogatari*.

Among Japanese art historians, the illustrations in the *Saga-bon* editions are considered very influential in book illustration as a whole. Certainly, they are the earliest known, non-Buddhist, printed illustrations in native works of literature. Tosa-style illustrations in the manner of the 1608 *Ise monogatari* came to be widely used in subsequent publications, especially before the mid-1650s, but it remains an open question whether this was due to the influence of *Saga-bon* illustrations themselves, or whether Tosa illustration was simply adopted as being the most suitable style for the themes portrayed.

TOSA ILLUSTRATION IN THE KAN'EI ERA (1624–44)

Illustrations of any kind, let alone Tosa, are extremely rare in printed books produced in the Keichō (1596–1615) and the Genna (1615–24) eras. Moreover, it is surprising that of all the works printed by movable type between the Keichō and the end of the Kan'ei era, only the following 40 contain illustrations: the *Saga-bon* editions of *Ise monogatari*, *Hyakunin isshu*, *Sanjū-rokka-sen* and *Nijūshi-kō* (Pl. 36); *Nijō-jō gyōkō-zu* (c. 1626); *Shijūni no mono-arasoi* (undated, but Kan'ei); *Shishō no uta-awase* (undated but Kan'ei); *Jūnidan sōshi* (various Kan'ei editions); *Shoreishū* (Kan'ei): *Sendenshō* (various editions); *Somon nyūshiki unki ron'oku* (1611); *Teikan zusetsu* (Kan'ei, though

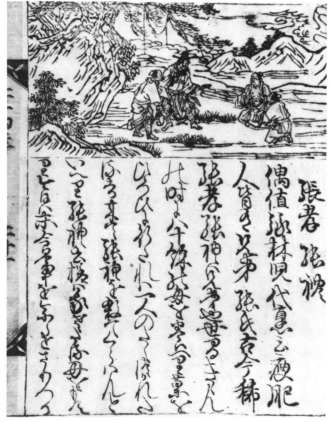

36. A block-printed edition of the *Nijūshi-kō* (c. 1624–44), containing the same illustrations as the movable type edition of the Keichō era (1596–1615).

there is a 1606 block edition with the same illustrations); *Dembō shōjūki* (1630); *Tokashi* (Kan'ei); *Fushimi tokiwa* (Kan'ei); *Kadensho* (probably Kan'ei); *Bussei biku rokumotsu-zu* (Kan'ei); *Kōshi kego* (1599); *Honchō kokon mei-zukushi* (Genna); *Mari no sho* (Genna or Kan'ei); *Rekidai kunshin zuzō* (c. 1610); *Atsumori* (Kan'ei); *Tsukishima* (Kan'ei); *Tsukimi no sōshi* (Kan'ei); *Jūshikei hakki* (Kan'ei); *Soga monogatari* (Kan'ei); *Gikeiki* (Kan'ei); *Kachō fūgetsu* (Keichō and Kan'ei); *Gigen yōkishū* (various editions); *Kan'ei gyōkōki* (Kan'ei); *Kyūshinan* (Keichō); *Manjū* (Kan'ei); *Biwakō chōgonka* (Keichō); *Chikubushima no honji* (Kan'ei); *Tsugimitsu no sōshi* (Kan'ei); *Iwaya no sōshi* (Kan'ei); *Hachikazuki* (Kan'ei); *Karaito no sōshi* (Kan'ei); *Shichinin bikuni* (Kan'ei); and *Kumo* (Kan'ei).

This list may seem substantial, but in fact only represents less than one-tenth of all the works known to have been printed on movable type during the same period, leaving out some of the *mai no hon* published in collections. A variety of illustrative styles are covered by them, ranging from copies of Chinese originals to reprints of pre-1600 Buddhist illustrations, but it is noticeable that out of all these, only works of native literature are illustrated in the Tosa style.

An examination of these works reveals some significant points. First, apart from *Saga-bon* editions, the *Soga monogatari* is the only pre-Muromachi-period fiction to have been issued in an illustrated movable type edition. Second, there is not one instance of a Tosa style illustration when the artist can be firmly attributed. Third, even though the texts were printed on movable type, the illustrations were always printed by block. And lastly, virtually all of these works were published in block-printed editions during the same period.

It is difficult to know what significance to attach to the anonymity of the artists involved, for the same anonymity also applies to most of the authors of these Tosa-style illustrated works. These are largely novels of either the *otogi-zōshi* or *kōwaka-mai* genres of the Muromachi period, with a few *kana-zōshi* of the Edo period. Several, such as the *Kachō fūgetsu* and the *Hachikazuki*, are also known in *Nara-ehon* manuscript versions of roughly the same period, although in these cases, too, the artists are unknown. Hence, it is difficult to avoid the conclusion that the role of the artist in the early seventeenth century did not have the same importance as later on. (We do not know of a single example of pre-1650 Tosa-style illustration in book form where the artist's identity is beyond dispute.)

There seems to be little aesthetic appeal in the Tosa illustrations of movable type editions, probably because they lack the single essential ingredient of color. The same is true of block editions with illustrations produced in the Kan'ei era, of which there are many. A block-printed edition of a Japanese literary work printed in the Kan'ei era without illustrations is an exception. It is not possible to list all of them here but basically such works can be divided into three types: editions of pre-Muromachi fiction; editions of *kana-zōshi* fiction; and editions of *jōruri-bon* fiction. Works of poetry were also published with illustrations, but there are comparatively few of them.

Under the heading of pre-Muromachi-period fiction, one includes works such as the *Genji monogatari*, the *Ise monogatari*, the *Taketori monogatari*, the *Yamato monogatari*, the *Heiki monogatari* and the *Hōgen monogatari*, all of which had existed for a long time in manuscript form and had earlier appeared in unillustrated movable type editions. By 1650, all these works had been block printed and illustrated, although the *Taketori monogatari* did not appear in an illustrated edition until 1646 nor the 60-volume *Genji monogatari* until 1650 (Pls. 33, 37). The *Heiki monogatari* and the *Hōgen monogatari* were both printed several times, often as paralled editions, the earliest illustrated example being the joint edition in six volumes published in 1626. Illustratively, there is little which distinguishes these works.

Kana-zōshi novels were descended from the *otogi-zōshi* and *mai no hon* fiction of the Muromachi period. Basically they are moral tales with strong Buddhist overtones, but incorporated a pronounced element of entertainment for its own sake. A great number of them were written in the Kan'ei era, mostly anonymously, but the authors commonly associated with the genre are Joraishi, Suzuki Shōzō (1579–1655), Asai Ryōi and Yamaoka Genrin. Among the most important works in illustrated editions until 1650 are:

37. This Tosa-style illustration by an unknown artist is from the 60-volume block-printed edition of the *Genji monogatari* (1650).

38.   An illustration by an unknown artist from the only extant copy of
the first edition of the *Taishokan* (1675), an anonymous *jōruri* play.
Here, Fujiwara Kamatari leads his forces against the demon soldiers of
the Dragon King of the Ocean.

the *Isoho monogatari* (various editions); *Fuji no hitoana-zōshi* (1627); *Usuyuki monogatari* (1632); *Nichiren shōnin chūgasan* (1632); *Shichinin bikuni* (1635); *Kirishitan
monogatari* (1639); *Ada monogatari* (1640); *Azuma monogatari* (1642); *Shiki-onron*
(1643); *Chikusai monogatari*; *Nise monogatari*; *Rokudai gozen monogatari*; *Wakashu
monogatari*; *Hana-zukushi* (1645); and *Kuyami-gusa* (1647). This list is by no means
exhaustive, but works not included here do not display important differences in the
style of illustration. Also deliberately omitted are all the *otogi-zōshi* and *mai no hon*
novels which were produced in illustrated editions in the same period, either individually
or in collections (such as the printed, illustrated collection of 36 *mai no hon* novels
published in the early 1630s).

The third category of books with Tosa-style illustrations are *jōruri-bon* novels (Pl. 38)
which fictionalized the plots of *jōruri* plays. *Jūnidan sōshi* (*Jōruri monogatari*) seems to
have been the earliest of these, although Mizutani Futō (*see* Bibl.) cites another 15 produced with illustrations in the Kan'ei era and 9 in the Shōhō (1644–48) and Kei'an
(1648–52) eras. *Takatachi* (1625), *Karukaya* (1631), *Hanaya* (1634), *Tomonaga* (1637),
Muramatsu (1637) and *Amida no honji* (1644), all with Tosa style illustrations, are
considered as representative early examples.

TANROKU-BON

Illustrated classical fiction, *mai no hon*, *otogi-zōshi*, *kana-zōshi* and *jōruri-bon* produced before 1650 have one major aspect in common apart from the style of illustration, and that is the method of illustration. All were originally done in *sumizuri*, but the vast majority are also known in *tanroku-bon* editions. This indicates that color was applied to the *sumizuri* illustrations by hand. The two primary colors from which the term *tanroku* derives were orange, obtained from red lead pigment (*tan*), and mineral green (*roku*), although sometimes other colors such as yellow and purple were added. However, the dominance of orange and green is the identifying characteristic of all *tanroku-bon*, distinguishing them from other examples of random hand-coloring. Curiously enough, a large number of illustrated books of the seventeenth and eighteenth centuries in particular, are crudely hand-colored at whim, it seems. This wide use of hand-coloring belies the traditional view that the reason color printing was delayed for so long was the excellence of black-and-white *sumizuri*. If this was so, people would not have resorted to hand-coloring (Pl. 39).

Tanroku-bon, however, differ from this kind of indiscriminate hand-coloring, since

39. This is from a *tanroku-bon* edition of the *Asagao no tsuyu* of the early or mid-sixteenth century, showing the rather crude attempts at hand-coloring.

they seem to represent the only type of work in which hand-coloring was systematized. The uniformity of the coloring suggests that it was done at the behest of the publishers and not of the individual owners. *Tanroku-bon* are traditionally closely related to *Nara-ehon* in as much as they attempt to reproduce *Nara-ehon* colors in printed illustrations. It should be remembered, however, that *Nara-ehon* were basically an extension of Tosa illustration and painting and, therefore, *tanroku-bon* are best seen as an attempt to supply color, the missing ingredient of Tosa illustration in printed books. This technique seems to have been first used in books of the Keichō era, but despite the fact that those books are usually undated, it can be stated with reasonable certainty that they did not survive beyond the 1650s. Though a disaster aesthetically, achieving only a sad parody of Tosa color schemes, *tanroku-bon* are much prized in Japan on account of their rarity.

TOSA ILLUSTRATION AFTER 1650

The year 1650, while of no outstanding significance to the development of Tosa illustration, marks the virtual end of movable type and the beginning of a decade that saw a substantial transformation in book illustration. It was the year in which the massive

40. This Tosa-style illustration, reflecting some ukiyo-e influences, notably in the figure of the samurai in the boat, is from the *kana-zōshi* novel *Shichinin bikuni* (c. 1660).

119

41. An example of late Tosa book illustration by an unknown artist, from Volume 5 of Toda Mosui's work on *waka* theory entitled *Nashinomoto-shū* (1700).

60-volume edition of *Genji monogatari*—the first printed, illustrated edition of the work —was published. It contains illustrations that are as fine as any produced by the Tosa school before then, but it marks no real advance in style or technique compared to the 1608 *Saga-bon* edition of the *Ise monogatari*. This very stylistic stagnation combined with the new forces in art and society under the Tokugawa to render the demise of the Tosa domination of book illustration inevitable.

In the following chapter, we shall examine the rise of ukiyo-e and its subtle and eventual transformation of the Tosa style as the seventeenth century progressed, but up to 1680, that transformation was still only partial (Pl. 40). Between 1650 and 1680, there was a considerable boom in publishing and a great number of illustrated books were produced. Most of the important illustrations produced in this period show the emergence of ukiyo-e elements, this factor alone accounting for their importance. However, probably the majority of books produced continued to have illustrations in the pure Tosa style. The *Hōgen monogatari* (1657), *Amayadori* (c. 1658), *Izayoi nikki* (1659), *Utsubo monogatari* (1660), *Shichinin bikuni* (c. 1660), *Amida hadaka monogatari* (c. 1660), *Ominaeshi monogatari* (1661), *Nembutsu sōshi* (c. 1665), *Enkō daishi go-denki* (1666), *Gikeiki* (1670), *Ikkyū shokoku monogatari* (c. 1670), *Ono no Komachi kashū* (c. 1675),

Utsubo monogatari (1677) and *Usuyuki monogatari* (1678) are all random but representative examples of Tosa illustration of the time, with no alteration of pre-1650 styles.

The significant aspects of these works is that they are either classical fiction, *waka* poetry, or *kana-zōshi* novels, which were first printed with illustrations prior to 1650. Clearly the Tosa style was still considered appropriate for such works, especially the *waka* anthologies (Pl. 41). Throughout the Edo period, *waka* remained the domain of the Kyoto aristocracy, who clung not only to traditional poetic form but also to traditional Tosa illustration. Thus the Tosa style was to dominate the illustration of *waka* until the eighteenth century and beyond. (One also finds editions of classical fiction published in the eighteenth century with Tosa illustrations, but these were very often reissues of older publications.)

There is little more to be said about the general significance of Tosa illustration in

42. The *Taiheiki taizen*, by Nishi Dōchi, which examines the exploits of warrior heroes in the *Taiheiki*, was published in 50 volumes in 1659. This sort of theme was to become a favorite with later ukiyo-e artists.

the latter half of the seventeenth century. By the time of the death of the ukiyo-e artist Hishikawa Moronobu, probably in 1694, Tosa illustrative style had been supplanted, or perhaps it would be better to say transformed. It had, however, become deeply ingrained in the illustration of classial fiction and occasionally, in addition to *waka* books and reprints of classical fiction with the original illustrations, one finds glimpses of it later, often where one might least expect it. There is, for example, a markedly Tosa-influenced color-printed illustration in the 1796 edition of the *Kyōka waka ebisu*, produced by none other than Utamaro. There is no doubt that the golden age of Tosa illustration was the years between 1624 and 1644, but as has been mentioned, in no case is the artist's identity certain, a remark also applicable to pure Tosa illustration between 1650 and 1700. In view of the rather flat uniformity of these works, the general anonymity is perhaps fitting.

8 | THE UKIYO-E SCHOOLS

A definition of ukiyo-e, the best known in the West of all the Japanese schools of art, poses problems, particularly in relation to seventeenth-century book illustration. The term *ukiyo*, or "floating world," Buddhist in origin, denotes simply the transience and ephemeral qualities of life. During the Edo period, with the rise of the new townsman society, its meaning came to be associated not with the transience of life, but with the pleasures of that transient life. It was with the depiction of these pleasures in the bustling cities of Edo and Osaka—courtesans of the Yoshiwara quarters, the *kabuki* theater, boating on the rivers, sumo wrestling—that the ukiyo-e ("pictures of the floating world") artists concerned themselves. The breadth of subject matter provided by daily life in the big cities gave scope for an infinite variety of themes in painting, prints and book illustrations, and these were fully explored by the ukiyo-e artists. However, just as that bustling society did not develop overnight, so ukiyo-e did not emerge suddenly but was the result of a gradual evolution.

THE EARLY DEVELOPMENT OF UKIYO-E

Unlike the Tosa, Kanō, Nanga and other schools to which a founding artist can usually be ascribed, there was no true founder of the ukiyo-e school. Some historians attribute it to artists such as Iwasa Matabei (1578–1650) or Hishikawa Moronobu (c. 1618–94), but the arguments put forward are not convincing. Ukiyo-e evolved slowly and a study of book illustrations provides a good mirror of that evolution. Its origins in painting can be traced to the end of the sixteenth century with the emergence of the new feudal nobility. Whereas the declining Kyoto aristocracy at this period continued to support and patronize artists of the Tosa school, the new feudal nobility tended to favor the Kanō school. Perhaps conscious of their own humble origins and anxious to establish a separate cultural identity from the Kyoto aristocracy, the feudal lords employed artists, usually of the Kanō school but occasionally of the Tosa school also, for murals and screen paintings to decorate their castles and residences. This new class had tastes which differed from those of the old aristocracy, and from early on it showed a greater interest in common people and in paintings of ordinary daily life.

It should not be thought that the Tosa artists ignored these themes in their own paintings or book illustrations, but their treatment of them always seems more aloof, less involved. When common people appear in seventeenth-century Tosa book illustration, they are usually depicted as incidentals rather than as central figures. Of course, one is here treading on dangerous ground in assessing the artistic motives of seventeenth-century Japanese artists from a twentieth-century Western viewpoint, and conclusions should not be pushed too far. Gradually, however, in the course of the seventeenth century one sees the inclusion of "modern" and "contemporary" elements in traditional Tosa illustrations, most often in the types of people represented and the prominence they are given in the painting. Very gradually, the Tosa cloud formations rolled back both literally and figuratively, for the traditional aristocratic figure was supplanted by the feudal samurai and scenes from the lives of the ordinary people were introduced.

The emergence of ukiyo-e in the seventeenth century should not be seen as a conflict with existing tradition, but as a natural development of art engendered by changes in the social structure of Japan. The decline of the old aristocracy, the rise of the samurai and the new, large urban areas with their working population of townsmen all conspired to undermine traditional concepts in art. There arose a desire for something fresh and original with which the newly dominant classes of society could identify and which they could find relevant to their lives. The rise of ukiyo-e reflects this change in society, but there is a substantial danger of regarding it as art "for the people, by the people," which it was not, or only partially so. Rather it reflected the tastes and interests of a large group of people in the cities, principally the samurai and the *chōnin*. The samurai, often the primary producers of art and literature, were a kind of aristocracy themselves, and the pleasure quarters of the cities, which formed both the principal subject and market for ukiyo-e art, were subworlds and not wholly representative of society. The peasant, the backbone of Tokugawa economy who formed the bulk of the population of Japan, is in some senses just as minor a figure in ukiyo-e as the samurai was in earlier Tosa illustration. Thus, although ukiyo-e was a popular art form supported by a large plebeian population, one should beware of regarding it as the art of the common people. Appreciation of ukiyo-e art in many of its forms demanded considerable sophistication.

In terms of printed book illustration, the early innovators of what might be called "ukiyo-e elements" were for the most part anonymous, especially before 1650. One finds occasional glimpses of these elements in some *jōruri-bon* novels and in such works as *Kumano no honji* (c. 1630), a semifictitious history of the Kumano shrine written in the Muromachi period. Such examples, however, are few and far between and often difficult to evaluate, but it is possible that some ukiyo-e style illustrations were produced in Edo before 1650. As the original Edo Yoshiwara was destroyed by fire in 1657, it is probable that many works of art in it perished, including perhaps some ukiyo-e art. This suggestion, however, is highly speculative in terms of book illustration since no book is recorded as having been printed in Edo before the *Daizō-kyō* of 1637–48, mentioned in Chapter Four.

In ukiyo-e book illustration it is possible to identify a formative period which lasted from approximately 1650 to 1750, with the Genroku era (1688–1704) acting as a watershed. During the first part of this era, the names of very few artists are known, and there has been a tendency to attribute anonymous works to the few known artists on stylistic grounds. In the years 1650–80, Kyoto remained the center of the publishing business, and it is to Kyoto that one must look for major evidence of the rise of ukiyo-e. It is significant that of the three major names in book illustration at that time—Hinaya Ryūho, Yoshida Hambei and Hishikawa Moronobu—the first two were from Kyoto and Moronobu received his early training in Kyoto.

Before the 1680s ukiyo-e elements in novel illustration are detectable, but there is basically little advance on the position prevailing in the Kan'ei era. Editions of classical fiction continued to be produced, but the illustrations were invariably in the Tosa style. It is noticeable that works of this type with which Ryūho is credited, such as *Jūjō Genji* (1661), *Eiga monogatari* (c. 1665) and *Osana Genji* (1666), and Moronobu's *Soga monogatari* (1663), *Hōgen monogatari* (1666), *Heiji monogatari* (1667) and *Ise*

43. En route to the hot springs of Arima, an illustration by Yoshida Hambei, from the *Arima ko-kagami*, an anonymous guide to the Arima area near Kobe, published in 1685.

44.   The Great Edo Fire of 1657, from the *Musashi abumi* (1661), written by
Asai Ryōi, artist unknown. An example of a Tosa-trained artist adapting to
a contemporary theme.

monogatari (1678) appear to show no ukiyo-e influence whatsoever. The same is true to
a lesser extent with *kana-zōshi* novels, although a distinction has to be made between
kana-zōshi works written and first published before 1650 but reissued after 1650, and
new *kana-zōshi* written in the 1660s and 1670s, which have more ukiyo-e influences,
usually in the change of subject matter. For example, *Shichinin bikuni*, a *kana-zōshi*
first published in 1635 was reprinted with new illustrations in c. 1660, but the style of
the illustrations was pure Tosa, while that of a *kana-zōshi* account of the Great Fire in
1657, *Musashi abumi*, written by Asai Ryōi and published in 1661, despite the obvious
Tosa stylistic influence, bears no resemblance to earlier *kana-zōshi* illustrations. The

artist of *Musashi abumi* is unknown, but clearly he was of the Tosa school who adapted his style to cover contemporary events (Pl. 44). Such developments were an important ingredient in the early progress of ukiyo-e.

Jōruri-bon novels, based on the plots of *jōruri* plays, developed an illustrative style of their own in the 1660s and, particularly, in the 1670s. They began to be produced in a much smaller format, and the pages were crowded with depictions of fierce samurai warriors. In a sense, they formed an independent development within ukiyo-e and it was about this time that, in book illustration at least, theatrical ukiyo-e began to emerge. Later, groups of ukiyo-e artists began to specialize in theatrical illustration, not only as prints but also in books. The novel, at least before 1680, was not a major vehicle for the advance of ukiyo-e trends. Basically, by this period both the classical and *kana-zōshi* forms of fiction were archaic, outmoded in the lifestyles depicted as well as in the styles of illustration employed. It was only with the advent of the *ukiyo-zōshi* genre of fiction, generally thought to date from the publication of Saikaku's *Kōshoku ichidai otoko* in 1682, that the ukiyo-e style of illustration began to dominate the novel, which it did until the Meiji Restoration in 1868.

The same lack of ukiyo-e trends in illustration characterizes the illustration of poetry before 1680. Despite Matsuo Bashō's (1644–94) creation of a new and popular *haiku* form of verse and the rise of comic *kyōka* poetry in the latter part of the seventeenth century, neither of these new forms appeared in printed, illustrated editions on a meaningful scale until the eighteenth century, and even then they were not monopolized by the ukiyo-e schools. The principal poetic form of the latter part of the seventeenth century was the Heian-period *waka*, and it comes as no surprise, therefore, to find the Tosa style of illustration in editions of *waka* poetry of that time and until well into the eighteenth century.

It was two semiliterary genres of writing that provided the major vehicle for the advance of ukiyo-e in the period 1650–80; the gazeteers generically known as *meisho-ki* ("records of famous places") and books on etiquette known as *ōraimono*. The former ranged from guidebooks for pilgrims visiting temples and shrines to illustrated accounts of places of interest in and around the leading cities, with specific attention paid to the pleasure quarters. These last were not truly *meisho-ki* works according to the normal use of the term but belong to the same "guidebook" category. The already mentioned *Kumano no honji* (c. 1630) and *Shiki-onron* (1643) were early examples of the illustrated *meisho-ki* genre, but the most important work of this type of the 1650s from both the content and illustration viewpoints was *Kyō warabe* (Pl. 45)—the first guide of its kind to places of interest in and around Kyoto written in 1658 by the physician Nakagawa Kiun (1638–1705). The six volumes contain over eighty *sumizuri* (black-and-white line) drawings by an unknown artist of a wide range of views in Kyoto: from Buddhist temples and portrayals of festivals to women washing clothes in the river. The illustrations have been attributed to Moronobu and to Hambei, as are many quality works of this period, but one contemporary Japanese source claims

45. The Kibune shrine of Kyoto, from Volume 5 of Nakagawa Kiun's guide to places of interest around Kyoto, the *Kyō warabe* (1658). The artist's identity has never been ascertained, but the ukiyo-e influence is obvious.

that they were done by Hinaya Ryūho (1595–1669), whose original surname was Nonoguchi. The fact that all Hinaya's known work is in pure Tosa style must cast doubt on the authenticity of this claim, and so it is best to regard the artist as unknown. The significant point about *meisho-ki* is that since they concentrated on contemporary life in places of interest, they permitted artists to produce contemporary illustrations, and for the first time we begin to see how people lived at the time the book was printed instead of several centuries earlier. This was of key importance in the development of ukiyo-e.

In the period following the publication of *Kyō warabe* until the end of the seventeenth century more than fifty other *meisho-ki* works were published, virtually all of which had illustrations depicting contemporary life, recognizable as early ukiyo-e works. One of the most prolific contributors to the illustration of these works was Hishikawa Moronobu, regarded by some as the founder of the ukiyo-e school. An indication of where Moronobu himself thought he stood in the tradition of Japanese painting is shown by the fact that he used to sign his works *Yamato-e shi*, "Master of Yamato-e."

HISHIKAWA MORONOBU (c. 1618–94)

Moronobu was arguably the greatest book illustrator of the seventeenth century and the most prolific known artist of the period. Allowing for the fact that books have been wrongly attributed to him, he was responsible between 1658 and 1694 for illustrating approximately 130 books of varying size and subject matter, many more than Yoshida Hambei, who can most closely be compared with him. The meager details known about Moronobu's life have been recounted numerous times and do not bear repetition here. It suffices to say for present purposes that he was born (probably in 1618) the son of an embroiderer at Hoda in Awa province, and at a comparatively early age began to study painting in Kyoto under a Tosa master. Around 1660, he began to study under the master Kanō Tan'yū (1602–74) in Edo. He is normally regarded as an Edo artist, although many of his books, particularly in the early period, were in fact published in Kyoto. At any rate, it is clear that he received a thorough training in both the Tosa and Kanō styles of painting. As prolific in print-making as in book illustration, Moronobu, if not the founder of ukiyo-e, was responsible for shaping the diverse elements of early ukiyo-e and giving them substance. Significantly, later in his career he took pupils and left behind him a school of artists who produced works in his style.

There is not much to say about Moronobu's contribution to the illustration of classical *jōruri-bon* and *kana-zōshi* fiction. However, with his adaptable style he could reproduce pure Tosa illustrations whenever they were applicable to the subject matter. Thus a great deal of his work in these fields and in the illustration of *waka* is representative of Tosa-style illustration of the period. This does not mean that Moronobu began his painting career in the Tosa style and then progressed to ukiyo-e, for some of his earliest works were in ukiyo-e style. On the other hand, *Waka no tebiki*, a poetry collection in five volumes published in 1686, eight years before his death, is illustrated in pure Tosa. With the rise of the new *ukiyo-zōshi* novel, Moronobu also contributed ukiyo-e illustrations to fiction, although he was less active in this field than Yoshida Hambei.

Moronobu's most creative work in book illustration is to be found not in novels or poems specifically, but in *meisho-ki*, *ōraimono* and *ehon*. Among the works of *meisho-ki* that he was responsible for were: *E-iri Kamakura monogatari* (5 vols., 1659); *Takuan oshō Kamakura-ki* (2 vols., 1659); *Edo suzume* (12 vols., 1677); *Tamatsu-shima honji* (1 vol., 1677); *Waka meisho-kagami* (2 vols., 1682); *Shokoku meisho uta-suzume* (2 vols., 1682); and *Tōkaidō bunken zue* (5 vols., 1690). Of these the best known is *Edo suzume* (*Sparrows of Edo*), a guide to the sights of Edo which could have been written as well as illustrated by Moronobu. This short list omits many works possibly attributable to Moronobu such as *Kyō warabe* and *Arima shigure* (5 vols., 1672).

Ōraimono were not new to the Edo period but were a legacy of the earlier *yūsoku-kojitsu* works, consisting of advice on correct costume, behavior, etc., at court. *Ōraimono* themselves were of two types: those aimed at cultivating the moral sense, which were often used for educational purposes in Buddhist temple schools in the sixteenth century; and those of a more practical nature which set out to teach correct behavior on certain occasions. The usual audience for *ōraimono* were women, and in these books practical advice was often combined with injunctions relating to moral behavior. These lessons were couched in entertaining stories of all kinds on womanly virtue taken from Chinese and Japanese antiquity. The more practical *ōraimono* were of illustrative significance in that they provided the opportunity for artists to portray contemporary life and customs, and while they were produced for women of high birth (who could read), they depict how the people lived. Moronobu's principal works in this genre were *Onna kagami* (3 vols., 1659) and *Onna shorei-shū* (7 vols., 1660), although there are doubts about them being Moronobu's (the majority of historians, however, seem to accept them as such). *Onna shorei-shū* is particularly interesting, showing scenes from events such as bridal processions and ceremonies following the birth of a child.

Despite these works, Moronobu's principal contribution to the history of book illustration lay in his development of the native Japanese *ehon*, or "picture books." These existed before his time only in works copied from Chinese books or adapted from them. Probably the reason for the initial popularity of *ehon* was the growth of a semiliterate audience in the cities who preferred books with pictures to solid text. The closest approach to this concept before the development of *ehon* proper can be seen in *waka* anthologies such as *Hyakunin isshu* and *Sanjū-rokka-sen*, which were produced with a portrait of the respective poet on each page. Such books, however, with their long tradition in manuscript form, almost exclusively used the Tosa style of illustration in printed editions, and were not meant for a mass audience, least of all a semiliterate one. Moronobu himself produced a considerable number of such works, of which *Hyakunin isshu zōsanshō* (1 vol., 1678) (Pl. 46) is notable. It was only a short step, however, from *meisho-ki*, which combined text with illustration, to *ehon*, which concentrated on the pictorial aspect and could be enjoyed by those not able to read well. An obvious subject matter for books of this type was everyday life in the cities, and in particular, the Yoshiwara pleasure quarters.

Moronobu's first step in this direction was the celebrated and erotic *Yoshiwara makura*, or *Yoshiwara Pillow*, of 1660, which contained illustrations of forty-eight traditional lovemaking positions. Eroticism of this type was to become an important feature of ukiyo-e art, perhaps inevitably, due to its close association with the Yoshiwara district. Very many ukiyo-e artists of the highest reputation—Utamaro, Harunobu, Hokusai, Shigemasa and Hiroshige—took pride in this kind of work, although it was always frowned on by the authorities. These books, usually in the form of *hyōban-ki*, or critiques of courtesans, were designed for the use of patrons of the pleasure quarters. The illustrations in *Yoshiwara makura* are not thought suitable for reprinting even in today's permissive age, and it is interesting to note that modern Japanese editions of this type of work are also censored. However, Moronobu and his fellow artists did not confine themselves to this type of depiction, and other works of his dealt with the social customs of the Yoshiwara district. *Yoshiwara sode kagami* (1 vol., 1666);

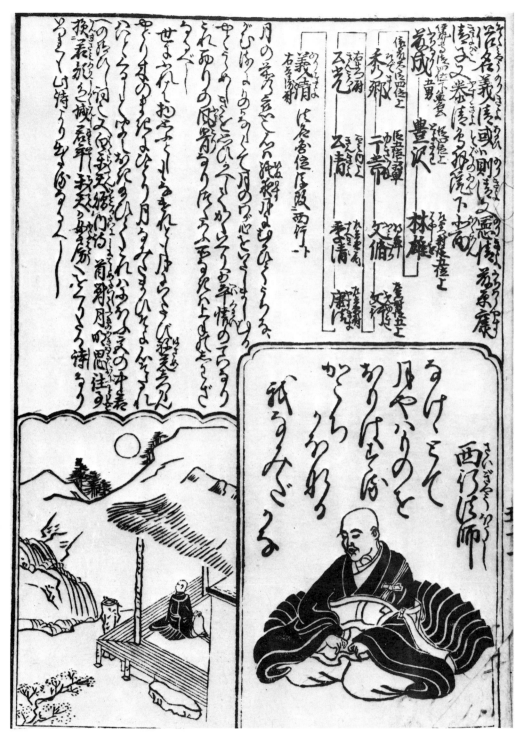

46. Hishikawa Moronobu working in the Tosa style depicts the poet Saigyō Hōshi (1118–90) together with a scene from one of his poems, from the *Hyakunin isshu zōsanshō* (1678).

Yoshiwara koi-no-michibiki (1 vol., 1678); *Yoshiwara daizu tawara hyōban* (1 vol., 1683); *Imayō Yoshiwara makura* (1 vol., 1685); and *Yoshiwara Genji gojūshi-kun* (1 vol., 1687).

Apart from these specialized productions, Moronobu was also responsible for many interesting *ehon* which displayed a variety of styles ranging from Tosa through Kanō to ukiyo-e. These were books made up almost entirely of pictures, sometimes accompanied by notes on each page. Classic examples of Moronobu's *ehon* of this type are: *Yamato-e zukushi* (1 vol., 1680, collected literary scenes in Tosa style) (Pl. 47); *Ehon tokiwa no matsu* (3 vols., 1682, Tosa-style designs for screens and *kakemono* paintings); *Kachō-zukushi* (1 vol., 1683, plants and birds in Kanō style); *Wakoku shoshoku e-zukushi* (4 vols., 1685, pictures of artisans and craftsmen from all over Japan in ukiyo-e style); *Iwaki e-zukushi* (3 vols., 1682); and *Kokon bushidō e-zukushi* (1 vol., 1685, portraits of famous warriors).

That Moronobu was a master of many different styles is obvious, but toward the end of his career, he showed a marked preference for ukiyo-e and left his pupils to carry on with that style. It can be said that Moronobu's works marked a watershed in the development of ukiyo-e, since they contain elements of Tosa, Kanō and ukiyo-e, but, as suggested earlier, he was responsible more than any other artist for giving shape to

47. The priest Nichiren praying for rain, by Hishikawa Moronobu, from the *Yamato e-zukushi* (1 vol., 1680).

a rather shadowy concept. Whatever his role in the development of ukiyo-e itself, Moronobu was certainly the first artist to work in the field of *ehon*. Whether the genre was a product of his genius or simply the result of the demands of a new audience, it did not exist before his time, but by the time of his death it was going from strength to strength.

YOSHIDA HAMBEI (active 1665–88)

In comparison to Moronobu, Yoshida Hambei is an obscure, and comparatively minor, artist who acquires importance because he is one of the few known artists of the second half of the seventeenth century. His birth and death dates are unknown, but his earliest illustrations date from the mid-1660s, so he was probably a slightly younger contemporary of Moronobu, although whether the two were ever acquainted is not known. Hambei was a Kyoto artist, and since Moronobu spent a part of his early career in Kyoto, it is quite likely that they did know each other. Hambei illustrated some sixty or seventy books, the vast majority of which were novels, and his chief contribution to ukiyo-e comes through the illustrations he did for several of Saikaku's *ukiyo-zōshi* novels.

By no means as prolific as Moronobu, Hambei's career, nevertheless, parallels that of his more famous contemporary in that he worked in more than one style. That he was trained in Tosa painting is clear from his two earliest extant works, the illustrations in *Yamato nijūshi-kō* (12 vols., 1665, biographies of twenty-four Japanese famed for their filial piety) and *Otogi-bōko* (13 vols., 1666, mostly tales of the supernatural by Asai Ryōi), both of which are in almost pure Tosa style. Despite the development of a rather unorthodox landscape style which was neither truly Tosa nor truly Kanō, Hambei continued to work in the Tosa style, particularly, as one would expect, in his illustration of *kana-zōshi* novels such as *Ikkyū shokoku monogatari* (5 vols., 1671) and of *waka* such as *Karin kinyōshō* (3 vols., 1695) (Pl. 48). This was undoubtedly due to the subject matter represented and reinforces the view that ukiyo-e at this period was denoted principally by content. During the 1670s, however, he illustrated five *meisho-ki* (Pl. 43), the best known of which is *Dekisai kyō-miyage* (7 vols., 1678). Here, in a work considered a sequel to and an improvement on *Kyō warabe*, one finds several scenes from popular life in what may be regarded as primitive ukiyo-e style in addition to conventional ones of temples and shrines. Unlike Moronobu who made extensive use of the *ehon* format, Hambei continued to work in novels, no doubt due to circumstance rather than to any specific preference, and produced no *ehon*, with the possible exception of pictorial *ōraimono* encyclopedias for women, such as *Kōshoku kimmō zui* (3 vols., 1685).

It was the *ukiyo-zōshi* genre of fiction that provided the opportunity for Hambei to produce the illustrations for which he is best remembered. *Ukiyo-zōshi* novels, fashionable around 1682 to 1741, were romances, or often collections of stories, set in large cities (usually Edo or Osaka) recounting the lives, deeds and amorous encounters of

133

48. An example of Yoshida Hambei's work in the Tosa style, from the *Karin kinyōshō* (1695), a work on *waka* theory by Ichijō Kanera.

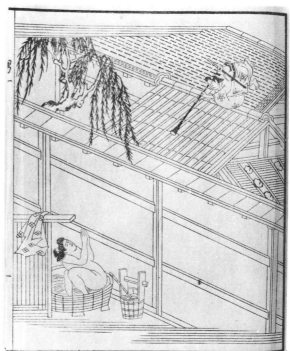

49. A scene from the *Kōshoku ichidai otoko* (1682), a *ukiyo-zōshi* tale by Ihara Saikaku, illustrated either by Hambei or by Moronobu.

the townsmen. They were filled with vivid detail of how people of this class lived, were usually humorous, often bawdy, and subject to frequent attack by the authorities on grounds of indecency. In other words, *ukiyo-zōshi* were the literary equivalent of ukiyo-e and the two went hand-in-hand. The most famous authors of *ukiyo-zōshi* novels were Ejima Kiseki, the Hachimonjiya brothers Kishō and Jishō, and Ihara Saikaku (1642–93), son of a wealthy Osaka merchant and the most esteemed author today. Indeed, he is generally regarded as the founder of the genre with his novel *Kōshoku ichidai otoko*, published in eight volumes in 1682 (Pl. 49). There is considerable debate about which artists were responsible for illustrating these early Saikaku *ukiyo-zōshi*; some were either definitely by or attributed to Moronobu, some to Saikaku himself, but there is no doubt that Hambei was the major contributor. Mizutani Futō (*see* Bibl.) lists a total of 21 *ukiyo-zōshi* novels, not all by Saikaku, which, in his view, were definitely illustrated by Hambei. Of these the best known are: *Kōshoku ichidai onna* (6 vols., 1686); *Kōshoku gonin onna* (5 vols., 1686); *Kōshoku sandai otoko* (5 vols., 1686); and *Nippon eitai-gura* (6 vols., 1688). The former two are particularly well known in the West under the titles *The Woman who Loved Love* and *Five Women who Loved Love*. Perhaps most representative of all is *Nippon eitai-gura*, which contains illustrations of samurai and samurai life, peasants, courtesans, *chōnin* tradesmen and

50. This depiction of a whale hunt is most probably by Yoshida Hambei; from Volume 2 of Saikaku's *ukiyo-zōshi* novel *Nippon eitai-gura* (6 vols., 1686).

135

a dramatic, humorous whale hunt (Pl. 50). *Nippon eitai-gura* is an appropriate example of what ukiyo-e was all about and, fittingly, it was published in 1688, the first year of the Genroku era, when ukiyo-e began to flourish.

KAMIGATA ARTISTS OF THE GENROKU ERA (1688–1704)

Art historians in Japan tend to divide the Genroku and immediate post-Genroku development of ukiyo-e into two separate branches, the Edo and the Kyoto-Osaka (or Kamigata) branch. Although this is a somewhat artificial distinction since the influences were mutual, the tradition is adhered to here.

In Kyoto and, to a greater extent, in Osaka both during and after Hambei's time, the traditions of ukiyo-e were upheld by a number of minor and major artists whose biographical details are often obscure. One such was "Makie-shi" Genzaburō, or "Lacquer-master" Genzaburō. He was born on an unknown date in Nara where he trained in lacquer work, which presumably he continued to practice when he moved to Kyoto later. We know nothing of his training in painting, but Mizutani Futō (*see* Bibl.) ascribes to him thirty to forty books published between 1690 and 1709. Most of these, however, are only speculative attributions. One that he was definitely responsible for was the encyclopedia *Jinrin kimmō zui*, published in seven volumes in 1690, containing a number of illustrations in ukiyo-e style. Virtually everything else ascribed to him is done so on purely stylistic grounds (and this is always a highly contentious area), but these attributions include some important works, such as Saikaku's *ukiyo-zōshi* titled *Kōshoku nishiki* (1692) and *Kōshoku jūninin otoko* (1696). To a large extent, the importance of Genzaburō rests on how many of these books he actually illustrated, and this is impossible to say.

A less prolific but more important Kyoto illustrator of this period was Ōmori Yoshikiyo. Virtually nothing is known of his origins, but to judge from his extant works he flourished between the late 1690s and the 1710–20 period. Although he illustrated less than twenty books, if they are all indeed his, some fine examples of ukiyo-e are included in them. The most outstanding of these is *Kyō Shimabara yūjo ningyō-zukai* of 1702, a series of double-page illustrations of scenes from the Shimabara (Kyoto's equivalent of the Yoshiwara), with the figures drawn largely and boldly. The exceedingly rare *Shidare yanagi* (one *orihon* album, 1703) is one of two books of Yoshikiyo's which actually bears his signature. This again depicts the courtesans of Shimabara and gives an example of the early use of the *orihon* format for *ehon*, which was to be so favored by Utamaro later in the century. The other book bearing Yoshikiyo's signature is *Shin usuyuki monogatari* (5 vols., 1716). This work by Rankei is generally described as an *ukiyo-zōshi* novel, but the story has earlier antecedents and the style employed by Yoshikiyo is best described as Tosa-ukiyo-e. Among other works attributed to Yoshikiyo are *Ayane-dake* (3 vols., 1702), *Hime kagami* (31 vols., bound in 8, 1709–12) and *Kiso shōgun Yoshinaka ki* (10 vols., bound in 5, 1712), none of which are truly ukiyo-e.

NISHIKAWA SUKENOBU (1671–1751)

The greatest of the early Kamigata ukiyo-e artists was the Kyoto-born Nishikawa Sukenobu. Like so many of his contemporaries, Sukenobu studied painting of both the Kanō (under Kanō Einō, 1634–1700) and Tosa (under Tosa Mitsusuke, 1675–1710) schools but evolved a style of his own, and he came to be regarded in his lifetime as the greatest ukiyo-e master. Sukenobu was in many ways an interesting artist, not least because unlike so many of his contemporaries he evinced no enthusiasm for single sheet prints. In fact, virtually all his best work is to be found in the many *ehon* he produced, prompting Nakada Katsunosuke (*see* Bibl.) to say that "he was born for *ehon*."

The most prolific book illustrator in the first half of the eighteenth century, Sukenobu is believed to have produced more than one hundred *ehon* in approximately three hundred volumes in addition to other works that he illustrated. Unless a great deal of his work has been unaccountably lost, Sukenobu's training must have taken a long time, since no work by him was published before 1699. Although Sukenobu worked almost exclusively in the ukiyo-e style, his technique, if not his style, owes a great deal to both the Kanō and Tosa schools. He began his career as an illustrator for the famous Kyoto Hachimonjiya fiction publishing house. His earliest known work is found in a *kyōgen-bon* entitled *Kyō hiinagata* published by Hachimonjiya in 1699 and a *yakusha hyōban-ki* (critiques of actors, parallel to those of courtesans mentioned earlier) entitled *Yakusha kō samisen* of the same year. There may be some validity in the idea proffered by Mizutani that Sukenobu supplanted Makie-shi Genzaburō as the principal illustrator for Hachimonjiya at this time. The end of the seventeenth and beginning of the eighteenth centuries marked the zenith of Hachimonjiya activity, and before 1699 many of their *ukiyo-zōshi* novels by men such as Ejima Kiseki were illustrated by Genzaburō, while after that date his role seems to have been taken over by Sukenobu. One can only guess at possible reasons for this. A number of *kyōgen-bon*, *yakusha hyōban-ki* and *ukiyo-zōshi* were published by Hachimonjiya in the next fifteen to twenty years which are believed to be illustrated by Sukenobu, but without signatures this is still speculative. What is significant is that during this period Sukenobu does not appear to have worked at all in the Tosa style, no doubt due to the waning popularity of novels and poetry requiring this style of illustration.

Despite the sheer quantity of *ukiyo-zōshi* novels that Sukenobu illustrated, the major consideration should be accorded to his *ehon*. Although he produced a few *ehon* before 1716, probably including the celebrated *Ehon shi-nō-kō-shō*, the picture-book survey of the four classes of society, most of his best work in this field falls between 1716 and 1741. (It should be said here that first editions of many of Sukenobu's books are exceedingly rare, and only later reprints of the originals have survived.) Judging from these *ehon*, Sukenobu evidently had an obsessional interest in the portrayal of women of all classes of society. Although this interest has always been an integral part of ukiyo-e, he was perhaps the first major artist of this school to adapt his technique of painting to each individual subject and to make occasional statements about his techniques.

51.   Dancers and blind musicians are portrayed in Sukenobu's *Hyakunin
jorō shina-sadame* (2 vols., 1723).

52.   Sukenobu depicted women of all classes, including flour-millers,
from the same work as Pl. 51.

In the preface to *Ehon tokiwa-gusa* (3 vols., 1730) he states that for ladies of the court it is best to follow the classical (Tosa) style, in particular that of Tosa Mitsunobu, while ordinary women should be treated more "realistically." There is here the implicit assumption that the Tosa school was not "realistic," and, therefore presumably, was "idealistic." *Ehon tokiwa-gusa* itself was designed as a book of instruction in painting, a comparatively rare attempt for a ukiyo-e artist of his period. It contains portraits of court ladies, common ladies and courtesans in the first, second and third volumes respectively. Each volume has a page of notes on the theory of the portraits included. In this way this work repeated an experiment conducted by Sukenobu in several earlier *ehon*, such as *Hyakunin jorō shina-sadame* (2 vols., 1723) (Pls. 51, 52), which also includes studies of women of all classes. Indeed in Volume One there is the portrait of an empress and a female firewood-seller, a breadth of interest typical of ukiyo-e. The significant point is not that Sukenobu found interest in the portrait of a firewood-seller but that he had equal enthusiasm for that of an empress. Other important works of this type were: *Sanjūni-sō sugata kurabe* (1 vol., 1717); *Onna manyō keiko sōshi* (3 vols., 1728); *Ehon tamazakura* (2 vols., 1736); *Ehon chiyomi-gusa* (3 vols., 1740) (Pl. 53); *Ehon hana-momiji* (3 vols., 1748); *Ehon masu-kagami* (3 vols., 1748); and *Ehon makuzu-hara* (3 vols., 1759, published posthumously, with studies of non-female subjects also).

53. The most prolific book illustrator of his time, Nishikawa Sukenobu was responsible for over one hundred *ehon*, including this, the *Ehon chiyomi-gusa* (3 vols., 1740).

These were in addition to a number of *ōraimono* for women such as *Onna kakun* (3 vols., 1729). Sukenobu's work is not of even quality, but at his best his women are typified by grace and elegance, while the finest of his figure studies, whether men or women, are larger than usual, with the composition showing a use of space unequaled, in our view, in any other artist, apart from Utamaro.

In addition to this obsession Sukenobu also had a profound awareness of history, and historical subjects are an important ingredient in his work. His most important work of this type is *Ehon Yamato hiji* (10 vols., 1742), which took three years to complete, filled with poets and painters from history, famous women and historical personalities. The illustrations in this work are generally regarded as Sukenobu's best, and certainly his most extensive. He produced many other similar works drawn from historical legends and anecdotes, of which the following are notable: *Ehon tōwa kagami* (3 vols., 1729); *Ehon Tsukuba-yama* (3 vols., 1730); *Ehon tatoe-gusa* (3 vols., 1731); and *Ehon hana no kagami* (3 vols., 1769, published posthumously). Works such as *Ehon miyako-zōshi* (3 vols., 1746) are historically important for showing the life of ordinary Kyoto people, who always received less attention from ukiyo-e artists than their Edo equivalents.

Sukenobu spent his entire career after 1730 in Osaka (though he was buried in Kyoto on his death in 1751) and was thus a true Kamigata artist. More important, he was the only Kamigata artist of the eighteenth century working in ukiyo-e to have made a considerable impact on Edo, the spiritual home of ukiyo-e. It is interesting to quote a few lines from the artist Yanagisawa Kien (Rikyō) (1706–58), which Kenji Toda includes in his brief account of Sukenobu (Ryerson Catalogue, p. 129): "In ukiyo-e, Hanabusa Itchō is good. There are men like Okumura Masanobu, Torii Kiyonobu, Hanegawa Chinchō, and Kaigetsudō, but the master in painting is Nishikawa Sukenobu. Nishikawa Sukenobu is the saint in ukiyo-e." Naturally the judgment of a Chinese-style painter on ukiyo-e artists is suspect and these words may mean no more than that Sukenobu came nearest, in Yanagisawa's view, to what a ukiyo-e artist ought to be, but even so such a description could only have been accorded to an outstanding artist.

Sukenobu had several followers and pupils including his own son Suketada (1706–62), Nishikawa Sukeyo, Nishikawa Sukenari, Kawashima Nobukiyo and, most important, Hasegawa Mitsunobu. Suketada, Sukeyo and Sukenari were all minor figures who imitated Sukenobu's style. Suketada in particular was responsible for *Ehon mitsuwa-gusa* (1 vol., 1758), no more than a copy of a previously unpublished work by his father Sukenobu. Nobukiyo, more of a friend and contemporary than a pupil, was responsible for some illustrations to novels in ukiyo-e style published between 1711 and the 1720's, particularly in connection with *ukiyo-zōshi* novels of Ejima Kiseki. Very little is known of Mitsunobu's life except that he was from Osaka, and contemporary sources indicate that he was a pupil of Sukenobu. He also seems to have been well acquainted with Ōoka Shunboku, of whom more will be said in the next chapter. Mitsunobu at any rate illustrated twenty or thirty books, many of which were in the style of Sukenobu, and he displayed a certain penchant for warriors as found in *Eiyū gafu* (1 vol., date unknown). Probably his most famous work, however, was the five-volume *Nihon sankai meibutsu zue* (*Illustrations of the Famous Products of Mountain and Sea in Japan*), published in 1754. His career was evidently a long one (unless L. N. Brown's hypothesis that there were two artists with the same name is correct), for examples of his work dating from the 1720s are also known.

EDO ARTISTS OF THE GENROKU ERA (1688–1704)

Despite the achievements of Sukenobu and his contemporaries in the Kamigata region, Edo was still the center of ukiyo-e throughout this period. Moronobu (Kichibei) had a considerable following there, among which were his sons Hishikawa Morofusa and Hishikawa Moronaga, who both followed his style. Morofusa and Moronaga were probably too overshadowed by their father to make any impact of their own, although Moronaga had a reputation for skillful hand-coloring of his and Moronobu's illustrations. The most gifted of Moronobu's immediate pupils was Furuyama Moroshige (Tarōbei), who may have been his nephew. Only four known works bear his signature (although others are attributed to him on stylistic grounds) and these were executed between 1686 and 1691. His most famous work was the obscene *Kōshoku Edo murasaki* about the Yoshiwara, published in five volumes in 1686, which so antagonized the authorities that the blocks were ordered to be burned. A similar book, *Shika no maki-fude*, published in the same year, resulted in the banishment of the author, one Shikano Bunzaemon, while Moroshige himself was compelled to leave Edo for a time.

Of Moronobu's other minor pupils, all of who are listed in L. N. Brown's work, the artist Ishikawa Ryūsen (active 1680–1720) is worthy of mention. Ryūsen was also an accomplished novelist and writer, but is better known for his illustrations. These include several *hyōban-ki* and, most notably, *Yamato kōsaku e-shō* (4 vols., c. 1694) and *Kōshoku e-zukushi* (1 vol., 1698), both of which feature the arts, crafts, festivals and agriculture of Japan. Ryūsen probably wrote these works as well as illustrated them. He was influenced by Moronobu's style, though there are certain differences in their work, for Ryūsen used a thinner brushstroke and his figures are smaller. This may also be said of another minor pupil of Moronobu, Sugimura Masataka, who was responsible for the illustrations in *Goseibai shikimoku e-shō*, published in one volume in 1697, showing the influence of Torii Kiyonobu.

We have looked briefly at the early development of ukiyo-e in the Kamigata region and more briefly at the immediate pupils of Moronobu in Edo. What becomes clear at this point is that by the late Genroku era ukiyo-e had become sufficiently important not only to be recognized as an independent development within Japanese art but also for it to become divided within itself. The Moronobu line, or Moronobu-ha, was the earliest recognizable ukiyo-e school of illustration, remembering of course that ukiyo-e was not confined to book illustration. The other schools of ukiyo-e which arose in Edo at this period were not so different from one another, although they are sufficiently distinctive to be recognized as subdivisions of the ukiyo-e movement as a whole. To a large extent, therefore, the subsequent history of ukiyo-e can be viewed in terms of these various schools, or *ha*. These are the Torii-ha, the Okumura-ha, the Nishimura-ha, the Katsukawa-ha, the Kitagawa-ha, the Kitao-ha, the Utagawa-ha and the artists who drew their inspiration from Hokusai. Apart from these principal schools there were also subdivisions in each and not all artists can be firmly associated with one school or another. One of the major problems of a brief survey of an artistic development as vast as ukiyo-e is that some kind of framework of discussion is necessary, although such a framework is ultimately self-defeating. Bearing this *caveat* in mind, we can look briefly at each school in turn.

THE TORII SCHOOL

The Torii-ha was founded by the Osaka artist Torii Kiyonobu (1663–1729), also known as Torii Shōbei, whose father, Torii Shōshichi, was a rather celebrated *kabuki* actor specializing in female roles. This strong theatrical connection was to play an important part in the development of the school. Kiyonobu first studied painting under his father, also a painter and designer of theatrical posters and playbills, and in 1687 both father and son moved to Edo where they set up a studio. In the same year Kiyonobu's illustrations appeared for the first time in the novel *Iro-no-someginu*, and no other book was illustrated by him until 1693. Kiyonobu was not prolific as a book illustrator, producing at most 26 works between 1687 and 1728. During this period he concentrated on designs for advertisement posters for *kabuki* theaters in Edo as well as on single-sheet actor prints. In his work in book illustration, he was drawn toward *kyōgen-bon*, the illustrated summaries of *kabuki* plays equivalent to the earlier-mentioned *jōruri-bon*. The majority of his surviving works are of this type, setting a pattern for later artists of his school. Although these extremely popular books have not withstood the test of time as well as some others, what has survived of Kiyonobu's work in this field indicates enormous power but little delicacy. Yet he also produced exquisite picture books, two of which, *Kokon-shibai hyakunin isshu* (1 vol., 1693) and *Keisei ehon* (1 vol., 1700) (Pl. 54), are outstanding. The former book is a collection of 100 portraits of *kabuki* actors accompanied by *kyōka* poems, while the latter is a collection of 19 portraits of courtesans. In both of these works the delicacy lacking in the *kyōgen-bon* illustrations is present and the courtesans are depicted as graceful, although a certain fullness of face is noticeable, probably reflecting the taste of the times. Kiyonobu also experimented with color printing and produced several *beni-e* prints, although he did not use color in his book illustrations.

The Torii line descended from Kiyonobu is exceeded in complexity only by the Utagawa school. Artistically, it was extremely closeknit and the styles of individual

54. Torii Kiyonobu's depiction of a graceful courtesan comes from the *Keisei ehon*, published in 1700.

artists within the school are often hard to tell apart. The school as a whole, which continued until after the Meiji Restoration in 1868, always concentrated on theatrical material, but also became closely involved with four new types of fiction which evolved from the 1730s, namely *aka-hon*, *kuro-hon*, *ao-hon* and *kibyōshi*, particularly the first three. *Aka-hon*, *kuro-hon* and *ao-hon* were rather similar in content and differed from one another only in terms of the colors of their covers: namely red, black and blue respectively. They were picture books with very little text, intended for children or semi-literate adults who could not cope with the wordier *ukiyo-zōshi* books. They consisted of stories that were highly fanciful, often dealing with supernatural events and appropriately illustrated. The fourth new genre, *kibyōshi*, or "yellow" books, was also rather similar in content but contained more text than the others and was introduced at a slightly later date. The dating of *aka-hon*, *kuro-hon* and *ao-hon* poses many problems, since undated reprints are common and the originals themselves are not clearly dated. There is some argument as to the time these books first appeared, but the decade after 1740 is usually given as the starting point, although examples are known from the earlier Kyōhō era (1716–36). In general, the authors are anonymous but occasionally, when an artist's name does appear, it invariably belongs to the Torii school, confirming the close association between this genre of fiction and the school. Unfortunately, the

143

illustrations in them are repetitious and lack any distinctiveness to mark them for collectors. Although *aka-hon* and *ao-hon* were not produced in great numbers, *kuro-hon* were, mostly by the Urokogataya and Yamamotoya houses of Edo, and new discoveries are constantly being made in this complex bibliographic field.

The artists principally involved with illustrating these books were Torii Kiyonobu II (active late 18th century), Torii Kiyomasu II (1706–63), Torii Kiyomitsu (1735–85), Torii Kiyoshige (active early–mid-18th century), Torii Kiyohiro (active mid-18th century), Torii Kiyohisa (active mid–late 18th century), Torii Kiyotsune (active c. 1780), and Torii Kiyonaga (1753–1815; principally for *kibyōshi*). A typical example of Torii illustration of *kuro-hon* is the five-volume *Raikō ichidaiki* (c. 1730), almost certainly the work of Kiyonobu II. This story of a Heian-period warrior is filled with heroic feats of war with a leavening of the miraculous, such as the provision of magic saké by the gods Hachiman, Sumiyoshi and Kumano. Such was the staple fare of *kuro-hon* novels, which in length seldom exceeded ten pages per volume. Kiyonobu was also responsible for four other similar works. All the above-named Torii artists, together with minor artists of the same school, devoted their talents to the illustration of *aka-hon*, *kuro-hon* and *ao-hon* in addition to the production of actor prints and theatrical playbills, but there is little point here in listing all these works typified by *Raikō ichidaiki*, for a good, though not comprehensive, list can be found in *Nihon shōsetsu nempyō* (*Chronology of Japanese Fiction*) (*see* Bibl.).

Three Torii artists deserving more specific discussion here are Kondō Kiyoharu (active early 18th century), Hanegawa Chinchō (1679–1754) and Torii Kiyonaga. Kiyoharu is usually regarded as a pupil of Kiyonobu I, but as Mizutani Futō (*see* Bibl.) suggests, one can also see the influences of Okumura Masanobu and Furuyama Moroshige in his work. He may have been a pupil of Torii Shōshichi and belonged to the Osaka branch of the Torii tradition, although he worked as a copyist before engaging in book illustration. A prolific designer of advertisement posters for the famous Nakamuraza theater, he, like many Torii artists, concentrated on theatrical works in book illustration. The *Hachikazuki* of 1710 was probably the first work of this type that he illustrated, followed by *Chōsen taiheiki* (c. 1711) and some other similar works. He also illustrated three *kana-zōshi* novels, including the one-volume *Amayadori* of 1728, which reveals how much the Tosa style normally associated with such works had been subverted by this time. Before his death between 1730 and 1736, he worked on several *aka-hon* and was altogether one of the most prolific Torii illustrators, although Mizutani says "one finds no special distinguishing characteristics in his work."

Hanegawa Chinchō (real name Ōta Bengorō) was born to a wealthy samurai family at Kawaguchi in Musashi province in 1679 and was an ancestor of the distinguished novelist Kyokutei Bakin. He came to Edo early in his life and eventually studied painting in the ukiyo-e style with Torii Kiyonobu I. He did no commercial work for a time but was ultimately drawn by Kiyonobu into the inevitable Torii practice of designing posters. He was not a prolific book illustrator, working on approximately 14 theatrical books

55. An early example of color illustration used purely decoratively, this is one of four color-printed illustrations by Ogawa Haritsu from the *Chichi no on* (1730), a *haiku* anthology published to honor the memory of the actor Ichikawa Danjūrō I. This work also contains 66 black-and-white illustrations by Hanabusa Ippō.

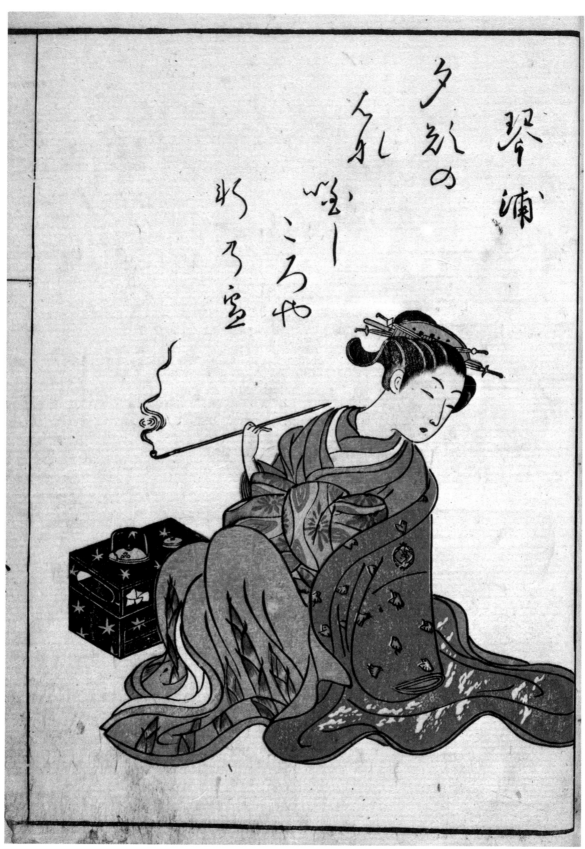

琴浦

夕永の

乱嗟し

ころや

新乃空

56. The courtesan Kotoura, by Suzuki Harunobu, from Volume 5 of the *Yoshiwara seirō bijin awase* (5 vols., 1770). This book is regarded not only as Harunobu's finest work of illustration but also as an inspirational example of the use of color in printing. This could be considered as the book that started the golden age of color printing in Japan. This portrait, like all the others, depicts a real person, and the collection is remarkable for the variety achieved in the costumes and poses of the courtesans.

仲見友成

遠山に
夕日をうけて
二すぢの
ふる滝ちとき
り立る空

57. A portrait of a *kyōka* poet, by Utagawa Toyohiro, from the *Jūsan-ban kyōka awase*, published in
1793. All the illustrations in this book are notable
for the richness of the colors as well as the humorous
poses of the poets.

田名武阿陵丸

みわたせは
邊と声節に
ちらも浜く
高田るらに

重丸を
雑台

請対人の多うも
らやき岩お多
ら田のら傍上
めらうろ

明根捨

郡々三田の
まてくのも
声成タよ雪庭の
あきのをこそ
細蟹人

こヽ了ヲのす
の易加成々そ
くやくろ
夢うそし時の
よろくり

雇　山法

もちサくちゑ出れ
島のつは妻
し

59. A woman and child weaving in the countryside with Mt. Fuji in the background, one of Hokusai's neglected masterpieces, showing the artist working in classical ukiyo-e style. From the *Shunkyō-jō*, published in 1798, at the end of the golden age of ukiyo-e.

◁ 58. This scene of spectators (*previous page*) at the racecourse at Takada (which is not depicted) is from the *Ehon kyōka yama mata yama* (1804), illustrated by Hokusai, who here combines figure studies with landscapes.

60.   A distant view of Enoshima in spring, by Hokusai (*above*), from the
kyōka anthology *Yanagi no ito* (1797), published by Tsutaya Jūsaburō. This is
a good example of the high quality of production of Tsutaya's illustrated
books. The work also contains illustrations by Tōrin, Eïshi and others.

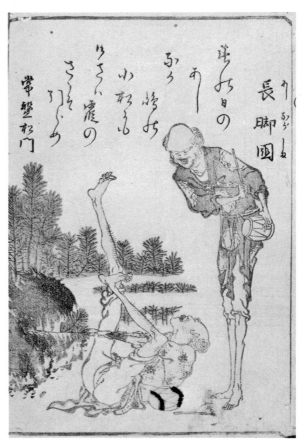

61.   The mythical land of the long-legged men (*right*), shows Hokusai at
his most imaginative and humorous. From the *kyōka* anthology *Shikinami-
gusa*, published in 1796.

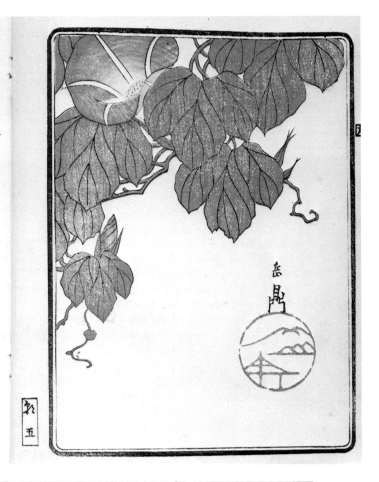

本曽

64. A bridge along the Kiso highway, by Yanagawa Shigenobu,
from the *kyōka* anthology *Kyōka meisho zue* (c. 1826). This illustration provides a good example of post-Shigenaga ukiyo-e.
Note the unusual soft colors of the landscape.

◁ 62. A morning glory, by Yashima Gakutei (*opposite above*),
from the *kyōka* anthology *Asagao hyakushu kyōka-shū* (1830).
It is noteworthy that in this kind of anthology the beauty of
the illustrations belies the comic and often vulgar nature of
the poems.

◁ 63. This depiction of a carp (*opposite below*) comes from the
Tatsu-no-miya tsuko, an anthology illustrated with fish and
crustaceans by Kitao Masayoshi, published in 1802.

65. A monkey trainer entertains courtesans during the New Year festivities. This illustration by Utamaro is from the *Ehon waka ebisu* (1786), published by Tsutaya Jūsaburō and believed by some to be the first *ehon* entirely illustrated by Utamaro. Evident are some typical features of the artist's style, notably the inclusion of a painting within a painting, the courtesans in silhouette and a symmetrically balanced composition. The cloud formations may be regarded as a deliberate attempt on the part of Utamaro to be archaic. All the illustrations in this book have some connection with early spring.

66. A boating scene, by the ukiyo-e artist Kubo Shunman ▷ (*opposite above*), from the *kyōka* anthology *Momo saezuri* (1797), published by Tsutaya Jūsaburō. Note how the distant perspective is only briefly sketched on the right-hand page, suggesting that what is not portrayed is as important as what is.

67. The *kabuki* actors Ichikawa Danzō, Ichikawa Dansaku and ▷ Ichikawa Danzaburō watching fishermen at work (*opposite below*), by Utagawa Toyokuni I for the *Yakusha sangaikyō* (1801) by Shikitei Samba. It is worth noting how much more prominence is accorded the actors than the fishermen. This illustration follows the tradition established by Katsukawa Shunshō of portraying actors away from the context of the theater.

共鼓蘭橈遊水
有星吹仙管遥
雲溪 山陰

69. This river scene by Chikudō Ki is from the *Chikudō gafu* (1803), one of the finest of all illustrated books produced by the Nanga school, typified by the Chinese poem and the *bunjin*-style scene.

◁ **68.** Feeding a caged bird (*previous page*), by Utamaro, from the *kyōka* anthology *Otoko dōka* (1798), published by Tsutaya Jūsaburō. The woman in the middle holding a pestle provokes laughter from the maidservant on the left, since the pestle was regarded among the lower classes as a phallic symbol. Note how by placing most of the figures on the right, Utamaro concentrates on the figure of the maidservant, who is the focal point of the illustration.

70. A mountain landscape in Nanga style (*above*), by Ike no Taiga, from the *Taigadō gafu* (1803). Despite the beauty and subtlety of the colors, there is a marked lack of realism, characteristic of all Nanga art.

71. Pine trees in Maruyama style, by Ōnishi Chinnen (*right*), pupil of Watanabe Nangaku, from the *Sonan gafu* (1834). An example of an artist trying to capture the spirit of the subject rather than its actual appearance.

72. A humorous *haiga*-style depiction of a street entertainer (*above*), by the otherwise unknown Kyoto artist Hosaku, from the *haiku* anthology *Tokai-jō*, illustrated by various artists and published in Kyoto in 1803.

73. This old man (*left*) is part of an illustration representing a memorial service for a dead badger, by Matsumura Goshun, founder of the Shijō school, for the *Shin hanatsumi* (c. 1784), the diary of Buson. This is one of few known book illustrations by Goshun and a classic example of the cursive *haiga* style.

74. A lively and humorous portrayal of courtesans (*opposite* ▷ *above*), executed in Maruyama style by Aoi Sōkyū, from the *Kishi empu*, published in 1803. The lack of realism provides a basic contrast with the courtesans of the ukiyo-e school (cf. Pl. 56).

75. Women admiring the cherry blossoms, by Yamaguchi ▷ Soken (*opposite below*), from the very rare collection of *haiku* poems, *Ranhō-chō*, published in 1806. The artist was one of the very few pupils of Maruyama Ōkyo to work creatively in book illustration.

78. A mountain and water landscape in light colors (*opposite* ▷ *above*), by Kawamura Bumpō for the *Bumpō sansui gafu*, published in 1824.

79. A haze of spring blossoms at Mimuro, by Kawamura Bumpō ▷ (*opposite below*), from the *Teito gakei ichiran* (1809–16), a collection of views of Kyoto.

76. Landscape with pagoda, by the Maruyama artist Fukuchi Hakuei, one of the most skillful colorists of his time, from the fourth book in the anthology entitled *Kyōka tegoto no hana*, published in 1813.

77. Enjoying the distant view in the cool, from the *Kyōchūzan* (1816), featuring mountain landscapes by the Nanga school artist Kameda Bōsai (Taihei Suimin). The soft colors and the figure surrounded by natural scenery are typical features of Nanga painting and book illustration.

御宝花露

82. A flight of birds, by Satō Suiseki, pupil of Matsumura Goshun, from the *Suiseki gafu nihen*, published in 1820. The variety, humor and intricacy of this illustration is self-evident.

◁ 80. Loquats on a branch (*opposite above*), illustrated in the Shijō style by Tani Bunchō for the *Shazanrō ehon* (1816). Bunchō was master of a bewildering variety of artistic styles, ranging from pure Nanga to pure Shijō.

◁ 81. A bird and flower study (*opposite below*), by the Nagoya artist Chō Gesshō, for the *Fugyō gaso* published in Nagoya in 1817. The impressionistic portrayal of the subject makes this both a typical and classical example of the Shijō style.

83. Cherry-blossom viewing along the banks of the Sumida River, by Ōnishi Chinnen, often associated with the Maruyama school, from the *Azuma no teburi* (1829), a work unusual for its collection of Edo street scenes as opposed to those of Kyoto, the spiritual home of the Maruyama school.

84. This study of a man and an ox (*opposite above*) by ▷ Kawamura Kihō is from the *Kihō gafu* (1 vol.), published in 1827. The colors, if not the style, owe a great deal to Kawamura Bumpō.

85. An old man fishing (*opposite below*), copied by Yamaguchi ▷ Soken, from the *En'ō gafu* (1837), a collection of paintings by Maruyama Ōkyo.

合衆國北亞墨利加
ガウシウユク
合衆國

合衆國此国北ハ新貌利太泥亜ニ接シ南ハ墨是可ニ至ル

86. An American naval officer and marine, by the otherwise unknown artist Tagawa Shundō, from the *Gaiban yōbō zue* (1854). This book is one of many produced in the 1850s following the visit of Commodore Perry, designed to inform the Japanese about people of the West. The uniforms are obviously based on observation, but it is curious to note that both figures have oriental features.

and *aka-hon*, of which *Yaoya o-shichi* (1 vol., c. 1720) is considered his most representative work.

Torii Kiyonaga was born in Sagami province in 1753 and later came to Edo to work for the publisher Shirokiya. He subsequently became the pupil of Torii Kiyomitsu, and when the latter died in 1785, he himself headed the Torii school. He died in 1815. Although best known as a fine print artist who exerted a profound influence on later artists including Shigemasa and Utamaro, Kiyonaga also illustrated books, principally *kibyōshi*. He is believed to have written as well as illustrated 30 *kibyōshi* novels, beginning with the two-volume *Fūryū mono-hazuke* in 1775. In addition, some 90 *kibyōshi* by other authors were also illustrated by him, making him the most prolific Torii illustrator, with the exception of Kiyotsune. He was certainly the most influential artist of *kibyōshi* books in the latter part of the eighteenth century and his style was consciously imitated by many other artists. It should be said, however, that his reputation deservedly rests on his prints rather than on his book illustrations, which were not remarkable in any way or distinguishable from those of other Torii artists working in the same field. Of his few *ehon*, the most noteworthy is *Ehon Edo monomi-ga-oka* (2 vols., 1785, color).

Book illustration was not the forte of the Torii artists, despite their prolificacy in this field in the eighteenth and nineteenth centuries, and their work compares unfavorably with contemporaries in other schools. In the main, like Kiyonaga, their best work was reserved for single-sheet prints and it is on these that they should be judged.

THE OKUMURA SCHOOL

It is misleading to speak of an Okumura school since the founder, Okumura Masanobu (1685–1768), had few pupils of any significance to continue his line. Nevertheless, he was an important and influential artist whose career spanned a good part of the eighteenth century and whose work showed considerable development. Since he did not belong to any other school, despite the influence of Moronobu in his early work it is permissible to speak of him in terms of an original line of ukiyo-e.

He appears to have been born in Edo, and in addition to his artistic activities ran a publishing business under the name Okumura Genroku. Opinions as to his artistic lineage differ, but the consensus of opinion seems to be that he took Torii Kiyonobu I for a master or, at least, fell heavily under his influence. During his long career he worked in a variety of genres including *ukiyo-zōshi* novels (which he possible wrote as well as illustrated under the name Bai-ō), theatrical books, erotica and *ehon*. His earliest known work, executed at the age of sixteen, was *Keisei ehon (Shōgi gachō)*, an album of portraits of courtesans, published in 1701. However, since this was merely a copy of the book of the same title previously attributed to Kiyonobu (published in 1700), it only demonstrates the close relationship between these two artists. Since Masanobu was only sixteen at the time, it is improbable that this relationship could have been anything other than that of master-pupil. L. N. Brown refers to a theatrical work entitled *Kyōtarō* (published in 1703) as Masanobu's earliest work, but *Keisei ehon* definitely preceded it and Japanese authorities, at any rate, do not recognize the existence of the other book.

During the next few years Masanobu concentrated on illustrating *ukiyo-zōshi* novels and theatrical books, of which no less than twenty (in 70 volumes) were produced between 1704 and 1710. Representative works of this period include the *ukiyo-zōshi* novel *Wakakusa Genji monogatari* (6 vols., 1707, where the influence of Moronobu is pronounced) and the theater books *Tōgensō* (1 vol., 1708) and *Hachiman Tarō* (1 vol., 1710), both of which are stylistically indistinguishable from similar works of Kiyonobu. After 1710, his interest in this kind of work terminated abruptly and he did not pursue it again until the Kyōhō era (1716–36).

In addition to these conventional works, Masanobu also produced 14 *ehon* in the early part of his career. All of them are undated, but they seem to have been done between 1702 and 1716. Most of them show a pronounced Kiyonobu influence, but evidence of an original Masanobu style is also apparent. Many of these *ehon* are untitled, but in these cases provisional titles (denoted in the following list by the letter *p.*) have been allocated by Japanese scholars. The works are as follows: *Shibai-e* (*p.*, late Genroku era); *Shibai-e Yamato irotake* (c. 1704); *Gōyū zue* (*p.*, c. 1704–10); *Shibai-e* (*p.*, c. 1704–10); *Yūkun midate Genji* (*p.*, c. 1711); *Yoshiwara hakkei* (c. 1710); *Chaban kyōgen* (*p.*, c. 1700–4); *Dōke midate* (*p.*, c. 1704–10); *Ukiyo fūzoku okashii kotobukuro* (c. 1711); *Shōjō Ebisu Daikoku* (*p.*, c. 1711–16); *Yoshiwara yūkun sugatami* (*p.*, c. 1704–10); *Yoshiwara kayoi* (*p.*, c. 1711–16); *Yūkun sakesui sankyō* (c. 1711–16) (Pl. 87); and *Jūnigatsu* (*p.*, c. 1704–10).

These titles give a fair idea of their contents. There is no text in the books and they are more like bound collections of prints, with actors, courtesans and their clientele as the principal subjects. Although the influence of Kiyonobu is evident, particularly in the earlier works, the figures of the courtesans, for example, are more slender and their faces thinner and more "beautiful." They also indicate that whereas Masanobu had earlier, under the influence of Kiyonobu, concentrated on actors, his interest veered toward courtesans, who were not a Torii specialty. Moreover, the treatment of the subject matter is much less confined than in Kiyonobu's work, and *Yoshiwara yūkun sugatami*, for example, contains an interesting picture of a courtesan receiving moxa treatment, a method of preserving youth and beauty.

Masanobu also had a passionate lifelong interest in *Genji monogatari* and constantly explored illustrative possibilities of this famous novel. The *Wakakusa Genji monogatari* has already been mentioned, and he illustrated another *Genji*-based *ukiyo-zōshi* novel, *Kōhaku Genji monogatari*, published in six volumes in 1709. After his period of concentration on *ehon*, he returned to the *Genji* theme in the 1720s with the novels *Zokkai Genji monogatari* and *Hiinagata* (*Hinazuru*) *Genji*, each published in six volumes in 1721. He was to approach the same subject again in a later *ehon*.

His later *ehon* present several problems since most of them have no printed date and

87. Saké-tasting, by Okumura Masanobu, from the *Yūkun sakesui sankyō* (c. 1712). Note the size and boldness of the figures.

others exist only in posthumous editions. What seems clear, however, is that he abandoned the large and more attractive format of the earlier *ehon*, so his later work suffers by comparison. Not outstandingly prolific in his youth, by the 1720s, when still comparatively young, Masanobu seems to have slowed down, working only sporadically. The most representative of his later *ehon* are *Kinryūzan Asakusa senbonzakura* (1 vol., probably 1734); *Shin Yoshiwara senbonzakura* (1 vol., probably 1734); *Ehon ogura nishiki* (5 vols., 1740); *Musha ehon kongō rikishi* (2 vols., c. 1752); and *Ehon sanjūni-sō* (*Edo o-yama ehon bijin fukutoku sanjūni-sō*, known only in a posthumous edition of 1778). The first two works were probably designed as complementary volumes, the first presenting scenes associated with the Asakusa shrines and the second showing courtesans engaged in flower arrangement and tea ceremony or playing musical instruments in the new Yoshiwara. Courtesans again are the subject of *Ehon sanjūni-sō*, a series of "ideal" beauties, with other women in various occupations such as dressmaking. All his courtesans are typified by a slenderness, showing how far Masanobu had deviated from Torii influence. *Musha ehon kongō rikishi* is a very different type of work showing the deeds of ancient warrior heroes, while *Ehon ogura nishiki*, regarded as the best of his later *ehon*, returns once more to the *Genji* theme. Basically, it is a combination of Fujiwara Teika's *Ogura hyakunin isshu* and *Genji monogatari*, borrowing poems from

171

each with humorous *kyōka* parodies. The illustrations in turn parody and "update" the classical illustrations so cleverly that the whole work may be described as satirical.

Of Masanobu's few pupils, Okumura Toshinobu, (active mid-18th century), Okumura Masafusa (active mid-18th century), Okumura Toshifusa (active mid-18th century) and Yoshimura Katsumasa (active mid-18th century) are all known to have illustrated books. Toshinobu worked on *kuro-hon* such as *Takasago tokai e-iri* (c. 1748) and Masafusa on *Tsuru-take nasakeno akibito* (1747). Both these artists produced too few books to allow worthwhile judgments, but what exists is very much in the Torii style. The same could be said of the more obscure Toshifusa, while Yoshimura Katsumasa is known to have produced only one book, *Taisei shūchō* (3 vols., c. 1720), a collection of sketches of animals, plants and shells, which was not of the ukiyo-e school at all.

THE NISHIMURA SCHOOL

Nishimura Shigenaga (1697–1756) is an obscure figure whose significance in book illustration lies more in the famous pupils he taught than in his own works, although he was an inventive print artist who pioneered early color printing. It is not known under whom he studied, although it is said that he was influenced by Torii Kiyonobu I, Okumura Masanobu and, indirectly, Nishikawa Sukenobu. Certainly during the Kyōhō and Gembun eras (1716–40) he is believed to have illustrated a number of *aka-hon* and *kuro-hon* very much in the Torii style. His prints, however, display a broader range of interest, for he depicted not only actors and courtesans but also flowers and birds. He is also said to have made use of Western perspective. His earliest book illustrations appear in the novel *Shiryō gedatsu monogatari* (2 vols., 1712), published when he was fifteen, with the last illustration bearing the signature "Senkadō Nishimura Shigenaga *fude*" (painted by Senkadō Nishimura Shigenaga). His reputation as a book illustrator rests, apart from the few *aka-hon* and *kuro-hon* which he may or may not have illustrated, on two *ehon*: *Ehon kokinran* (3 vols., 1762, with Harunobu) and, more particularly, *Ehon Edo miyage* (3 vols., 1753). The former will be mentioned again in the account of Harunobu's work, but the *Ehon Edo miyage* was an extremely important and influential book. Its three volumes contain a series of Edo views at various times of the year, and, significantly, the figures are small and do not dominate the landscape. One of the most obvious features of ukiyo-e up to this time and throughout its history is the prominence given to figures, and although *Ehon Edo miyage* did not reverse this trend even in book illustration, it may have opened up possibilities for a more landscape-oriented ukiyo-e style that was seized on by later illustrators like Hokusai and Hiroshige. Certainly this title was used by several later artists for similar productions, which clearly indicates its influence.

Suzuki Harunobu (1724–70), the best known and most respected today of Shigenaga's pupils, particularly in the West, was born in Edo. He came under Shigenaga's influence at quite a late age, adopting the surname Suzuki (Shigenaga's original name) as a token of respect for his master. Virtually nothing is known of his early life except that his own name was Hozumi Jihei and that he may have worked as a brush-seller in his youth. However, from the early 1750s he was known as an artist of considerable talent who made effective use of color at a time when color printing was still in its infancy. His favorite subject was the courtesan, both in prints and books, and although little distinctiveness can be perceived in the faces of his subjects, he achieved a remarkable variety in the pattern and arrangement of their costumes and poses in his color prints.

Unlike most artists of his period, he completely avoided the novel and concentrated on *ehon*. Working almost exclusively in black and white (even the celebrated color *Yoshiwara bijin awase* also exists in a black-and-white edition), he produced 14 *ehon* between 1762 and 1770, almost all published by Yamazaki Kinbei, and another 4 published posthumously. These works were: *Ehon kokinran* (3 vols., 1762); *Ehon shogei nishiki* (3 vols., 1762); *Ehon hana-kazura* (3 vols., 1764); *Ehon kotowaza-gusa* (3 vols., 1765); *Ehon sazare-ishi* (3 vols., 1766); *Ehon haru no tomo* (3 vols., 1767); *Ehon chiyo no matsu* (3 vols., 1767); *Ehon buyū nishiki no tamoto* (3 vols., 1767); *Ehon warabe no mato* (3 vols., 1767); *Ehon zoku Edo miyage* (3 vols., 1768); *Ehon yachiyo-gusa* (3 vols., 1768) (Pl. 88); *Ehon take no hayashi* (3 vols., 1769); *Ehon ukiyo-bukuro* (3 vols., 1770);

88. An illustration from one of Harunobu's finest examples of black-and-white book illustration, the *Ehon yachiyo-gusa* (3 vols., 1768). The small dog is particularly associated with Harunobu.

173

Yoshiwara seirō bijin awase (5 vols., 1770) (Pl. 56); *Ehon haru no nishiki* (2 vols., published posthumously in 1771); *Ehon iroha uta* (1 vol., published posthumously in 1775); *Ehon misao-gusa* (2 vols., published posthumously in 1778); and *Ehon haru no yuki* (3 vols., date unknown).

In addition, he contributed a frontispiece to Ishikawa Toyonobu's *Yoshiwara taizen* and is sometimes credited with the illustrations in *Tōto meisho* (c. 1765–70), an album of color-printed scenes of Edo similar to *Ehon Edo miyage*. Otherwise only his *Yoshiwara seirō bijin awase* and *Ehon haru no nishiki* are in color. *Ehon kokinran*, his earliest work of this type, was produced in collaboration with Shigenaga and consists of miscellaneous illustrations of peoples' lives in spring and summer, occasionally drawing on Chinese themes for inspiration. Several of the themes are also taken from Japanese literature, notably *Ehon hana-kazura* and *Ehon sazare-ishi*, both of which are based on the *Sanjū-rokka-sen*. A pleasing feature in some of the books is the occasional use of gray wash for added dimension and grading.

Undoubtedly the most famous and influential of Harunobu's works is the *Yoshiwara seirō bijin awase*, a collection of 166 color portraits of courtesans, each accompanied by a *hokku* poem. It is impossible to gauge accurately the influence of this finest example of early color illustration in books, but there is no doubt that the soft, delicate greens against a gray or gray-green background, and the intricate working of the courtesans' kimono, to say nothing of the varied poses and activities of the subjects, served as a mine of inspiration for his contemporaries. The golden age of color printing in Japanese book illustration is generally regarded to have lasted from 1770 to 1830 or shortly after, and there is no doubt that this book marks the beginning of that age. Books with color-printed illustrations had been produced before Harunobu's time, but none achieved such harmonious and effortless integration of color to subject as this.

Isoda Koryūsai, whose life is very obscure, was either a fellow pupil of Harunobu under Shigenaga or, as some believe, a pupil of Harunobu. His prints, for which he is best known, show clear signs of Harunobu's influence, but they also encompassed landscape and traditional Kanō specialties of birds and flowers. He left only four examples of illustrated books: *Azuma no nishiki tayu-kurai* (1777); *Ehon yakusha te-kagami* (1 vol., 1779); *Konzatsu Yamato sōga* (3 vols., 1781); and *Hokuri no uta* (1 vol., c. 1784). Of these, the first two are so rare that even Nakada (*see* Bibl.) had not seen any copies. *Konzatsu Yamato sōga*, a collection of humorous sketches of animals and birds, shows pronounced Kanō influence and is reminiscent of the work of Hanabusa Itchō. *Hokuri no uta* is a collection of Chinese poems with appropriate illustrations again displaying a pronounced Kanō influence, particularly in the landscapes.

Shiba Kōkan (1738–1818) was a pupil of Harunobu and even possibly his adopted son, who executed a number of prints either in Harunobu's style or copied directly from his works. He apparently became weary of this kind of work, perhaps a reason for his eventual journey to Nagasaki in 1788, where he studied European painting (as far as it was possible with the limited facilities possessed by the Dutch) and copper-plate engraving. This had a profound effect on his artistic career, drawing him away from both the traditional ukiyo-e subject matter and styles. His one major book was *Seiyū ryodan*, a collection of his sketches from his travels, which he published, apparently at his own expense, in five volumes in 1790. Revised and enlarged editions of the same work were subsequently published under the titles *Gazu seiyū ryodan* (1803) and *Seiyū nikki* (6 vols., 1815). All three works were substantially the same with a number of interesting studies not only of Japanese landscapes (where the use of Western perspective is noticeable) but also of various activities of the Dutch, with special emphasis on Dutch sea vessels and whale-hunting. Apart from book illustrations and prints, Shiba Kōkan also left several copper engravings. He is sometimes not regarded as a true ukiyo-e artist, but in fact it is more correct to say that he was a ukiyo-e artist who chose unusual subjects for his times—subjects that were subsequently picked up by several other ukiyo-e artists in the Bakumatsu period (c. 1830–68).

The most senior pupil of Shigenaga was Ishikawa Toyonobu (1711–85), who had studied under Kiyomasu II before coming under the influence of Okumura Masanobu and, finally, Shigenaga. His artistic activity in book illustration spanned the decades 1750–80. His earlier *ehon* show clear Torii influence, but works done at the end of his career such as *Ehon chiyo no haru* (3 vols., 1769) and *Ehon oshie-gusa* (2 vols., 1779) are almost inseparable in style from the *ehon* of Harunobu.

THE KITAGAWA SCHOOL

The Kitagawa-ha takes its name from Kitagawa Utamaro, who adopted this name out of respect for his patron, the Edo publisher Kitagawa (Tsutaya) Jūsaburō, but the school itself was founded by Utamaro's master Toriyama Sekien (1712–88). Sekien came from a wealthy cultured background and gained recognition as a *haiku* poet as well as a painter. His formal instruction was received from Kanō Gyokuen (1688–1743) and the Kanō influence remained dominant throughout his working life. He is known to have produced only eight illustrated books, virtually all on the subject of demons and ghosts, a theme on which Japanese artists have always displayed great inventiveness. His known *ehon* are as follows: *Sekien gafu* (2 vols., 1774); *Ehon hyakki yagyō* (3 vols., 1776); *Suiko gasenran* (3 vols., 1777); *Eji hiken* (3 vols., 1778); *Konjaku zoku hyakki* (3 vols., 1779); *Hyakki yagyō shūi* (3 vols., 1780); *Gato seiyūdan* (3 vols., 1783); *Gato hyakki tsurezure-bukuro* (3 vols., 1784); and *Kamakura no chikabito kashū* (1 vol., 1787, with Sekiryū and Utamaro).

The two most interesting of these are *Sekien gafu* and *Gato hyakki tsurezure-bukuro*, a most imaginative ghost and demon book. The extremely rare *Sekien gafu* is a collection of a variety of subjects including several landscapes in the Kanō style, which although ordinary are enhanced by the soft and light colors resulting from the use of the *fukibokashi* technique of applying color to the block, which Sekien is believed to have devised and which was used by later artists for landscapes in book illustration.

Gato hyakki tsurezure-bukuro is a collection of 48 studies of demons transformed from all sorts of household utensils, and displays remarkable inventiveness, although it is difficult to regard it as an example of ukiyo-e illustration. In fact, although Sekien is normally regarded as a Kanō artist "converted" to ukiyo-e, his heart was never really in the new movement and his traditional association with ukiyo-e derives from the work of his pupils.

The most notable of these was Kitagawa Utamaro (c. 1753–1806), one of the few artists in the history of ukiyo-e to achieve the pinnacles of success in both prints and book illustration. As a print artist he concentrated on *bijin-ga* and thus invites comparison with his near-contemporary Harunobu. In book illustration, however, while Harunobu produced *ehon* in black and white, Utamaro worked almost exclusively in color. Little is known of his origins, but for a time he studied Kanō-style painting under Sekien until 1770, when the two parted company for unknown reasons. It is suggested that Sekien disapproved of Utamaro's dissolute way of life, but there is every reason to believe that the two remained on good terms, for we find a postscript written by Sekien in Utamaro's *Ehon mushi-erami* (1788).

The break with Sekien led Utamaro to form a close association with the young publisher Tsutaya Jūsaburō (1748–97), who later became a noted patron of ukiyo-e artists and of the novelists Santō Kyōden and Jippensha Ikku. Around 1775, Tsutaya took Utamaro into his house, and when the rising publisher moved to new premises in 1783, Utamaro went with him and stayed there until Tsutaya's death in 1797. Tsutaya seems to have been more of a boon companion to the dissolute Utamaro than a patriarchal figure, and the two frequently went on jaunts in the Yoshiwara with friends. Tsutaya had a natural gift for recognizing genius in others and this association led to the publication of some of the finest prints and illustrated books of the age. Utamaro's earliest illustration is to be found in a theatrical book dated 1775, and throughout his career, he illustrated a series of *kibyōshi* and *share-bon* novels including the works of Santō Kyōden. These were naturally produced in black and white, and in the earlier examples, at least, one finds the inevitable Torii influence.

After Tsutaya Jūsaburō moved his premises to those of Maruya Jihei, a publisher whose business he took over and operated under his own name in 1783, he became involved, probably through his friend Ōta Nampo (1749–1823), the noted humorist, in the publication of anthologies of comic *kyōka* poetry, and from that time on he concentrated on this field, with Utamaro as principal illustrator. As Tsutaya's *kyōka* anthologies were designed for an audience of connoisseurs, a great deal of effort went into these publications: not only were illustrations almost always in color, but the paper, calligraphy and binding were of the highest quality and works of art in themselves. Utamaro's most important work of this type in chronological order (the dates of some are contentious) are as follows: *Ehon waka ebisu* (1 *orihon* album, 1786, color); *Ehon Edo suzume* (3 vols., 1786, black and white); *Ehon kotoba no hana* (2 vols., 1787, black and white); *Ehon mushi-erami* (2 vols., 1788, color); *Ehon tatoe no bushi* (3 vols., 1789, black and white); *Ehon kyōgetsubō* (1 *orihon* album, 1790, color); *Shioi no tsuto* (1 *orihon* album, 1790, color); *Momo-chidori kyōka awase* (2 *orihon* albums, 1791, color); *Ehon fugenzō* (1 *orihon* album, 1791, color); *Ehon gin sekai* (1 *orihon* album, 1791, color); *Ehon azuma asobi* (3 vols., 1791); *Ehon suruga-mai* (3 vols., 1791, black and white); and *Ehon shiki no hana* (2 vols., 1801, color). In addition, he was responsible for the non-*kyōka* work *Yoshiwara seirō nenjū gyōji* (2 vols., 1804) and contributed single illustrations to several *kyōka* anthologies published by Tsutaya including *Otoko-dōka* (1 *orihon* album, 1798, color) (Pl. 68). All these, with the exception of *Ehon shiki no hana* and *Yoshiwara seirō nenjū gyōji*, are books of *kyōka* and all, with the same two exceptions, were published by Tsutaya.

It may be unreasonable to single out any of these books for special comment, but it must be said that *Ehon waka ebisu*, *Ehon mushi-erami*, *Ehon kyōgetsubō*, *Shioi no tsuto*, *Momo-chidori kyōka awase* and *Ehon gin sekai* are outstanding and significant in the enormous range of styles they encompass. *Ehon waka ebisu* (Pl. 65), for example, has five double-page color illustrations of New Year ceremonies, including two in archaic style imitative of *Nara-ehon* and one extraordinarily beautiful study of a courtesan in the spring snow of the Yoshiwara. The special feature of this, in addition to the soft and delicate colors, lies in the use of space—an outstanding quality of Utamaro's work—which gives the impression that what is not represented is as important as the subject itself. *Ehon mushi-erami*, *Shioi no tsuto* and *Momo-chidori kyōka awase* together form a series, the first depicting insects and reptiles, the second seashells and the third birds. These were all successful attempts at treating non-ukiyo-e subjects in a realistic manner, a challenge to the stereotyped Kanō studies of the same subject. These subjects were all subsequently used by other ukiyo-e artists, but none even approached Utamaro's success, particularly in the subtlety of the colors, seen to their best advantage in the soft blues and pinks in *Shioi no tsuto*. *Ehon kyōgetsubō* contains a series of five scenes in color, including the use of gold and silver, with the moon as a linking theme. However, the most effective one is a landscape, which in true Kanō manner contains two silhouetted figures dwarfed by the grandeur of nature. In *Ehon gin sekai*, Utamaro returned to a theme he first used in *Ehon waka ebisu*, the beauties of snow. One shows children playing in the snow, the vivid colors of their clothing contrasting pleasantly against the white background, but the most interesting of the scenes is his opening snowscape, which has no color but achieves its effects by careful graded tones of white, gray and black.

That Utamaro was a ukiyo-e artist there is no doubt. A glance at any of his prints or his numerous erotic books such as the *Uta-makura* (1788) will confirm this, but nevertheless he incorporated a strong Kanō strain in his illustrations and achieved an imaginative balance in his work which transcends categorization.

Another pupil of Sekien was Koikawa Harumachi II, who was also known as Utamaro II, a signature he adopted after marrying Utamaro's widow in 1806 and completing many of Utamaro's prints. He is known to have illustrated a few *kibyōshi*, some of which he wrote himself, mostly dating from the mid-1770s. The connection between Sekien and the artist Hosoda (Chōbunsai) Eishi (1760–1829), however, is less clear. It is known that he studied under Kanō Eisen (1730–90), Torii Bunryūsai (active mid–late 18th century) and Kitao Shigemasa (1739–1820), and that he illustrated a few *kibyōshi* between 1785 and 1795. Toward the end of that century, he began to produce single illustrations for *kyōka* anthologies such as *Yanagi no ito* (1 *orihon* album, 1797, color) and *Otoko-dōka* (1 *orihon* album, 1798, color). Utamaro also made contributions to these albums, and since Eishi's work here bears strong resemblances to Utamaro's, he may have fallen under the former's influence. This is, however, pure conjecture, for Eishi, particularly later in his career, concentrated on painting and prints and produced only a few book illustrations.

The short-lived Eishōsai Chōki (active c. 1770–1810) was probably a pupil of Utamaro rather than of Sekien, although there is some doubt about this since not all sources agree on the date of his birth. He is better known as a print artist than an illustrator, although he produced illustrations for no less than 36 *kibyōshi*, 8 *share-bon* and 3 *yomi-hon* between 1789 and 1809. Minor Utamaro pupils include Yukimaro, Tsukimaro, Shikimaro and Toyomaro, all of whom concentrated on *kibyōshi* novels in book illustration.

THE KATSUKAWA SCHOOL

Although the Katsukawa school was founded by Katsukawa Shunsui (1680–1752), the pupil of Miyagawa Chōshun (1683–1752), the artist who really established it was his pupil Katsukawa Shunshō (1726–92). Shunshō's first published work, *Ehon butai no ōgi* (3 vols., known in both color and black-and-white editions), produced in collaboration with Ippitsusai Bunchō, did not appear until 1770. This was a collection of color portraits of actors on fans (although a black-and-white edition is also known), and also Shunshō's first attempt at a subject that was to make his reputation. The book itself was such a success that in 1778, he produced a similar, smaller collection under the title *Ehon zoku butai no ōgi* (2 vols., in both color and black-and-white editions). Shunshō's principal contribution to this already well-worn ukiyo-e theme was in his realistic treatment of the subjects, taking the actors away from the context of the plays. This was evident in the color-printed *Ehon yakusha natsu no Fuji* (1 vol., 1780), where actors were shown engaged in all kinds of non-theatrical pursuits and recreations, a theme taken up later by Utagawa Kunisada in the almost identically titled *Yakusha sugao natsu no Fuji* (1827). Actors were the theme of several other of some twenty *ehon* produced by Shunshō between 1770 and 1790, but ironically his three most celebrated works were on entirely different subjects.

The earliest of these works was *Nishiki hyakunin isshu azuma-ori* (1 vol., 1774, color), a collection of portraits of poets and poetesses in the *Hyakunin isshu*, where no attempt was made at authentic reproductions of costume and so forth. The garb of the poets is strictly contemporary, highly varied as well as richly colored, and the whole work may be regarded as a ukiyo-e version of a Tosa theme. The *Sanjū-rokka-sen* (1 vol., 1789, color) was similarly and even more successfully treated by him, and both works, like the *Ehon yakusha natsu no Fuji*, proved extremely influential at the time. His best work, however, was imitative rather than original. This was the *Seirō bijin awase sugata kagami*, a collaborative work with Kitao Shigemasa, published in three volumes in 1776 by Yamazaki Kinbei and Tsutaya Jūsaburō. It was a collection of color portraits of groups of courtesans corresponding to different seasons of the year. Both the title and the portraits are highly suggestive of Harunobu's *Yoshiwara seirō bijin awase* published six years earlier by Funaki Kasuke, and it is very likely that Shunshō and Shigemasa intended to follow up the success of Harunobu's original, especially since Yamazaki Kinbei was the original publisher of most of Harunobu's *ehon*. Shunshō's other *ehon*, which include *Ehon Ibukiyama* (3 vols., 1778, color) and the interesting sericultural work *Sanyō zue ehon takara no itosuji* (1 vol., 1786, color, with Shigemasa), were less successful.

Apart from Kitao Shigemasa, Kitao Masayoshi and Kitao Masanobu, who will be dealt with as a separate school, Shunshō's immediate pupils, Katsukawa Shunchō (d. c. 1820) and Katsukawa Shun'ei (1762–1819), were not distinguished in the field of illustration. Shunchō illustrated a few *kibyōshi* in the Torii style in the 1780s and the *kyōka* anthology *Kyōka chiyo no aki* (1 vol., 1790, black and white) on the celebration of the Chrysanthemum Festival in the Yoshiwara, cleverly working a chrysanthemum design into each illustration. Shun'ei, better known for his actor prints, also illustrated a number of *kibyōshi*, but his most famous work was the theatrical encyclopedia *Shibai kimmō zue*. This was a humorous parody of the encyclopedia *Wakan kimmō zui* and was written by Shikitei Samba (1775–1822) and published in eight volumes in 1803. The volumes include many theatrical illustrations of interest by Shun'ei, while Utagawa Toyokuni produced the actor studies in Volume Seven. Shunshō's other pupils include Shunkō (1743–1812), Shunjō (d. 1787), Shunzan (active late 18th century), Shuntei (1770–1820), Shundō (active late 18th century) and Shunsen (active late 18th century), who left little of note in the way of book illustration apart from a few *kibyōshi*. As has been mentioned previously the school is much better known for its wide range of theatrical prints.

THE KITAO SCHOOL

Kitao Shigemasa was born in 1739, the son of the Edo publisher Suwaraya Saburōbei, and died in 1820, living through the most exciting period of ukiyo-e development. Little is known of his artistic lineage; most historians opt either for the theory that he was self-taught or that he was a pupil of Nishimura Shigenaga, even though his works bear little relation to those of the latter. His own pupils included Kitao Masanobu (the novelist Santō Kyōden), Kubo Shunman and the celebrated Kitao Masayoshi. Like most artists of his period in the ukiyo-e schools, especially as a result of his publishing

179

connections, Shigemasa began his career illustrating *ao-hon, kuro-hon, kibyōshi* and the-atrical books, and his earliest works were published in 1765. Between 1765 and approx-imately 1809, when his talents began to fail, Shigemasa illustrated almost 200 works of this type, including some novels by Kyōden and Bakin, but since this kind of work was always executed hurriedly, little noteworthy is included.

Shigemasa's *ehon*, produced at approximately the same time were, however, numer-ous and varied, and although they do not compare favorably with those of Harunobu and Utamaro to the modern eye, there is no doubt that he was considered a great master in his lifetime. His early *ehon* produced in the 1760s and including *Ehon asa-murasaki* (2 vols., 1769), *Ehon azuma no hana* (2 vols., c. 1769) and *Ehon isaoshi-gusa* (3 vols., 1769) concentrate on popular Edo life with several studies of courtesans, but *Ehon isaoshi-gusa* is devoted to military heroes, which later became a Shigemasa spe-cialty. During the 1770s, Shigemasa's friendship with Katsukawa Shunshō led him to collaborate with the latter on the previously-mentioned *Seirō bijin awase sugata kagami* (1776) and *Sanyō zue ehon takara no itosuji* (1786), but he also found time to produce more fine warrior studies, notably in *Ehon yasoujigawa* (3 vols., 1786) and *Ehon musha-waraji* (2 vols., 1787, color). The latter work was published by Tsutaya Jūsaburō, and although he was not as dependent on Tsutaya as Utamaro was, he became closely involved with the publisher and contributed to several of his *kyōka* anthologies. Notable among these were *Kyōka ehon Amanogawa* (1 vol., c. 1790), *Ehon fukujusō* (1 vol., 1791, color) and *Ehon azuma karage* (3 vols., c. 1791); he also contributed to illustrative miscellanies such as *Otoko-dōka* (1798). The *Ehon azuma karage* is a collection of Edo views, not dissimilar to *Ehon asa-murasaki*, and resembles many other works of this type which were so popular in the last decades of the eighteenth century, while *Ehon fukujusō* is a more distinctive work based on Japanese and Chinese legends. This proved sufficiently popular to be reissued without the text in 1804, under the title *Ehon takara no nanakusa*.

There seems little doubt that during the period of his association with Tsutaya, Shigemasa became well acquainted with Utamaro and was particularly impressed with that artist's "naturalistic" experiments with plant, bird, fish and insect life. This is the conclusion gained from looking at Shigemasa's *Ehon tatsu no miyako* (1 vol., c. 1810, color) and *Kachō shashin zui* (first series, 3 vols., 1805; second series, 3 vols., 1827; both color), the former of which treats fish and shells and the latter plants, flowers and birds, both imitative of Utamaro's work. However, the former work bears an even closer resemblance to Katsuma Ryūsui's *Umi no sachi* (1 vol., 1762, color) and it is interesting to speculate whether that work and its companion volume on flowers and insects, *Yama no sachi* (1 vol., 1765, color), had any influence on Utamaro himself.

Of Shigemasa's three major pupils, Kubo Shunman (1757–1820) did little work in book illustration, but what he did achieve was quite outstanding. Virtually all his work was in color and he concentrated on *kyōka* (Pl. 66)—*Kyōka hidare domoe* (2 vols., 1802) and *Kyōka kotoba no takimizu* (2 vols., c. 1810)—and made contributions to *kyōka* miscellanies such as *Otoko-dōka* (1798) and the exceptionally rare *Haru no iro* (1 *orihon* album, 1794). In fact, all his work in book illustration is extremely rare and highly sought after. To Kitao Masanobu (1761–1816), another of Shigemasa's pupils, book illustration was of secondary importance to his major occupation of writing novels under the name Santō Kyōden. His illustrative work included the usual ration of *kibyōshi* novels and his *ehon* were derivative of both Shigemasa and Shunshō. Probably his best work is to be found in *Azuma-buri kyōka bunko* (1 vol., 1786, color) and *Kokon kyōka fukuro* (1 vol., 1787, color), both collections of portraits of *kyōka* poets in brilliant colors, and the poses of the poets are varied and amusing. Both books were published by Tsutaya. Much of the rest of Masanobu's illustrative work is in a humorous vein, although he also displayed a penchant for portraying the supernatural.

The most interesting of Shigemasa's pupils was Kitao Masayoshi (1764–1824), often known by the name he later adopted, Kuwagata Keisai. Masayoshi was the adopted son of a Suruga farmer, and when the family opened a *tatami* shop and moved to Edo, he was drawn into art. Probably in 1780 he became a pupil of Shigemasa, using the name Kitao Sanjirō, which in the following year he changed to Kitao Masayoshi. The number of ukiyo-e artists who began painting in the Tosa or Kanō styles is very large, but Masayoshi proved something of an exception in that he began his paintings in the field of ukiyo-e and to an extent moved away from it later. This change in motivation is generally attributed to his visit in 1786 to the Kamigata region, where he met several leading artists of the Maruyama and Shijō schools, including Maruyama Ōkyo (1733–95). Before this visit, Masayoshi's career in ukiyo-e was conventional, and he concentrated on the production of prints and illustrations for *kibyōshi* novels. In 1783 alone he illustrated 27 such novels, and between 1780 and 1796 (when he abruptly discontinued this kind of work) he illustrated over 60 *kibyōshi*. He also produced a few *ehon* in this period, mostly of popular views of famous places and city life, such as *Edo meisho zue* (1 vol., 1785).

His exposure to the Maruyama and Shijō techniques in 1786 profoundly altered Masayoshi's approach to art and life, and in the following decade he went through a period of absorbing what he had learned. Evidence of this comes through such works as *Ehon miyako no nishiki* (1 vol., 1787, color, a collection of views of Kyoto and a direct result of his visit to that city) and, more important, *Raikin zui* (1 *orihon* album, 1789, color). This rare book, which caused something of a sensation when it first appeared, is a collection of bird and plant studies very much in a native adaptation of the Chinese style, owing nothing to ukiyo-e and comparable with Utamaro's more famous efforts in the same direction only by its completely different approach. All that *Raikin zui* and Utamaro's *Momo-chidori kyōka awase* have in common is the subject matter, for the contrast between Utamaro's "realistic" approach and Masayoshi's adopted Chinese style is great.

The more Masayoshi's career developed, the less involved with ukiyo-e he became, although the break was never quite complete. For example, in the year 1797, when

Masayoshi entered the service of the Tsuyama daimyo as a painter and formally adopted the name Kuwagata Keisai, we find him working with Takehara Shunsensai on the Tōkaidō guide *Tōkaidō meisho zue* (6 vols.), which contained ukiyo-e illustrations. That to an extent he remained in ukiyo-e is further shown by his involvement with a few *kibyōshi* in the early 1800s. Generally speaking, however, Masayoshi's style at least moved away from ukiyo-e after 1795 with the publication of his celebrated *Ryakuga-shiki* (1 vol., color). This was the first of a series of eight works in which he, to quote the preface, "copied not the form but the spirit [of his subjects]." *Ryakuga-shiki* (or the *Simplified Picture Style*) is a miscellany of sketches of figures, birds, animals, flowers and fish, where the subjects are "stripped" of the adornment and embellishments normally associated with ukiyo-e. The characters from popular city life, whether they be courtesans or *chōnin*, are present but are portrayed in a style so removed from ukiyo-e that it comes much closer to the "impressionistic" Kyoto schools. The figures are simplified to the point where they could almost be termed caricatures. Over the next eighteen years Masayoshi fully explored this concept, notably in *Jinbutsu ryakuga-shiki* (3 vols., 1795–99, sketches of human figures); *Chōjū ryakuga-shiki* (1 vol., 1797, birds and animals); *Sansui ryakuga-shiki* (1 vol., 1800, landscapes); *Gyobai-fu* (1 vol., 1802, fish and shells); *Genga-en* (1 vol., 1808, miscellaneous); *Keisai ryakuga-shiki* (1 vol., 1809, miscellaneous); and *Sōka ryakuga-shiki* (1 vol., 1813, flowering plants). All these are in color. After a pause Masayoshi returned to this theme again, particularly in *Keisai soga* (5 vols., c. 1815–42) in collaboration with others, with himself probably responsible for the first volume. It may be thought that the concept of "copying the spirit and not the form" was alien to ukiyo-e, which was always, superficially at least, obsessed with form, but Masayoshi's work proved highly influential in ukiyo-e circles as much of Hokusai's later work testifies. Of several other *ehon* produced by Masayoshi, the most interesting is *Tatsu-no-miya tsuko* (1 vol., 1802, color) (Pl. 63), which contains studies of fish and sea creatures in the style of Ryūsui's *Umi no sachi*.

THE UTAGAWA SCHOOL

The Utagawa school was founded by Utagawa Toyoharu (1735–1814), one-time pupil of both Toriyama Sekien and Ishikawa Toyonobu, and thus indirectly of Shigenaga, and is associated more than any other school with the rapid decline of ukiyo-e in the nineteenth century. Although earlier Utagawa artists lived through the golden age of ukiyo-e in the last quarter of the eighteenth century, by the late 1830s the genre was so completely exploited that its decline was inevitable. Since the Utagawa artists remained prolific in painting, prints and illustrations throughout this period and beyond the Meiji Restoration of 1868, and since they produced so much mediocre work, they are generally regarded as representing the nadir of ukiyo-e achievement. They were, in a sense, victims of their own industry in an age when authority was rapidly crumbling, and more particularly, color printing lost all quality through the use of imported

Western dyes. Yet the early Utagawa masters were the equal of most of their contemporaries, and even in the nineteenth century the school did produce one artist of profound significance in Hiroshige, so the picture was not quite so black as has sometimes been painted.

Toyoharu was not a prolific book illustrator, and a typical example of his work, very much in the Shigenaga style, is *Ehon Edo nishiki* (2 vols., c. 1804), a collection of Edo views in color. Of Toyoharu's pupils the most prolific was Toyokuni I (1769–1825), who from 1786 until his death in 1825 was responsible for illustrating some 180 books as well as for producing a large number of prints. Many of these were *kibyōshi* novels, particularly those produced in the last decade of the eighteenth century (this was such a common phenomenon among young ukiyo-e artists that one feels that executing this kind of work constituted an apprenticeship). In general Toyokuni's illustrative work was derivative of the Shunshō and Kiyonaga style, but he was an able craftsman, and his actor studies in *Yakusha meisho zue* (1 vol., 1800, color), *Yakusha sangaikyō* (2 vols., 1801, color) (Pl. 67) and *Yakusha sanjūni-sō* (1 vol., 1802, color) are comparable with Shunshō's best work in book illustration. *Ehon imayō sugata* (2 vols., 1802, color) was probably his finest work in this field, containing a series of double-page studies of women of all classes, although here again the style shows the marked influence of Utamaro.

Utagawa Toyohiro (1773–1828) was another of Toyoharu's pupils. Less prolific than Toyokuni, he completely avoided actor studies, concentrating on portraits (Pl. 57) and landscapes (in the latter connection it should be mentioned that Hiroshige was Toyohiro's pupil). His landscape and courtesan studies are seen to best effect in *Ehon azuma warawa* (2 vols., 1804, in both color and black-and-white editions), which contains scenes from Edo life for each month of the year. Apart from his prints, Toyohiro's reputation rests on his illustrations of novels, chiefly in the *yomi-hon* genre. *Yomi-hon* novels first came to prominence in the last decade of the eighteenth century and were most popular in the first decades of the nineteenth century. They were usually quite lengthy with comparatively few illustrations, and their most popular theme was the deeds of famous warriors, since these books were aimed at the samurai. The most noted author of *yomi-hon* novels was the extremely prolific Kyokutei Bakin (1767–1848), many of whose early works were illustrated by Toyohiro, including the famous *Musō byōe kochō monogatari* (9 vols., 1809–10) and *Asahina shima meguri no ki* (30 vols., 1814–27). As warriors formed the principal subject for the illustrations, Toyohiro's work in this field clearly owed something to Shigemasa.

Of Toyokuni's pupils, the most conspicuous are Utagawa Kunisada (1786–1864), later known as Toyokuni III, and Utagawa Kuniyoshi (1797–1861). Like so many others of the Utagawa school, Kunisada suffered from being too prolific. In an extraordinarily active career he produced many thousands of prints and illustrated dozens of novels, primarily *gōkan-mono*, a variant on the traditional *kibyōshi* which first appeared in the early years of the nineteenth century. They were much longer than *kibyōshi*, borrowed themes and plots from history, *kabuki* and *jōruri* drama, and are readily identifiable by their bright, even garish, pictorial covers. They enjoyed a great vogue up to and beyond the Meiji Restoration. The most representative author of this literary genre was Ryūtei Tanehiko (1783–1842) and his most famous work, *Nise murasaki inaka Genji* (160 vols., 1829–42), was illustrated by Kunisada. Illustrations to this new genre became very much associated with the Utagawa school, but since they were hack productions, like *kibyōshi*, the illustrative work is never of a high standard. However, perhaps the crude and clumsy illustrations in *gōkan-mono* reflected the mood of the times, and whatever one's opinion of Kunisada's artistic skills, he was enormously popular with the mass audience. He also worked in *ehon*, but his best work of this type is found in actor studies such as *Yakusha sugao natsu no Fuji* (2 vols., 1828) and *Yakusha kijin-den* (4 vols., 1833), where the beneficial influence of Shunshō is apparent.

Kuniyoshi justifiably has a higher reputation than Kunisada, primarily because he used his talents in more diverse ways. He specialized in landscapes—where the influence of his studies in Western painting is pronounced—caricatures and portraits of warriors, working extensively in traditional actor studies and novel illustration. He was not outstandingly prolific as a book illustrator and his best work is to be found in *Ichiyū gafu* (1 vol., 1820, studies of warriors), *Ichiyūsai gafu* (1 vol., 1846, miscellaneous sketches of Ichiyūsai [i.e., Kuniyoshi]) and its sequel *Ichiyūsai manga* (1 vol., 1855, caricatures), *Kujaku tsuizen hanashi-dori* (1 vol., 1852, with Kunisada and others, a memorial volume for the actor Nakamura Utaemon IV) and the unusual *Ansei kemmon-shi* (3 vols., c. 1858–9, a pictorial account of the great Edo earthquake of 1855).

Space does not permit the discussion of the multitude of Utagawa artists who flourished with so little distinction in this period, but mention must be made of one, whose name is known even among those who have no interest in Japanese art—Hiroshige. As with Hokusai, Hiroshige's reputation owes much to the fact that his work was seized on by Westerners after the opening up of Japan in the early 1850s. His popularity was due to the availability of his prints as well as to their subject matter, landscapes, which was readily understood by foreigners. Utagawa (family name: Andō) Hiroshige (1797–1858) was born to an Edo fireman, a career which he himself followed until the age of 26, when he began his art training under Utagawa Toyohiro. Toyohiro was a noted landscape artist and undoubtedly woke Hiroshige's early interest in that field, although both Masayoshi and Hokusai had great influence on him too. Although he illustrated some novels early in his career, Hiroshige was primarily a print artist, and that side of his activity is too well known to bear repetition. However, he also illustrated a number of fine books with landscapes and caricatures in the fashion of Masayoshi (Keisai).

The following is a list of his most notable illustrated books in approximate chronological order: *Ukiyo gafu* (3 vols., c. 1836, color sketches and caricatures by Keisai and Hiroshige; Hiroshige was responsible for Volume Three only, later issued under the title *Ryūsai gafu*); *Ehon tebiki-gusa* (1 vol., c. 1848, color sketches of flowers and fish); *Sōhitsu gafu* (4 vols., 1848–51, a collection of *ryakuga-shiki* sketches in the Keisai style); *Ehon Edo miyage* (10 vols., 1851–67, color landscape views of Edo explicitly in the style of Shigenaga, the last two volumes being illustrated by Hiroshige II); and *Kyōka Edo meisho zue* (14 vols., c. 1856–60, landscapes and scenes of Edo life). The last of these is a *kyōka* anthology and Hiroshige was responsible for several minor books of this sort, often working in association with the poet Hinokien Umeaki. Hiroshige's pupils, Hiroshige II and Hiroshige III (*see* Pls. 2, 24), produced little of distinction, although Hiroshige II collaborated with his master on some quality productions including the above-mentioned *Ehon Edo miyage*.

HOKUSAI AND HIS FOLLOWERS

No Japanese artist enjoys such a high reputation in the West as Katsushika Hokusai (1760–1849), who produced so much in his lifetime that it is impossible to cover the full scope of his works, save in a specialized study. Like Hiroshige, Hokusai's fame in the West also sprang from the great number of his works available on subjects easily understood by non-Japanese. Hokusai cannot be regarded as Japan's foremost artist but neither does his work merit the harsh criticism to which he has been subjected in recent years, and it should at least be said of him that he showed great capacity for absorbing other artists' ideas and turning them to good account.

The number of ideas reflected in Hokusai's work probably resulted from the many masters he studied with, for he apparently found it hard to settle. His father, Nakajima Ise, was a mirror-maker to the Tokugawa court and Hokusai, who seems to have worked for a publisher from the age of twelve when he learned many printing techniques, began his artistic career under Katsukawa Shunshō in 1777. Soon after, he began illustrating a number of *kibyōshi* novels, but was expelled from the Katsukawa school in the mid-1780s, probably because of his refusal to adhere to the Katsukawa line. Over the next few years he studied under several artists including Tawaraya Sōri, Tsutsumi Tōrin, Kanō Yūsen and even Shiba Kōkan. It is believed that his studies with Yūsen were the reason for his expulsion from the Katsukawa school, but by temperament Hokusai was unable to stay long with any school. He quarreled frequently with his masters and was dogged by poverty and family troubles, which often caused him to leave Edo.

Accounts of Hokusai's life and career as a print artist are already well known. As a book illustrator his career was both prolific and varied, the product of restless energy and his ability to master and integrate various styles. Virtually all his work in the 1780s and 1790s was devoted to *kibyōshi* novels in the current style. However, in the last years of the eighteenth century Hokusai formed a friendship with Tsutaya Jūsaburō, probably on account of his acquaintance with the artists of the Kitao school, and contributed some fine color illustrations to Tsutaya's *kyōka* anthologies, continuing to do so even after the publisher's death in 1797.

The earliest of these works was *Shikinami-gusa* (1 vol., 1796), which contained inventive depictions of mythical lands, such as that of the long-legged men (Pl. 61), followed by

89. Landscape with poems, from the *Ehon ryōhitsu* (1 vol., c. 1800), a collection of landscape and figure studies in ukiyo-e style by Hokusai and Rikkōsai, published in Nagoya. The figures here are given less attention than the landscape.

Azuma asobi (1 vol., 1799, both color and black-and-white editions exist, as do editions with and without poems), a succession of landscapes in the Shigenaga style with greater emphasis on figure studies, *Tōto shōkei ichiran* (2 vols., 1800, color landscapes and city scenes with graceful courtesans) and *Ehon kyōka yama mata yama* (3 vols., 1804, color, similar to the previous work) (Pl. 58). This was in addition to his contributions to *Yanagi no ito* (1797) (Pl. 60) and his illustration of at least three conventional books of portraits of *kyōka* poets. These were produced for Tsutaya and the *Shunkyō-jō* (1 vol., 1798, color, publisher unknown, with three illustrations, the second of which is by Hokusai, an extremely effective study of country life with Mt. Fuji in the background) must be among the finest work he ever did (Pl. 59). In style they belong completely to the golden age of ukiyo-e—the age of Shunshō, Shigemasa, Harunobu, Utamaro—and with a few exceptions, such as *Ehon Sumidagawa ryōgan ichiran* (3 vols., 1801, color), Hokusai never again attempted to recapture it, but changed direction completely.

It has already been said that Hokusai's illustrative career began with *kibyōshi* novels, and throughout his life he never abandoned the novel. His best work was the product of his friendship and association with the *yomi-hon* novelist Takizawa (Kyokutei) Bakin, who was at his most prolific in the early years of the nineteenth century. *Yomi-hon* have already been briefly described above, but they represented a change in approach from *kibyōshi*, where the text and illustrations were mixed, for *yomi-hon* illustrations were fewer but each had a page to itself. In some ways this was a return to seventeenth-century practice, but due to the many illustrative styles in existence in the nineteenth century more variety was possible, and because of the increased relative importance of illustrations, much more care and attention was paid to them. Some of the best of Bakin's *yomi-hon* illustrated by Hokusai were: *Sumidagawa bairyū shinsho* (5 vols., 1807); *Shin kasane gedatsu monogatari* (5 vols., 1807); *Sanshichi zenden nanka no yume* (7 vols., 1808); *Aoto Fujitsuna moryōan* (10 vols., 1811–12); and *Chinsetsu yumihari-zuki* (29 vols., 1807–11).

During the same period several Chinese novels and collections of stories were translated and adapted into Japanese, such as *Ehon saiyūki* (40 vols., 1806–35, illustrated by Hokusai and several others) and *Shimpen suiko gaden* (101 vols., 1805–38), which demanded a different treatment. Hokusai displayed considerable skill in this and made repeated use of Chinese themes in his work, including the illustrations to *Ehon suiko-den* (1 vol., 1829, studies of the heroes of the Chinese novel *Shui-hu-chüan*) and especially sections of *Ehon tōshi-sen*, an extensive collection of Chinese T'ang poetry with appropriate illustrations. This huge work was published in eight parts, each containing a varying number of volumes by Kobayashi Shimbei of Edo, between 1788 and 1836. Several artists were involved in the work, but Hokusai was responsible for large parts of it, showing a remarkable versatility of style. It is also significant that few of these other artists were of the ukiyo-e schools, demonstrating that Hokusai did not regard himself as completely of that movement.

Apart from large numbers of undistinguished *ōraimono* and *hiinagata* ("pattern" books for kimono, combs and other objects), Hokusai's reputation as an illustrator rests on his sketchbooks and the occasional books of landscape design such as the famous *Fugaku hyakkei* (3 vols., 1834–5, one hundred views of Mt. Fuji). His principal sketchbooks were: *Ryakuga haya-oshie* (1 vol., 1812); *Hokusai gakyō* (2 vols., 1813, with Gakutei, Bokusen and Hokuyō); *Hokusai shashin gafu* (1 vol., 1814); *Santai gafu* (1 vol., 1815); *Hokusai gafu* (2 vols., 1820); *Hokusai soga* (1 vol., 1820); *Ippitsu gafu* (1 vol., 1823); and *Hokusai manga* (15 vols., 1812–78).

There is no space here to describe these books, but virtually all of them are printed in light colors, aesthetically rather unappealing, in Keisai's style. It certainly is no accident that Hokusai's work in the *ryakuga-shiki* style began in the second decade of the nineteenth century after the appearance of the best of Keisai's work. However, Hokusai developed Keisai's ideas considerably and although the basic themes of his sketchbooks —figures, birds, plants, animals—are Keisai's, Hokusai's treatment is broader in style and content. Nowhere is this more evident than in *Hokusai manga*, probably his most famous work of illustration. This remarkable work, which was published over an extremely long period (although only the last two volumes were published posthumously) encapsulates the whole of Japanese life in a series of sketches done in ukiyo-e,

Kanō and other styles. All the four classes of Japanese society are included, and the subjects range from plants, birds, animals and fish, through landscapes of the various provinces, architecture, artisans, samurai and entertainers engaged in their pursuits. The illustrations lose something through mediocre color work, but their designs are endlessly varied and wider in scope than anything done by Keisai. If variety and interest are the chief qualities in an artist, then Hokusai was an artist *par excellence*. If not, one is likely to be disappointed with his work. Hokusai's illustrations always seem to inspire either enthusiasm or criticism—people are seldom indifferent to his work—perhaps the result of a highly talented artist working in a period when ukiyo-e had been exhausted in terms of style and subject matter. In the time he lived, he stood against an overwhelming tide of mediocrity and the strain sometimes shows.

Hokusai took a great many pupils, too many to mention here, but something must be said about the most notable—Totoya Hokkei (1780–1850), Teisai Hokuba (1771–1844), Yanagawa Shigenobu (1780–1832) and Yashima Gakutei (active c. 1820–50). Other pupils including Hokuju, Bokusen, Hoku'un and Taitō also have their admirers, but they did little illustrative work and followed Hokusai's style too closely to be worthy of detailed comment.

His most interesting pupil and the cause of many of his troubles, was his son-in-law Yanagawa Shigenobu. Shigenobu seems to have shared Hokusai's restlessness, beginning his career with the Utagawa school and studying under the non-ukiyo-e artists Nanrei and Gyokuzan. It may be thought that this search for tuition outside ukiyo-e, already mentioned in connection with both Keisai and Hokusai, was partly a symptom of the exhaustion of the ukiyo-e movement. Much of Shigenobu's illustrative efforts were directed toward the novel, including Bakin's famous *Satomi hakkenden* (106 vols., 1811–42), although he also worked extensively on *kyōka* anthologies. His best book illustrations are to be found in landscapes, in *Kyōka meisho zue* (1 vol., c. 1826, where the designs are impressive and the colors delicate) (Pl. 64), and in his sketchbooks, *Ryūsen gajō* (2 vols., undated), *Ryūsen manga* (2 vols., undated) and *Yanagawa gafu* (3 vols., 1856).

Hokkei, a fishmonger by trade (his adopted surname Totoya means "fish-seller"), began painting under the Kanō school before joining Hokusai. Between 1806 and his death in 1850, he illustrated some 40 books, many of them *kyōka* anthologies such as *Fusō meisho kyōka-shū* (3 vols., 1824, color, later reissued with illustrations only under the title *Yamato meisho ichiran*). He was a faithful pupil of Hokusai in so far as his subject matter and style are concerned, and produced some fine landscape studies (usually accompanied by *kyōka*) and several sketchbooks in the *ryakuga-shiki* style such as *Hokkei manga* (2 vols., 1814, color, many of the designs were taken from his earlier *Kyōka banka-shū* of 1810).

Teisai (Arisaka) Hokuba was less prolific than Hokkei and was primarily a painter. Most of his illustrative work, which included *yomi-hon* novels such as *Yoshinaka kunkō zue* (10 vols., 1832), was undistinguished and imitative of Hokusai. Perhaps his best

新川酒問屋

90. A saké wholesaler at Shinkawa in Edo, from the first edition of the
Edo meisho zue (1834–36), a topographical guide to the city, illustrated
by Hasegawa Settan.

work in illustration is to be found in *Kyōka maku no uchi* (2 vols., 1802, black and white), which is closer to Hokusai's style of the 1790s, and *Kyōka shikishi ogura-gata* (1 vol., c. 1830), which contains some delightful small color sketches of birds, flowers and figures, done in collaboration with Hiroshige.

Gakutei, a writer as well as an artist, was a pupil of Hokkei rather than of Hokusai. He was sufficiently removed from Hokusai to escape from that artist's predilection for the *ryakuga-shiki* style. Like Hokkei and Hokuba, he illustrated several *kyōka* anthologies, and in books is best known for his landscapes, which on occasion (as in *Ichirō gafu*, 1 vol., 1823, color) show marked Western influence. He is also notable for the bold contours of his drawings. Other works by him are: *Asagao hyakushu kyōka-shū* (1 vol., 1830, with a color illustration of a morning glory) (Pl. 62); *Haikai waka suigyo-shū* (3 vols., c. 1840, color); and *Kyōka Nihon fudoki* (2 vols., 1831, color scenes from various parts of Japan, with the frontispiece showing a *kyōka* poets gathering which includes the artist himself).

In this brief outline of ukiyo-e book illustration, many artists have unavoidably been omitted, either because they were not important or distinctive enough or because their association with ukiyo-e is only marginal. A good example of the former category is Matsukawa Hanzan (active. c. 1840–70), a talented Osaka artist who was at the peak of his powers when ukiyo-e was on its way out. A prolific novel illustrator, Hanzan also left some distinguished (for the period) landscape and city life *ehon*, including *Naniwa meisho* (3 vols., 1855, color) and *Kyō miyage* (2 vols., 1866, color). Hasegawa Settan (1778–1843) is an example of the latter category and worked primarily in the *meisho-ki* field; his *Edo meisho zue* (20 vols., 1834–36) (Pl. 90) is considered the best of the genre. Although *meisho-ki* works were the province of ukiyo-e artists, and *Edo meisho zue* for example, can only be described as a ukiyo-e work, Settan and his followers were never completely in the ukiyo-e movement.

In conclusion, it should be said that ukiyo-e, although never unchallenged, dominated Japanese art for well over two hundred years. Most of the artists were men of humble backgrounds and the movement was an embarrassment to the more orthodox artists of the Kanō and Tosa schools who, throughout the period, were patronized by the nobility. In the eighteenth century, ukiyo-e illustration completely dominated the novel form, and during that golden century some of the finest works of popular art in the world were produced, not only in books but also in prints and paintings. This was the essence of ukiyo-e: its origins and subject matter were basically popular and it catered for a mass audience, which might well be described as the world's first true consumer society. In the end, however, it became more dependent on its audience than the reverse, and just as ukiyo-e was born and prospered in a period of social change, so a new era engendered by contact with the West gave birth to a new kind of audience and sounded the death knell of ukiyo-e.

9 | THE KANŌ SCHOOL

The origins of the Kanō school can be traced indirectly to the introduction of Zen Buddhism from China at the end of the twelfth century. The Zen sect had none of the elaborate ceremonial of Tendai and Shingon, and was primarily concerned with the achievement of enlightenment through meditation and intuitive cognition. Thus from the beginning, the art associated with Zen did not tend toward the iconographical portrayal of Buddhist divinities. Closely associated with nature, Zen painters in both China and Japan often took as their themes trees, flowers, water, birds, and the medium they normally employed was known as *suiboku*, or "black ink" painting. This method of painting, popular during the Sung and Yüan dynasties in China, was introduced to Japan with Zen Buddhism, and achieved its effects not through the use of color (as typified by Yamato-e) but through slow or rapid and flowing strokes drawn in Indian ink. The greatest masters of *suiboku* painting in the fifteenth century, when it was at its zenith, were the Zen priests Shūbun (active c. 1415–60) and Sesshū (1420–1506), and it was a pupil of Shubun, Kanō Masanobu (1434–1530), who founded the Kanō school.

The Kanō painters, beginning with Masanobu, contributed one major development by combining traditional *suiboku* themes with the rich colors of Yamato-e, a splendid and distinctively Japanese style, although the stark and subtle simplicity of the Chinese masterpieces was consequently lost. The Kanō artists used the *suiboku* technique, but gradually Masanobu, his son Motonobu (1476–1559), and later Kanō masters began to add Yamato-e color schemes to their work while adhering to traditional landscape themes. Although their affiliation with Zen weakened as time went by, that connection was responsible for the later success of the school.

One reason for this was that Zen became the adopted philosophy of the military rulers of Japan, who in asserting a separate cultural identity for themselves turned away from the Tosa school, with its long-established connections with the old aristocracy. When it came to decorating their castles and homes, the new nobility instinctively turned toward the Kanō school, whose masters were able to supply their demand for magnificence, where color was a vital ingredient, without the taint of former court tradition. Since Kanō artists were employed by the new social class which governed

Japan until the Meiji Restoration in 1868, it was natural that the Kanō school should also become dominant.

At the same time, the association with daimyo and samurai, whose family origins were often humble, led to a broadening of Kanō themes in art as well as an increased concern with scenes of everyday life. As we have already seen, it was precisely this concern with daily living that laid the foundation for the ukiyo-e schools in the seventeenth century. The Kanō school, however, was never as popular as the ukiyo-e schools, for it developed into an "establishment," where artists through their official positions became monitors of orthodoxy. Just as the Tosa school lapsed into mannerism, so the Kanō school, with its unending concentration on the same themes, particularly flower and bird (*kachō*) studies, and its tendency to imitate old masters, became trite and tedious.

Kanō book illustration also suffered the same disadvantage as Tosa illustration through the inability at that time to reproduce the rich colors in printed form. Unlike Tosa illustration, however, Kanō work was not confined to the novel and *waka* poetry, and its influence on other schools is much more evident than that of Tosa. Owing to the nature of most of the printed material from 1600 to 1675, there was little demand for

91. A simple Chinese-style landscape attributed to Kanō Tan'yū, from the *Shiji yūshō* (1668), a work containing descriptive passages of the seasons.

Kanō-style illustration in books, and despite the school's dominance during that period, its artists showed no interest in books as an art form. There are tentative exceptions to this: the normally reliable *Kokusho sō-mokuroku* (*see* Bibl.) attributes the fine Kanō-style illustrations in the 1668 first edition of *Shiji yūshō* (Pl. 91) to Kanō Tan'yū, although the book itself does not support this. But generally, it was not until the eighteenth century that Kanō artists turned to books. When they did so it was in a very different manner from the ukiyo-e artists. The latter, one feels, used the book as an art form parallel with the print and painting, but Kanō artists used it primarily as a means of reproducing copies of famous paintings to serve as models for instruction. Therefore, from the creative viewpoint, Kanō illustrated books are something of a disappointment, and although the Kanō artists were gifted, their books do not show them to full advantage. (There is, however, the more academic virtue of preserving copies of paintings, the originals of which have long since been lost, that provide valuable source material for the art historian.)

The various branches of the Kanō tradition are complex and confusing, and what follows is no more than a brief summary of the ones most important in book illustration.

THE LINE OF KANŌ TAN'YŪ

It is unlikely that Kanō Tan'yū (1602–74), the greatest artist of the school in the seventeenth century, illustrated any books, but copies of his work and that of his foremost pupil Tsuruzawa Tanzan (1655–1729) can be found in several eighteenth-century collections. Copies of Tan'yū's paintings for example can be found in more than one of Ōoka Shunboku's collections and in works such as *Kyōga-en* (2 vols., 1775, caricatures by Tan'yū and others, copied by Suzuki Rinshō) (Pl. 92), *Gato hyakkachō* (5 vols., 1729, one hundred *kachō* studies of Tan'yū, copies by Sekichūshi Morinori) and *Gazu senyō* (3 vols., 1766, copies by Fujiwara Gyokusuisai), while Tanzan's work can be seen in *Unpitsu soga* (3 vols., 1749, copies by Tachibana Morikuni).

It is Tachibana Morikuni (1679–1748), a pupil of Tanzan, who was one of the earliest Kanō artists to work extensively in book illustration and to use that medium as a creative vehicle. Morikuni was born and lived his life in Osaka. His earliest work of illustration was probably *Ehon kojidan* (9 vols., 1714), designed as a supplement to Hasegawa Tōun's *Ehon hōkan* (6 vols., 1688), an illustrated collection of stories and anecdotes from ancient China. Despite the preface which disclaims it as a textbook of painting, *Ehon kojidan* was undoubtedly used as such, although its significance lies in its expansion of the *Ehon hōkan* to include Japanese tales. The illustrations in it seem to be originals, although copies, not always acknowledged as such, figure prominently in much of Morikuni's other works which include: *Morokoshi kimmō zui* (15 vols., 1719, an encyclopedia of Chinese matters); *Ehon shahō-bukuro* (10 vols., 1720); *Gaten tsūkō* (10 vols., 1727); *Ehon tsūhō-shi* (10 vols., 1729); *Honchō gaen* (6 vols., 1729); *Utai gashi* (10 vols., 1732); *Fusō gafu* (5 vols., 1735); *Ehon ōshukubai* (7 vols., 1740); *Ehon jikishihō*

(10 vols., 1745); and *Unpitsu soga* (3 vols., 1749). All these works have their points of interest, but the cumulative effect is somewhat tedious. Since so much of his work was in the form of copies, it is difficult to assess Morikuni's creative talent, but his meticulous attention to detail in his plant studies is noteworthy, as is his scrupulous effort to reproduce the original ink wash tones in printed form. One saving feature, however, is his realistic and humorous treatment of animals, monkeys in particular, and when examples of his illustrations are reproduced, an animal is almost invariably chosen (Pls. 93, 94).

Morikuni's most important pupil was his son Tachibana Yasukuni (1715–92), whose two principal works of illustration were *Ehon noyama-gusa* and *Ehon eibutsu sen* (5 vols., 1779). The latter is undistinguished and follows the style of Morikuni, but the former enjoys a considerable reputation. Originally designed as a supplement to the flower section in Morikuni's *Ehon ōshukubai*, it contains almost two hundred "field and mountain" flower pictures, some of which include birds. Again the attention to detail, a characteristic of so many Kanō flower and bird studies, is notable.

Minor pupils of Morikuni include Sekichūshi Morinori (active early 18th century), who was responsible for the copies of Tan'yū's work in the previously mentioned *Gato hyakkachō*; and Tachibana Minkō (active mid–late 18th century), who after a journey

92.   A demon, copied by Suzuki Rinshō, from the *Kyōga-en*, published in 1775.

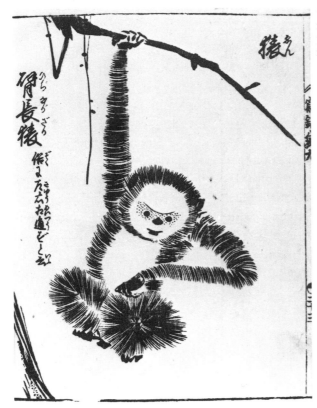

93. Tachibana Morikuni is celebrated for his humorous depiction of animals, particularly monkeys. This illustration is from the *Ehon shahō-bukuro* (10 vols., 1720).

94. This bull, by Tachibana Morikuni, is from Volume 1 of the *Unpitsu soga* (3 vols., 1749), a work of instruction in painting technique.

195

to Edo in 1760 severed his links with the Kanō fold in favor of ukiyo-e. Minkō's most famous work was the highly regarded collection of studies of artisans at work, *Saiga shokunin burui* (2 vols., 1770, color) (*see* Pl. 1).

THE LINE OF HANABUSA ITCHŌ

Hanabusa Itchō (1652–1724) was the son of an Osaka doctor, and although he received his initial training in art under Kanō Yasunobu (1613–85) in Edo, he is not normally regarded as a Kanō artist but as the founder of a new school with Kanō associations. It is likely that his individuality led to his expulsion from the Kanō school, which resulted in explorations further afield, particularly in his search for new subject matter. Itchō was also a pupil of the *haiku* poet Matsuo Bashō, and since *haiku* was regarded as a lowly poetic form by those prominent in the Kanō movement, this furthered his estrangement, although Itchō's *haiku* studies had a beneficial effect on his painting.

As with Kanō Tan'yū, it is likely that Itchō never illustrated books and his surviving work in this form is the result of copies made by later artists. Itchō's work, for example, appears in Ōoka Shunboku's *Wakan meiga-en* (6 vols., 1750), but the most prolific copyists of his paintings were his pupil Hanabusa Ippō, and Kanō Eisen's pupil Suzuki Rinshō. The principal sources of Itchō's paintings are the following books: *Ehon zuhen* (3 vols., 1751, copies by Ippō); *Hanabusa-shi* (*Eishi*) *gahen* (3 vols., 1754, copies by Ippō); *Ryōtorin* (1 vol., 1758, copies by Ippō); *Eihitsu hyakuga* (6 vols., 1758, copies by Ippō and Rinshō, normally only found in the 1773 edition); *Eiga zukō* (3 vols., c. 1770, copies by Rinshō); *Itchō gafu* (3 vols., 1770, copies by Rinshō); *Eirin gakyō* (3 vols., 1773, copies by Ippō); and *Gunchō gaei* (3 vols., 1778, copies by Rinshō) (Pl. 95). It seems likely in some cases that Rinshō's copies are taken not from Itchō originals, but from Ippō's copies.

Itchō was something of an Edo man-about-town and a noted wit with a gift for caricature, which led to his banishment when he rashly satirized the shogun in a caricature. Although Itchō's brushwork belongs to the Kanō school, his choice of subjects is wider than most Kanō artists. When one thinks of the Kanō school of painting, the inevitable association is with landscapes and bird and flower studies, but Itchō concentrated a great deal on figure studies and street scenes of Edo, which are more in line with the ukiyo-e schools. Humor is the keynote of Itchō's work, and often the extremely expressive features of his figures, whether *chōnin*, peasant or Chinese sage, are wreathed in smiles. All the books quoted above containing Itchō's work in copies by Ippō or Rinshō are miscellanies which do not relate to any particular theme, and inevitable Kanō subjects are also included. Itchō's plant studies are simply and extremely carefully executed with a fine regard to overall composition, but it is his bird and animal studies that are most compelling. Probably no other artist in Japanese history contrived to give so many different humorous facial expressions to animals. Particularly notable are his comic portrayals of tigers, such as the one in the final volume of *Ehon zuhen*, and owls, and in other animal works, notably *Gunchō gaei*, Itchō displays a fine sense of the dramatic as well as the humorous. Itchō was extremely well served by his copyists, who managed to reproduce the artist's bold lines and subtle tones in printed form exceptionally well, and these collections of his work are among the finest illustrated books ever produced.

Ippō (1691–1760) did little work in book illustration apart from his copies of Itchō's paintings, but he was the main illustrator of *Chichi no on* (2 vols., 1730), an anthology of *haiku* produced to commemorate the death of the actor Ichikawa Danjūrō I. These illustrations are very much in Itchō's style, but the book is more notable for the early color illustrations by an artist called Ogawa Haritsu (*see* Pl. 55). Suzuki Rinshō (d. 1802), a pupil of Kanō Eisen (1730–90), was a gifted amateur painter in the Kanō tradition, but like Ippō, most of his illustrations were copies of other artists' paintings, particularly of Itchō's. He seems also to have moved in the circle of the publisher Tsutaya Jūsaburō,

95. A street entertainer with his monkey, from Volume 1 of the *Guncho gaei* (3 vols., 1778). The illustrations are Suzuki Rinshō's copies of the works of his teacher, Hanabusa Itchō.

and contributed illustrations to some of Tsutaya's *kyōka* anthologies. Itchō's minor followers include his two sons, Hanabusa Itchō II and Hanabusa Isshū, neither of whom contributed much to book illustration. Katsuma Ryūsui (active mid-18th century), although not strictly of the Kanō line, is sometimes associated with it through his joint efforts with Ippō on the *Hokku-chō* anthology of *haiku* (1 vol., 1756). He is best known for *Umi no sachi* (2 vols., 1762, color) and *Yama no sachi* (2 vols., 1765), which have been briefly mentioned in the previous chapter.

Thus it could be said that Hanabusa Itchō's line in book illustration is represented only by his own work, since none of his pupils used the book as a creative medium. Nevertheless, Itchō's work was highly influential, and echoes of it can be found in the illustrations of other unconnected artists, particularly in *haiga*, the illustrations to *haiku* poetry.

THE LINE OF ŌOKA SHUNBOKU

Not a great deal is known about Ōoka Shunboku (1680–1763), but he was a self-taught Osaka artist who worked in the Kanō style. A prolific painter and a man of wide interests, Shunboku did not turn to book illustration until his middle years. Possibly as a result of being self-taught, he displayed a considerable awareness of all the nuances of Kanō tradition, and his three major compilations of copies of old masters, both Chinese and Japanese, reflect diligent academic study. These are *Ehon te-kagami* (6 vols., 1720), *Wakan meiga-en* (6 vols., 1750) and *Gashi kaiyō* (6 vols., 1751), all of which were designed as painting textbooks. Perhaps Shunboku's most famous book of copies, however, was *Minchō seidō gaen*, originally published in two volumes in 1746, and later reissued in a larger format under the title *Minchō shiken* (3 vols., 1812). The paintings in this are reproduced in color, and the first two volumes are based on two famous Chinese painting manuals, *Shêng-tung hua-yüan* and *Chieh-tzŭ-yüan hua-chuan* (*Kaishien gaden*). Flowers form the principal subject, and the work is regarded of considerable importance in the history of Japanese color book printing.

Shunboku displayed considerable talent, attested to by examples of his own work in *Ehon te-kagami*, for Toba-e, a low form of cartoon caricature which is named after the Heian priest and painter Toba Sōjō (1053–1140). Toba-e were not the monopoly of any particular school, and the most noted artist of this genre was one Jichōsai (active late 18th century), who is classified by some Japanese authorities as a ukiyo-e artist and is included by others in the Shijō-Maruyama fold. It may be thought that Toba-e are a kind of equivalent to *kyōka* poetry in the sense that they were designed for amusement with no artistic pretensions, and certainly should not be compared with the subtle caricatures of Itchō. However, Shunboku clearly had a liking for this kind of work and imparted it to more than one of his pupils. Otherwise, he was not especially prolific, and examples of his work in *Ramma zushiki* (3 vols., 1734) and *Tansei kinnō* (6 vols., 1753) are not very striking.

Of Shunboku's pupils, his son Ōoka Shunsen (1718–73) was better known for his work in lacquer painting, but also left a few illustrated books. His *Ehon fukujusō* (3 vols., 1737) was a standard collection of plant designs very much in the Kanō manner, with instructions for coloring, while *Sekiga* (1 vol., date unknown) was a collection of sketches in cursive style, some of which were originals and some copies.

Ōoka Michinobu (active mid-18th century) was another of Shunboku's pupils who seldom worked in book illustration. His most interesting publication was *Oshi-e te-kagami* (3 vols., 1736), a set of model designs of landscapes, figures and flower and bird studies for the making of *oshi-e* (pictures made of cloth-covered cardboard cutouts). Takehara Shunchōsai (d. 1800), a one-time pupil of Shunboku, is best known as a most capable illustrator of *meisho-ki*. His works of this type include *Miyako meisho zue* (6 vols., 1780), *Yamato meisho zue* (7 vols., 1791) and *Settsu meisho zue* (8 vols., 1796–98), guides to Kyoto, Yamato province and Settsu province (modern Osaka region) respectively. Landscapes form the principal subject matter of these works together with scenes from the life of the regions. Shunchōsai is not usually regarded as a Kanō artist, but from Shunboku he did absorb a liking for Toba-e caricatures, and his *Toba-e akubi dome* (3 vols., 1793) is an outstanding example of this genre.

Yoshimura Shūzan (d. 1776), a pupil of Kanō Mitsunobu and a friend and contemporary of Shunboku, left about six illustrated books, the best of which are *Wakan meihitsu gaei* (6 vols., 1749) and *Wakan meihitsu gahō* (6 vols., 1767), both collections of copies of famous Chinese and Japanese paintings. Shūzan's illustrative work reflects Kanō tradition in a much more orthodox fashion than that of Shunboku does, and despite the fact that Shūzan did not use the book as a creative medium, his reputation in his lifetime rivaled that of the now more famous Shunboku. This yet again demonstrates the greater emphasis placed on painting by the Kanō tradition and the secondary importance of the illustrated book.

THE LINE OF KANŌ EINŌ

Kanō Einō (1634–1700) made his most important contribution to the printed book as a writer rather than an illustrator. Copies of his paintings can be found in more than one collection including Shunboku's *Wakan meiga-en*, but it is Einō's history of Japanese painting, *Honchō gashi* (6 vols., 1693, a collection of biographies of nearly 400 artists), by which he is best remembered today. However, although Einō does not feature prominently in the history of Japanese illustration, his direct and second-generation pupils made a considerable impact on the illustrated book.

The Jōdo sect Buddhist priest Kokan (1653–1717) was a noted follower of Einō's painting, and is famous for his figure studies, especially of Daikoku, one of the gods of wealth and happiness. His direct involvement with book illustration is doubtful since virtually every book bearing his name as artist was published after his death (but with no mention of a copyist). Most of the books he was either directly or indirectly responsible for, such as *Yakushiji engi* (4 vols., 1716) and *Kōa shōnin den* (2 vols., 1787, there may well have been an earlier edition), were related to Buddhist subjects, in particular biographies of Buddhist "saints," but his reputation as an illustrator rests on his caricatures. Although Kokan produced many, the only existing source of his caricatures in printed form is *Jinbutsu soga* (3 vols., 1724, also known as *Keisai soga*). Since Kokan died in 1717, these caricatures must have been copies of his own paintings or of his designs for wood blocks. Kokan's name is not mentioned in the 1724 edition, but does appear in the 1735 second edition, and the omission from the earlier production was probably intentional from the publisher's view that this type of work was unfitting for a priest. Examples of Kokan's other paintings in printed form may be found in *Wakan meiga-en* and *Meisū gafu* (4 vols., 1810, a collection of copies of paintings by numerous artists, compiled by Ōhara Minsei).

Kokan's pupil, Takada Keiho (1674–1755), was another Kanō artist whose book illustrations exist in the form of copies made by later artists. Keiho was born the son of an apothecary in Ōmi province and studied painting under Kanō Eishin before becoming a pupil of Kokan. Copies of his work may be seen in the previously mentioned *Meisū gafu*

96. The Chinese immortal Bashiko, famed for performing acupuncture on the throat of a dragon, by Takada Keiho, student of Kanō Eishin, from the *Keiho gafu* (1804).

and *Meika gafu* (probably published in 3 vols. in 1814; the second is no longer extant and there is doubt whether it was ever published), but the principal collection of his work is in the *Keiho gafu* (4 vols., 1804, also known as *Chikuin gafu, Chikuinsai gafu* and *Chikurin gafu*) (Pl. 96). This fine book was edited by the minor Kyoto artist Tanida Hakuyū, and although the copyist is not known, it contains copies of paintings by Keiho and some of his pupils. The first two volumes are devoted to the works of Keiho, where figure sketches influenced by Itchō predominate, but there is one flower study and several magnificent landscapes, where Keiho's strong brushwork, reputedly modeled on Sesshū's, is faithfully reproduced. The latter two volumes contain copies of the work of numerous pupils and cover a much wider range of subject and style, with a few landscapes displaying a distinct Nanga flavor. However, despite the book's claim that it contains the works of Keiho's pupils, many of the paintings included were not done by his pupils at all. In one instance, an example of Kokan's work appears. The standard of reproduction is extremely high, and the subject matter represented is skillfully arranged to achieve a varied and interesting result.

One of the most influential of Takada Keiho's pupils was the artist Tsukioka Settei (1710–86), who was also born in Ōmi province but who lived in Osaka. Settei was one of those artists whose work is impossible to classify. Reference books describe him sometimes as a Kanō artist and sometimes as a ukiyo-e artist, whereas paradoxically he was both and neither—in other words, he was yet another artist who was influenced by a variety of styles and who worked happily in all of them. It is important to realize, as has been suggested, that both the Tosa and Kanō schools of painting formed part of the basic training of almost all the Japanese artists in the Edo period, and quite naturally few ever entirely escaped from these early influences, however historians categorize them.

Between 1753 and the early 1780s Settei was responsible for illustrating some 30 books, and the majority of his work could be described as of ukiyo-e type. *Yūjo gojūnin isshu* (2 vols., 1753, portraits of courtesans) is a typical example of Settei's work in this style, but he also produced *meisho-ki* works such as *Tōgoku meisho-ki* (5 vols., 1762, a guide to the eastern provinces) and was noted for many effective studies of warriors such as *Ehon musha tazuna* (3 vols., 1759). *Onna buyū yoso-oi kurabe* (3 vols., 1757) was an interesting variant on the traditional warrior theme so favored by artists catering to a samurai audience, for it depicted the deeds of heroines in Japanese history and legend. Even in such works as *Ehon musha tazuna* and *Onna buyū yoso-oi kurabe*, however, one usually finds the deliberate insertion, often at the end of a volume, of a conventional Kanō plant or flower and bird study, although this is often irrelevant to the other illustrations. Settei's most orthodox illustrations are in (*Wakan meihitsu*) *kingyoku gafu* (6 vols., 1771), a collection of copies of old Chinese and Japanese paintings, and from this it is clear that although Settei concentrated on subjects normally associated with ukiyo-e, he was never truly of that school.

Shitomi Kangetsu (1747–97) was a pupil of Settei who was not particularly prolific in book illustration but who gravitated toward the illustration of *meisho-ki*. He left one work of warrior studies in *Ehon musha roku* (3 vols., 1768), which was produced early in his career when Settei's influence was at its strongest, but his most representative books were published shortly after his death—*Nippon sankai meisan zue* (5 vols., 1799) and *Ise sangū meisho zue* (8 vols., 1797). The late eighteenth century was a golden age of *meisho-ki* works, and the same year that saw the publication of the relatively ordinary *Ise sangū meisho zue* (a record of famous places on the pilgrims' road to the Ise shrine) also saw the publication of the more ambitious *Tōkaidō meisho zue* (6 vols., 1797). This latter work contained illustrations by nearly 30 artists, representing a complete cross-section of painting schools, and can almost be used as a textbook of landscape styles of the period. Both *Ise sangū meisho zue* and *Ōmi meisho zue* (4 vols., 1797, jointly illustrated by Kangetsu and Nishimura Chūwa) are typical of the work done by Kanō artists in *meisho-ki*. In these it is the guidebook objective that governs subject matter and style, but Kanō artists still tended to make landscape dominate all else in the picture in the Chinese manner, unlike ukiyo-e artists who gave the figure study much more prominence. Kangetsu's work has a reputation for close detail, but an examination of both these *meisho-ki* indicates that much of this detail is reserved for the settings rather than for the figures. In *Nippon sankai meisan zue*, Kangetsu's best work of illustration, the closer attention to figures gives the book much of its interest. Indeed this difference of emphasis is one of the most distinctive factors separating Kanō from ukiyo-e art.

Okada Gyokuzan (1737–1812) was a pupil of Settei, whose work has come to be identified with ukiyo-e. It is likely that he illustrated more than 30 books, which display great versatility of style, from orthodox Tosa, in *Ise monogatari zue* (3 vols., published posthumously in 1825), to a number of *yomi-hon* novels illustrated in ukiyo-e style, the most famous of which is *Ehon taikōki*, a vast semifictional account of the life of Toyotomi Hideyoshi, published in 84 volumes between 1797 and 1802. This work was written by Takenouchi Kakusai and banned by the Tokugawa shogunate in 1804 because of its depiction of the period leading up to the seizure of power by the Tokugawa in the 1600s, but nevertheless, a considerable number of volumes have survived. Okada Gyokuzan's most orthodox work in Kanō style is found in two *meisho-ki* books, *Sumiyoshi meishō zue* (5 vols., 1794) and *Morokoshi meisho zue* (6 vols., 1805, with Ōhara Minsei and Oka Bunki). The latter is a guide to places of interest in China, but although landscapes and temples form the primary subject matter, there is also some emphasis on the depiction of objects and scenes relating to Chinese art and history. Since none of the artists involved ever visited China, the views contained in *Morokoshi meisho zue* must have been copies or adaptations of the work of prior Chinese artists.

Hayami Shungyōsai (d. 1823) was born either in Kyoto or Osaka and studied painting under Gyokuzan. He became a prolific writer and illustrator of novels and was compelled to follow the ukiyo-e style, since its domination of the novel was so complete. Between 1801 and 1823 he illustrated some 24 novels, of which *Ehon ken'yū roku* (10 vols., 1810, a *yomi-hon* novel written and illustrated by Shungyōsai) is typical. Inevitably, Kanō influences are apparent in these illustrations and this also applies to Shungyōsai's most popular book, *Nenjū gyōji taisei* (6 vols., 1806). This ambitious illustrated account of festivals and customs throughout Japan, although concentrating on the Kamigata region, is basically in ukiyo-e style, but the attention to detail and the contrivance to subjugate the figures to the setting even when the former are central, are typical of the Kanō artists, especially of his master Gyokuzan. Despite the fact that what is normally regarded as Shungyōsai's representative work, *Miyako fūzoku kewai den* (3 vols., 1813, on beauty preparations of Kyoto women), is ostensibly in ukiyo-e style, Shungyōsai's involvement in orthodox aspects of Kanō and Chinese art tradition can be seen in his participation as editor rather than illustrator of several books of this type, such as *Hengaku kihan* (1 vol., 1819).

97. A rat, by Yamamoto Nobuatsu of Osaka, from the *Gazu zetsumyō*, a book of painting instruction published in Kyoto in 1772.

These are by no means all the Kanō artists who worked in book illustration, but there would indeed be little point in describing the work of minor artists closely imitating the masters previously mentioned. It must be noted that Kanō artists were never as involved with illustrating books as were artists of the ukiyo-e, Nanga, Shijō and Maruyama schools, and with the exception of Hanabusa Itchō, the books they produced are not particularly attractive, for their talents were more apparent in their paintings. In the nineteenth century their landscape and *kachō* studies became repetitious, especially in book illustrations, perhaps because Kanō artists virtually never used color. In addition to the previously mentioned fact that Kanō painting formed part of the basic art training, some of the freer spirits within the Kanō movement strove to escape to more fertile fields. The list of major artists who began painting in the Kanō style and moved on to challenge its orthodoxy with new and imaginative variations on Kanō themes is a long one, headed perhaps by Utamaro. Even comparatively minor Kanō figures such as Nakai Rankō (1766–1830, pupil of Shitomi Kangetsu) and Shimokōbe Shūsui (active late 18th century) participated in this exodus. Since the Kanō school drew its inspiration from both Chinese and native sources, the ultimate destinations of these artists were widely divergent. Yet, however hidebound the Kanō school was by orthodoxy, it did enrich Japanese artistic tradition and, unlike the ukiyo-e schools, it survived the upheavals of the Meiji Restoration (at any rate as far as painting is concerned), showing that sweeping social changes in themselves were not enough to destroy the movement. That said, it should be admitted that the full flowering of Kanō achievement was never satisfactorily adapted to the illustrated book.

10 | THE KŌRIN, NANGA, MARUYAMA, SHIJŌ AND KISHI SCHOOLS

Japanese art historians usually consider Hishikawa Moronobu, Hanabusa Itchō and Ogata Kōrin as the greatest painters representative of the late seventeenth century. This is slightly questionable since Itchō was not really typical of the school he nominally belonged to, but all three artists did represent major art movements in Japan. It is another example of the surprising results of Kanō influence, for Moronobu, Itchō and Kōrin all received their initial training from Kanō masters. Apart from that their work has little in common, and as far as book illustration is concerned, only Moronobu worked creatively in that medium. Two other factors separate Kōrin from the others: Kōrin was born into the vastly different Kyoto society, which resulted in a distinct form of artistic motivation; and Kōrin was talented in several other arts apart from painting.

THE KŌRIN SCHOOL

Ogata Kōrin (1658–1716), founder of the Kōrin school (sometimes called the Rimpa school), was born in Kyoto to the wealthy dyer and silk merchant Ogata Sōken, who in turn was the great-nephew of Hon'ami Kōetsu. The Ogata family were descended from a long and distinguished line which took part in the Heike wars, and although much of their wealth and position was lost after the fall of the Ashikaga shogunate, it was this distinction of birth that afforded the opportunity for marriage between Sōken's father, Ogata Sōhaku, and Kōetsu's sister. Kōrin thus came from a wealthy Kyoto background with a long artistic tradition, and perhaps because of this he inevitably avoided the popular ukiyo-e movement in art. In his youth Kōrin is believed to have received training in the Kanō style under Yamamoto Soken, and either Kanō Yasunobu or Kanō Tsunenobu. Although it is normally said that he became dissatisfied with Kanō and turned toward the "old Tosa" style of Kōetsu and Sōtatsu, there is no reason to suppose that this move was a consequence of his dissatisfaction, for Kanō subjects were prominent in Kōrin's work. It is certain, however, that Kōrin did not become a pupil of Tawaraya Sōtatsu as L. N. Brown states, for Sōtatsu died some years before Kōrin's birth, but as many of the works of Kōetsu and Sōtatsu were in the possession of the Ogata family, it is likely that Kōrin's artistic development was influenced by them. It was not only a style of painting that Kōrin acquired from these works but also a versatility in many other fields of art including lacquer work and pottery, both of which Kōetsu excelled in.

Little of Kōetsu's work has survived, but in painting Kōrin probably owed more to Sōtatsu, who like Kōetsu hankered for the refinement of Heian court culture and who, through the influence of Kanō Eitoku, introduced many Kanō themes into his painting. Sōtatsu is best known as a brilliant screen painter, and Kōrin, too, excelled in this decorative form of painting, making use of Kanō bird and plant themes that Sōtatsu had treated so successfully. Although he produced many figure studies, Kōrin's main talent lay in decorative art; he also produced large numbers of designs for pottery and displayed an enormous talent for gold lacquer work. This obsession with design and decoration became a hallmark of the Kōrin school, and his own work grew highly stylized, a feature which is especially pronounced in later books of his paintings and designs.

Kōrin himself never worked directly in book illustration, and all the books containing his work were produced, sometimes more than a century after the artist's death, in the form of copies done by his pupils. These fall into two types: books of patterns and designs for kimono, pottery, fans, boxes; and books of copies of his paintings. Pattern books were always a popular genre in Japan and many artists, including Hokusai, produced them in large numbers, although the intent of such works was decorative rather than utilitarian. Kōrin's designs are among the best of their type despite their stylization, and the addition of color in some later publications lends a pleasing dimension to the designs themselves. In his flower studies particularly, Kōrin's style is closer to the later evolving Shijō style than the Kanō. In this connection his most important follower, Sakai Hōitsu, was closely involved with the Shijō movement. Another feature of Kōrin's books of designs, and one which can be attributed to his copyists as well as to himself, is the use of the full width of the page for the illustration, heightening the decorative effect of the book without giving any feeling of overcrowding.

The list of Kōrin's most important pattern and design and painting books is: *Kōrin hiinagata suso moyō* (2 vols., 1727, kimono designs copied by Nonomura Chūbei, which may perhaps be the same book as *Kōrin hiinagata wakamidori* quoted by Nakada Katsunosuke [see Bibl.]); *Hiinagata some-iro no yama* (3 vols., 1732, kimono designs copied by Nonomura Chūbei); *Kōrin ehon michi-shirube* (3 vols., 1735, flowers and plant designs for cloth, *furoshiki* wrappers, pottery and fans copied by Nonomura Chūbei); *Hiinagata tatsutagawa* (3 vols., 1742, various designs copied by Nonomura Chūbei); *Kōrin-fū hiinagata taki no ito* (undated, mentioned only by Nakada as a design book copied by Ebishiya Chūshichi); *Kōrin gafu* (2 vols., 1802, a collection of flowers, landscapes and figure studies copied by Nakamura Hōchū and printed in light colors); *Kōrin hyakuzu* (4 vols., 1815–26, more than "one hundred pictures of Kōrin" to commemorate the hundredth anniversary of his death, with black-and-white copies by Sakai Hōitsu; its most interesting feature is the two prefaces by Kameda Bōsai and Tani

Bunchō, leading figures in the Nanga movement); *Kōrin manga* (1 vol., 1817, flowers and plants, possibly copied by Tatebayashi Kagei); *Ehon Kōrin* (1 vol., 1818, flower and plant motifs copied by Aikawa Minwa); *Kōrin gashiki* (1 vol., 1818, miscellaneous flower, plant, animal and figure studies copied by Aikawa Minwa).

Glancing at this list of copies of Kōrin's work, the hundredth anniversary of his death seems to have stimulated remarkable publishing activity, and it is to his credit that his designs were in such demand so long after his death. In fact, despite the stylization in Kōrin's work, his school was surprisingly enduring, attracting several artists of quality, although few worked in book illustration as anything more than copyists. All Kōrin's followers came from the Kamigata region and his work never made any substantial impact in Edo. It seems that his designs captured something of the spirit of Kyoto in the Genroku era (1688–1704), as historians suggest, but it is infinitely easier to make such a statement than to define what the "Kyoto spirit" was. Certainly, Kōrin's work was far less contemporary than Moronobu's, and it may simply be that Kyoto always trailed a little behind the fast-moving, more fickle city of Edo. The flavor of the old aristocratic society lingered long in Kyoto, and Kōrin's decorative designs appear to have captured that flavor remarkably well.

Ogata Kenzan (1663–1743), Kōrin's younger brother, is far better known as a potter and master of the tea ceremony than a painter, but he studied under Kōrin, and a book of his paintings copied by Sakai Hōitsu was published in 1823 under the title *Kenzan iboku* (1 vol., color). Stylistically, there is no truly discernible deviation in his work from that of Kōrin. Sakai Hōitsu (1761–1828) was the principal copyist of Kōrin's work and a fine artist in his own right, who at various stages in his career studied painting in the Kanō, Tosa, Shijō, Maruyama and even ukiyo-e schools before coming under the influence of Kōrin's style. Since he was subjected to many styles, it is not surprising that his representative work in two books, *Ōson gafu* (1 vol., 1817, color) and *Hōitsu shōnin shinseki kagami* (2 vols., undated, color, copied by his pupil Ikeda Koson [1801–66]), reveals substantial deviations from Kōrin's despite the similarity of themes. On the whole, his work is much closer to the Maruyama-Shijō styles. Other examples of his illustrations can be seen in *Un'yū buni* (5 vols., 1802), *Sakura* (1 vol., c. 1812) and *Ryōri-tsū daizen* (4 vols., c. 1822–34), all of which were not associated with the Kōrin school.

Of later Kōrin school artists, Nakamura Hōchū, Suzuki Kiichi (1796–1858) and Ikeda Koson (the latter two were pupils of Hōitsu) contributed to book illustration as copyists of Kōrin's and Hōitsu's work, and on their own participated occasionally in collections of illustrations of the Maruyama-Shijō schools. One artist who never studied under Kōrin but whose work shows some Kōrin characteristics was Itō Jakuchū (1716–1800), proprietor of a Kyoto grocery. Jakuchū began his artistic training under an unknown master of the Kanō school, but later studied Yüan and Ming Chinese paintings as well as the work of Kōrin on his own. He specialized in flowers and domestic fowl, and the two most famous collections of his paintings, *Jakuchū gafu* (4 vols., 1890, color) and

Jakuchū gajō (2 vols., undated, white on black) were not published until the Meiji period. His other works—*Gempo yōka* (1 *orihon* album, 1768, white on black), *Sōken-jo* (1 *orihon* album, 1768, white on black), *Shōshun-hō* (1 *orihon* album, 1777, white on black) and *Gakuga shōkei* (1 vol., 1836), all show his skills to good advantage.

THE NANGA, MARUYAMA, SHIJŌ AND KISHI SCHOOLS

The Nanga, Maruyama and Shijō schools can be treated as separate entities and developments in Japanese art, but they were very closely related. All were centered in Kyoto in their early periods, all continued to flourish into the nineteenth century when the Tosa, Kanō and ukiyo-e movements were in decline, all owed a great deal to Chinese painting tradition, and all were highly individualistic and subjective. The term "impressionistic" is frequently used to describe these three schools, and accurately so, provided that one can disassociate the word from its European overtones. Realism in Japanese painting, prints and book illustration is best represented by artists of the ukiyo-e school in the sense that they strove to depict exactly what they saw. This is not to say that artists such as Utamaro did not capture the spirit of the courtesans they depicted, but their aim was to produce recognizable portraits of the people and events of everyday life. Theatergoers of Edo wanted portraits, not artists' impressions, of their favorite actors and this is what ukiyo-e artists provided. It is this factor that makes ukiyo-e such a valuable source material for the social historian. Even in landscape painting ukiyo-e artists accurately depicted places familiar to all; the landscapes of the Nanga artists are recognizable as such, but the places more often than not are imaginary or else are Chinese scenes that the artists had never seen. Likewise, courtesans of the Maruyama school are recognizable as courtesans, but in no sense are they realistic; and the plants and flowers of Shijō artists are profoundly beautiful, but they are not the minutely observed, detailed portrayals of the Kanō artists.

Whatever the subject, artists of the Nanga, Maruyama and Shijō schools always sought to capture the inner spirit of what was depicted. The Nanga pioneer Yanagisawa Kien (1706–58), for example, wrote that the Kanō artists never got beyond the skin of their material. It is probably true that when Westerners in the late nineteenth century first saw Japanese art, they seized on what was most understandable as the best and the most representative, and ukiyo-e paintings and prints were ready-made to fit this need. In recent years, however, the work of the Nanga and Maruyama artists has come into its own in the eyes of Western connoisseurs (although, unfortunately, all too often this new appreciation has led to unjustified censure of ukiyo-e), and no critic of today would dream of dismissing the Nanga school, as Fenollosa did in the early years of this century, as "hardly more than a joke."

It has been said that the Nanga, Maruyama and Shijō schools owed much to China, and the growth of each was stimulated in Japan by a combination of historical circumstances. First, the Tokugawa authorities actively fostered Confucianism as a code of moral behavior calculated to keep the feudal nobility in a state of quiescence. Naturally, interest in Confucianism led to involvement with other aspects of Chinese culture, including painting. Second, although Japan was a "closed" country from the middle of the sixteenth century, Chinese books and paintings continued to reach those interested, primarily through Nagasaki. Two superlative examples of Chinese printed albums, *Hasshu gafu* (*Pa-chung hua-p'u*), published in China in the 1620s and in Japan in 1671, and *Kaishien gaden* (*Chieh-tzŭ-yüan hua-chuan*, or *Mustard Seed Garden Manual*), printed in Japan in 1748 but widely known by the end of the seventeenth century, were received and studied avidly. Finally, with the collapse of the Ming dynasty in 1644, some Chinese painters fled to Japan, where they established studios and taught painting, thus influencing the development of Japanese art. Curiously, Chinese painters such as I Fu-chiu and Shên Nan-p'in, who came to Nagasaki in the 1730s and 1740s respectively, did not enjoy high reputations in China and their influence in Japan was rather out of proportion to their individual talents.

Not all the Chinese painters who arrived in Nagasaki belonged to the same school of art, which was then broadly divided by Chinese historians into the "Northern" and "Southern" schools. These terms had no geographical significance but originated from the painter-theorist Tung Ch'i-ch'ang (1555–1636), who distinguished "Northern" artists, who were professional, loved detail, were relatively colorful but conservative, from "Southern" artists, who were less realistic (i.e., more "impressionistic"), deliberately awkward in style and amateurish. The term "amateur" was not one of opprobrium, since "Southern" artists were by tradition scholars of literature and philosophy who painted for recreation, combining their knowledge of literature and their calligraphic skills with their painting. It was the "Northern" tradition that was embodied in the Chinese stream of the Kanō school, and the "Southern" tradition, particularly prized in the Ming and Ch'ing dynasties, which developed into the Nanga school.

The Nanga school in Japan displayed certain differences from its Chinese parent. This was almost inevitable since the Japanese never received the complete training of the school at one time and were forced to reconstruct from paintings and books as well as through the teachings of men like I Fu-chiu. The movement made its first impact in Nagasaki and spread later to Kyoto and, much later, to Edo. Probably because of some misunderstanding of the Chinese distinction between Northern and Southern painting, and certainly because of native Japanese interpretation and inspiration, there was far less distinction between the two movements in Japan than there was in China, and although the principles of Southern painting were adhered to, there was a substantial amount of eclecticism in the work of Japanese artists practicing the new style. It was thus inevitable that within a very short time the new Chinese inspiration should bear fruit in unexpected ways, and the Nanga, Maruyama, Shijō and Kishi schools were all products of that inspiration manifested in different directions.

The Northern school lost much of its popularity in Ming China, but its influence and tradition in Japan endured for a long time, dating from the time of Sesshū (1420–1506).

98. A Nanga-style landscape, by Nakabayashi Chikutō, from the *Chikutō sansui gakō* (1812).

Since not all the Chinese artists who came to Japan in the late seventeenth and early eighteenth centuries were of the Southern school, there was naturally something of a Northern revival, manifested in what is sometimes called the Modified Northern school or the Modified School of Sesshū. This is principally represented by the work of Yamaguchi Sekkei (1644–1732) and his pupil Mochizuki Gyokusen (1692–1755). However, neither of these artists were prominent in book illustration, and it is extremely hard to assess the influence of this revival on book illustration.

Since the Nanga, Maruyama, Shijō and Kishi schools are so closely related, rather than attempt to follow each school as a separate entity, it is perhaps more logical to examine some of the leading artists in the "impressionistic" movement, the major innovators or faithful representatives of an identifiable tradition, and then to look at their followers. The nomination of these key figures is almost always a subject of contention, but we suggest the following artists be included: Ike no Taiga, Yosa Buson, Tani Bunchō, Maruyama Ōkyo, Matsumura Goshun, Kishi Ku (Ganku) and Tatebe Ryōtai. It is important to stress again that all these movements belong fundamentally to painting and thus are not perfectly represented in book illustration, especially since some of the leading artists (such as Yanagisawa Kien of the Nanga tradition) never worked directly in book illustration. Just as in Kanō book illustration, where copies outnumber original works, so in Nanga copies are more prominent, although this is less true of Maruyama work.

None of the three most distinguished artists to first take up the Nanga style—Gion Nankai (1676–1751), Yanagisawa Kien (1706–58) and Sakaki Hyakusen (1697–1752)—worked directly in book illustration or had their work reproduced in books on a meaningful scale. All, particularly Nankai and Kien, were scholars of Chinese literature and from similar feudal backgrounds typical of the scholar-painter (*bunjin*, the Nanga school was often known as the Bunjin-ga school), which also typified the Southern movement in China.

IKE NO TAIGA (1723–76)

The artist responsible for bringing the Southern style to full maturity in Japan and making it a viable entity in itself with a substantial native flavoring was Ike no Taiga. Unlike Nankai and Kien, Taiga did not come from a feudal background, for his father, who died when he was four, worked in the Kyoto mint. Taiga later opened a fan shop with his mother and sold fans decorated with his paintings copied from *Hasshu gafu*. This shop was not particularly successful and little else is known about Taiga's early life except that he was a child prodigy, adept at calligraphy and painting at the age of seven. In his early teens he is believed to have received training under the master Tosa Mitsuyoshi (1700–72) before going to live and study with Yanagisawa Kien in 1738. Kien trained him in finger painting (the application of ink to paper with fingers, nails and hands), at which Taiga excelled, and in 1750 Kien introduced him to Gion Nankai, by then a very old man. This meeting with Nankai was probably too short to leave any profound influence, but Taiga certainly studied and respected his work as much as that of Kien and the Chinese Southern artist I Fu-chiu. By the early 1750s Taiga had developed a style of his own firmly based on Chinese Southern technique. Nanga was fundamentally a school of landscape painting in which literary associations played an important part (often paintings were based on events from Chinese literary history), and even in Japan artists continued to produce Chinese rather than native landscapes. Although Taiga usually painted Chinese landscapes he had never seen, he was also fond of nature and frequently ventured into the countryside. This led him to portray Japanese scenes in his famous series of paintings *The Six Sights of Kyoto*, produced in the early 1750s, and his observations of nature had the effect of expanding his work and making it much more than simple imitation of Chinese style.

In Taiga's work we see the expression of native genius applied to transform a foreign style, and it enables us to obtain a fairly clear idea of Japanese Nanga. As the aim of Nanga artists of Japan (and for that matter Chinese Southern artists too) was to capture the inner meaning of the scene, not only are landscapes suggested rather than portrayed, but the light colors frequently used by Taiga and other Nanga artists, however subtle

211

and beautiful, are not in any sense naturalistic or real. Two distinctive features of Taiga's style were the repeated use of dot patterns, a Chinese technique, and the very non-Chinese use of gold for decoration, perhaps borrowed from Kōrin. Some critics see the dot technique (not, of course, unique to Taiga) as an influence on the European pointillists. A great deal more has been said, notably by James Cahill (*see* Bibl.), about Taiga's technique of painting, but since we are more concerned with book illustration, it suffices to say that Ike no Taiga was a great deal more than a proficient copyist of a foreign style. His work was popular and influential in his own lifetime, and although he did not work directly in book illustration, copies of his work can be found in several collections published after his death in 1776. He has far more claim than any of the other earlier Nanga artists to the title of "founder" of Japanese Nanga.

Apart from occasional copies of his paintings in anthologies such as the previously mentioned *Meika gafu* and *Gakuga shōkei*, Taiga's work in book illustration is confined to three books, *I Fukyū Ike no Taiga sansui gafu* (2 vols., 1803), *Taigadō gahō* (3 vols., 1804, with reprints, notably that of 1835) and *Taigadō gafu* (1 *orihon* album, 1804, color, one of the most beautiful illustrated books ever produced in Japan). In the first work, Volume One consists of copies of I Fu-chiu's paintings and Volume Two of copies of Taiga's paintings by Kan Dainen, in black and white. The juxtaposition of the work of these two artists indicates that at that time I Fu-chiu and Taiga were seen to have much in common. However, the collection reveals certain differences. I Fu-chiu's designs are simple, with the traditional massed whorllike lines in the mountains, a distinct feature of Nanga art in both China and Japan, while Taiga's paintings are thematically more varied (in one case figure studies are given preeminence), emphasizing trees more than mountains. As the *sansui* ("mountain and water") of the title implies, the works are nearly all landscapes, and in traditional Nanga style small houses in the mountains form the focal points around which the landscapes are framed. The volume devoted to Taiga's work includes designs for fans, where once again plants and trees are prominent, and the last illustrations are composed almost entirely in massed blocks of ink with the occasional use of gray wash, which gives a substantially different effect from I Fu-chiu's traditional approach. The second book, *Taigadō gahō*, is a more extensive collection of Taiga's landscapes, enhanced by the greater use of gray wash and occasional light colors, but it does not begin to rival the fascinating *Taigadō gafu*, which, although containing fewer illustrations, is a triumphant transference of Nanga landscape style in color to the printed book, a work which has few parallels in book illustration in its quiet beauty (Pl. 70).

The copies for this album were made by Taiga's pupil Sō Geppō (1760–1839), who managed to capture not only the wide range of Taiga's landscape style, but also his soft and delicate colors. Taiga had numerous other pupils, including the notable painters Aoki Shukuya (d. 1808), Kuwayama Gyokushū (1746–99) and Noro Kaiseki (1747–1828), all of whose works appear occasionally in printed books in the form of copies, but none worked directly in books to justify a "Taiga" school in book illustration.

Yosa Buson (1716–83)

Yosa Buson was a friend of Ike no Taiga rather than his pupil, and occasionally collaborated with him on paintings. Buson was basically a Nanga artist, since his landscape paintings are in Nanga style, but his talents were more diversified than those of Taiga. Buson (original family name Taniguchi) came from a wealthy farming family and first studied *haiku* in Edo under Uchida Senzan. His talents in *haiku* have earned him recognition as one of Japan's three greatest *haiku* masters, with Bashō and Issa, and his abilities as a calligrapher were scarcely less, as is evidenced in the edition of *Shin hanatsumi* of 1784. We shall return to this work later as an example of the illustration of Buson's pupil Matsumura Goshun; discounting the illustrative content, the book is a *haiku* diary by Buson and the calligraphy used in the printed edition is a copy of Buson's own handwriting. Many Westerners find it hard to understand the subtleties of Japanese calligraphy, but this book can be appreciated by all as an example of the beauty of written Japanese (*see* Pl. 4).

In the early 1750s Buson moved from Edo to Kyoto, where he set up a studio and began work as a painter, although he never abandoned *haiku*. As indicated earlier, Buson's landscapes are very much in Nanga style, sharing similarities with the work of Taiga, but often his brushstrokes were thicker and his work seems more impressionistic than Taiga's. He concentrated far more on Japanese subjects, and figure studies occupy a more prominent place in his works. He was also influenced by the realism of Shên Nan-p'in and executed a number of plant, bird and animal paintings in this style. In book illustration, in which he may have worked directly on occasion, Buson was primarily concerned with the illustration of *haiku*, and his approach in this ranged from orthodox studies of *haiku* poets to the cursive *haiga* style. His direct contribution to book illustration, however, was small and consists principally of *Yahanjō* (1 vol., 1764, portraits of 36 *haiku* poets in cursive style, giving "impressions" rather than likenesses, which was an essential feature of *haiga*) and the exceedingly rare *Kachō hen* (1 vol., 1782, bird and flower studies). Even in these two cases there is some question about Buson's direct involvement. Other books which include Buson's illustrations, copied from paintings, are *Haikai sanjū-rokka-sen* (1 vol., 1799, portraits of *haiku* poets in light colors in *haiga* style); *Haikai Buson shichibu-shū* (2 vols., 1809) and *Zoku haika kijin dan* (3 vols., 1832, illustrated by Buson and others).

Like Taiga, Buson had many pupils in painting and in *haiku*, including Matsum_a Goshun, founder of the Shijō school. They also include notable Nanga painters such as Yokoi Kinkoku (1761–1832), but his only pupil who worked promine___ly in book illustration was Ki Baitei (1744–1810). Baitei's painting was so similar in style to that of Buson that contemporaries called him Ōmi Buson, the Buson of Ōmi province. Copies of Baitei's work appeared in several anthologies including *Sanuki buri* (1 vol., 1798), *Yume no inano* (1 vol., 1801), *Tokai-jō* (1 *orihon* album, 1803, color) and *Ariwara bunko* (5 vols., 1810), but the only book consisting entirely of copies of his paintings is *Kyūrō gafu* (1 vol., c. 1795, studies in Nanga style with augmented reprints in 1799 and 1824).

TANI BUNCHŌ (1763–1840)

With Tani Bunchō we come to one of the greatest geniuses in the history of Edo-period painting, a man who is also credited with introducing the Nanga style to Edo. The son of a feudal retainer of the lord of Tayasu fief, Bunchō began to study painting at an early age, and in due course mastered a bewildering variety of styles. His earliest teacher was Katō Bunrei (1706–82), who was himself converted to Nanga from the Kanō school, and whose work is pleasantly represented in collections such as *Bunrei gasen* (3 vols., 1779). Over a period of years Bunchō studied both Southern and Northern Chinese styles, Ch'ing-dynasty bird and flower painting as represented by Shên Nan-p'in's work, Tosa, Kanō, ukiyo-e, Western art, and ultimately, Maruyama and Shijō painting.

The result of such a plethora of influences was that Bunchō could paint in any style at will, so that he becomes completely unclassifiable in normal school terms. He was prolific, which in some senses affected his work adversely, for many of his paintings were inferior in quality, but he was astonishingly popular in his own time and his influence was manifested in many directions. Tani Bunchō also worked directly in book illustration, alone or with collaborators, for some thirty or forty books. He was perhaps most skilled as a landscape painter who combined Nanga and Northern styles, and unlike other Nanga artists concentrated on accurate observation and detailed sketching, particularly of mountains. His greatest triumph in landscape and mountain painting in illustrated books was the *Nihon meisan zue* (3 vols., 1804), a collection of mountain scenery in Japan, in which the realistic influence of the Northern Chinese style is apparent. The illustrations in it are far more recognizable as real places than those in Taiga's *Taigadō gafu*.

Bunchō also worked on several *meisho-ki* books in the same style including *Gokinai sambutsu zue* (5 vols., 1813) and *Itsukushima ema kagami* (5 vols., 1832), but nothing demonstrates his breadth of interest and his versatility more clearly than *Shazanrō ehon* (1 vol., 1816, color) (Pl. 80). This work is generally recognized, with *Nihon meisan zue*, as Bunchō's masterpiece of book illustration, but in style and subject matter the two could hardly be more different. This is a collection of fruit, flower, bamboo and insect studies in what can only be described as Maruyama style, a style which Bunchō seems to have imbibed through the studies of his adopted son Tani Bun'ichi (1787–1818) under the Maruyama artist Watanabe Nangaku (1763–1813). Other important books to which Bunchō contributed, mostly in the form of landscapes, were *Meika zusan* (1 vol., 1805), *Nikkō san shi* (5 vols., 1837, the mountains of Nikkō) and *Enshū gafu* (1 vol., 1846, a posthumous collection including the work of Bun'ichi, Kita Busei and others).

There is some confusion about Bunchō's pupils, since the two artists Watanabe Gentai (1749–1822) and Suzuki Fuyō (1749–1816) are cited, in different sources, as Bunchō's masters and as his pupils. In the case of Fuyō, it seems likely that Bunchō was both his master and pupil at different times in his life. Watanabe Gentai was the son of Watanabe Shinsui, one of the first Japanese artists to study under Shên Nan-p'in in Nagasaki and whose bird and flower studies reflect this. It seems likely, in view of their relative ages, that Gentai was Bunchō's master rather than his pupil. Gentai's landscape studies are so similar to Bunchō's that he must have had a strong influence on Bunchō, assuming that the master-pupil hypothesis is correct. Gentai contributed to a number of illustrated books including *Yomo no haru* (1 *orihon* album, 1796, curiously appearing together with the work of Kitao Masanobu), and his most typical work is found in *Henshi gafu* (5 vols., 1799, copies by Gentai of his father Shinsui's work, with some examples of his own). This is also known as *Gentai gafu* and *Gentai sensei gafu*, and is a miscellany ranging from landscapes and figure studies to building designs. Suzuki Fuyō was a relatively minor artist, whose principal works in illustration are *Hi Kangen sansui gashiki* (3 vols., 1789, copies of the Chinese artist Fei Han-yüan) and *Gazu suifuyō* (3 vols., 1809).

It is impossible to pursue in detail the works of all of Bunchō's pupils, who included the distinguished Tanomura Chikuden (1777–1835), an artist who never worked in book illustration, and Ōnishi Chinnen (1792–1851), whose work was much closer to the Maruyama style. However, Kita Busei and, more particularly, Watanabe Kazan are worthy of attention. Kita Busei (1776–1856) received his early training from Bunchō and executed a number of paintings and illustrations in Nanga style, also contributing to *Nikkō san shi* and other Nanga landscape albums. However, he was never truly of the Nanga fold, being a close friend of Hokusai and an admirer of Kanō Tan'yū's works, which led him away from Nanga. None of his three best-known books were in Nanga style. *Kasen e-shō* (1 vol., c. 1810, color) is a collection of portraits of the *Sanjū-rokka-sen* in conventional style, while *Kottō-shū* (4 vols., 1814) is a book of art objects and antiques that also contains illustrations by the ukiyo-e artists Masanobu and Toyohiro. His best work, however, was the *Ehon isaoshi-gusa* (10 vols., 1839), which contains selected passages from Japanese classics on the deeds of warrior heroes. The curiosity of this book lies both in its style, which ranges from almost pure ukiyo-e to Tosa with the occasional impressionistic landscape, and in the coloring, which is bold and bright without being overwhelming as was commonly the case in ukiyo-e works of the time.

Watanabe Kazan (1793–1841) is both the ablest and best known of Bunchō's pupils. A retainer of the impoverished Tawara fief, he took up painting as a means of earning a living, although he remained poor all his life. He became the pupil of Bunchō in 1809, and at the same time studied Dutch, and was eventually responsible for the coastal defence of his fief, presumably a position awarded him for his interest and proficiency in European affairs. Ultimately this interest proved to be his undoing since he fell victim to a government purge of Dutch specialists and was put under house arrest. After two years of enforced confinement he took his own life.

As a painter Kazan was a faithful follower of Bunchō, who always cited him as an example to other pupils in as much as he studied the methods of many schools. His landscapes were more truly in Nanga style than his master's and he also excelled in the painting of bamboos and orchids, and, rather unusually, portraits, where he used Western techniques. In addition, Kazan wrote several books of poems and essays, enjoying the friendship of Bakin, whose essay collection, *Gendō hōgen* (6 vols., 1820), he illustrated. Regarded in later times as something of a hero, several collections of his work were issued in book form during the Meiji period, but several examples of his illustrations published in his lifetime were in *haiku* and *kyōka* books such as *Haikai shiyō-chō* (2 vols., 1835–37), which do not show him at his best.

Kazan had numerous followers, the most important of whom was Tsubaki Chinzan (1801–54), but none of them made anything other than small contributions to the Japanese illustrated book. The most active in this field was Chinzan who, apart from contributions to *Nikkō san shi*, collaborated with others on a series for the Momonoya Haiku Group entitled *Momonoya shunchō* (published almost annually in the 1840s by the Momonoya Haiku Group with poems and illustrations composed by its members). A close friend of Kazan was the minor Nanga artist Kameda Bōsai (1754–1826), whose one contribution to the illustrated book was the exquisite *Kyōchūzan* (1 vol., 1816, light colors) (Pl. 77), a collection of landscapes somewhat in the manner of Kawamura Bumpō.

MARUYAMA ŌKYO (1733–95)

Ōkyo occupies an honored place in the history of Japanese painting. Of farming stock from Tamba province, he took up a number of occupations before studying painting under the Kanō artist Ishida Yūtei (d. 1785), one-time pupil of Tsuruzawa Tanzan, in Kyoto. In addition to his studies in Kanō technique, which did not leave a profound mark on his later work, Ōkyo also studied the work of Chinese artists including Shên Nan-p'in, Ch'ien Hsüan (1235–c. 1290), a noted Yüan-dynasty flower painter and Ch'iu Ying (c. 1522–60), a celebrated Ming-dynasty figure painter. His major contribution to Japanese art is his theory that painters should not copy the works of earlier masters, but produce their own based on an accurate observation of nature and through the sketching of the subject before painting it. It is an open question whether this was as revolutionary as is usually suggested, and one feels that it was advice not needed by ukiyo-e painters, for example; perhaps it was more valuable to painters of the Nanga and the Kanō schools, who tended to spend too much time copying earlier works. Ōkyo added a perplexing second theory, that a painter who had mastered his subject through observation and sketching should then seek to interpret its spirit to the beholder. What this means in abstract terms is hard to define, but in practical terms one sees the effectiveness of this in Ōkyo's bird and flower or landscape and figure studies which, in contrast to the stylized efforts of Kanō artists on the same theme, have life and vividness. They are realistic pictures which transcend simple realism, and this is a characteristic of all great Japanese art, applying just as much to the work of Utamaro as it does Ōkyo. Whatever its truth, Ōkyo's work transformed the Japanese approach to the painting of nature and, fortunately, Ōkyo was also a lucid and capable teacher, which is reflected in the distinguished work of so many of his pupils.

Ōkyo did little, if any, direct work in book illustration, but *En'ō gafu* (2 vols., 1837, color, copies by Yamaguchi Soken) and *Ōkyo gafu* (1 vol., 1850, color) contain studies of Chinese figures (Pl. 85), plants, birds and landscapes that show up his style well. Of his many pupils, ten were later classified as the ablest: Nagasawa Rosetsu (1755–99), Komai Ki (1747–97), Yamaguchi Soken (1759–1818), Oku Bummei (d. 1813), Yoshimura Kōkei (1769–1836), Mori Tetsuzan (1775–1841), Maruyama (Kinoshita) Ōju (1777–1815, Ōkyo's second son), Hatta Koshū (1760–1822), Yamaato Kakurei (active early 19th century) and Kameoka Kirei (active early 19th century). Other notable figures in Ōkyo's circle were Minagawa Kien (1734–1807), Maruyama Ōshin (1790–1838), Maruyama Ōzui (1766–1829), Nishimura Nantei (1755–1834), Watanabe Nangaku (1763–1813), Matsumura Goshun (1752–1811) and Sō Gessen (1741–1809).

Virtually all these talented artists had their work represented in illustrated books to some degree, but of the ten only Rosetsu, Soken, Bummei and Koshū were significant in this respect. Rosetsu was a free and rebellious spirit, who was later expelled from the Maruyama school for insubordination. One tradition even has it that he was murdered (he died from poisoning) by a group of artists jealous of his enormous talent. Although he did some landscape painting, he excelled at figure studies and was famous for his magnified paintings of insects. The only book exclusively illustrated by Rosetsu was the biographical work *Daimon-mura kōshi den* (1 vol., 1786), but he made distinguished contributions to *Tōyūki* (5 vols., 1795, stories and views from the eastern provinces), *Meika gafu* and *Itsukushima ema kagami*.

Yamaguchi Soken was probably Ōkyo's most significant pupil as far as book illustration is concerned, since he not only produced copies of Ōkyo's paintings but also produced books of his own (Pl. 75). In addition to his contributions to collections such as *Ariwara bunko*, he was responsible for illustrating the novel *Hadaka yakan* (4 vols., c. 1795), a very rare thing for a Maruyama artist, *Shindai yamabuki-iro* (5 vols., 1799, another novel), *Yamato jinbutsu gafu* (3 vols., 1800, ukiyo-e scenes from popular life in Maruyama style), *Yamato jinbutsu gafu kōhen* (3 vols., 1804, a sequel to the previous work), *Soken gafu sōka no bu* (3 vols., 1806, sketches of plants) (Pl. 99) and *Soken sansui gafu* (2 vols., 1818, "mountain and water" landscapes). Soken therefore not only understood Ōkyo's teachings, but had considerable talent for detailed work, particularly in plant studies. He was also one of the earlier Maruyama artists to borrow the themes of ukiyo-e artists. It is probable that Aoi Sōkyū, the artist of the brilliant Maruyama work *Kishi empu* (1 vol., 1803, studies of courtesans) (Pl. 74), was a pupil of Soken. Oku Bummei, believed to have been a priest, was not solely responsible for any illustrated books, but his ability for landscape and figure work is shown in *Tōkaidō meisho zue*, *Miyako rinsen meishō zue* (6 vols., 1799, scenes from Kyoto life with landscapes and figures in ukiyo-e style executed in collaboration with the ukiyo-e artist Nishimura Chūwa) and *Wasure-gusa* (4 vols., c. 1810, color), to which Bummei contributed a study of a flower. His work also appears in *Bijin awase* (1 vol., 1807), a *haiku* anthology containing studies of courtesans in Maruyama style.

Despite Hatta Koshū's contributions to other books, his main illustrated book was

217

99. Two cranes in flight, from the plant and flower section of Yamaguchi Soken's sketchbook, the *Soken gafu sōka no bu*, published in 1806.

the *Koshū gafu* (1 vol., 1812, color), a collection of studies of birds, plants, animals and figures (principally from Chinese legends) which has been rather overrated. A superior artist in book illustration was Koshū's pupil Fukuchi Hakuei (active c. 1800–50), whose work is comparatively rare but always interesting. He executed landscape studies for the *Kyōka tegoto no hana* series of *kyōka* anthologies (1810–34, 5 series, color) (Pl. 76) and notable figure studies for another *kyōka* anthology, *Kokin wakashū* (2 vols., 1805), but his best work is found in *E-naoshi gafu* (1 vol., 1808, reissued in color in the 1850s under the title *Sōseki gafu*) and *Ririn gafu* (2 vols., 1834, color). The former work is an interesting example of a popular pastime among Kyoto artists, where an entire picture was begun by a single dot or stroke, while the latter is a miscellany of landscape, plant and figure studies to accompany *kyōka* poems. The colors of *Ririn gafu* are particularly striking and effective and, indeed, Hakuei was reputed to be one of the most skilled colorists of his time.

Watanabe Nangaku probably studied under Kishi Ku (Ganku) as well as Ōkyo, and his work shows some influence of Kishi, although in reality the Maruyama and Kishi groups were closely related. Nangaku visited Edo for three years in the first decade of the nineteenth century and taught Ōkyo's methods, thereby gaining credit for introducing Maruyama to Edo. He was especially skilled in the painting of carp and *bijin-ga*, and his work appeared in several of the printed collections mentioned previously. His most famous book, however, was *Kaidō kyōka awase* (1 vol., 1811, light colors), a collection of *kyōka* poems by Ueda Akinari, illustrated jointly by Nangaku and Kawamura Bumpō. In it, themes from everyday life are treated in Maruyama style, providing yet another example of Maruyama encroachment on ukiyo-e subject matter. Nangaku, too, had several distinguished pupils, the two most important being Ōnishi Chinnen (1792–1851) and Suzuki Nanrei (1775–1844). Chinnen was responsible for a number of delightful books printed in color, the most famous being *Azuma no teburi* (1 vol., 1829, a collection of sketches of popular Edo life, also known as *Taihei ushō*) (Pl. 83) and *Sonan gafu* (1 vol., 1834, miscellaneous subjects in humorous style). Nanrei specialized in birds and flowers and contributed to several albums, notably *Shoga-chō* (1 *orihon* album, 1830, color).

Nishimura Nantei was an artist who showed a predilection for figure studies, and his ability in this is seen in his most famous books, *Nantei gafu* (3 vols., 1804, color) (Pl. 100)

100. Two courtesans, by Nishimura Nantei, pupil of Maruyama Ōkyo, from the *Nantei gafu* (1804).

and *Nantei gafu kōhen* (1 vol., 1826, color, a supplement to the previous book). Sō Gessen was not really of the Maruyama fold although he studied under Ōkyo. He received his early training under Sakurai Sekkan and devoted much time to the study of Yüan and Ming painting as well as to the works of Sesshū and Buson. His concentration on Chinese painting and Chinese-derived painting led him, in illustration, toward formal studies of Chinese subject matter, and his most famous book, *Ressen zusan* (3 vols., 1784), was a collection of paintings of Taoist immortals, probably copied from Chinese exemplars. His other major work of illustration was *Wakan gasoku* (5 vols., 1776), also a collection of copies of the works of Chinese masters.

MATSUMURA GOSHUN (1752–1811)

Matsumura Goshun was another artist like Buson, who combined a wide range of talents. Although principally recognized as a painter, he was also a competent *haiku* poet, calligrapher and even musician. He was born in Kyoto and spent part of his early life as a scribe for the courtesans of the Shimabara, which earned him a reputation for dissipation, although in 1782 he became a Buddhist monk. His earliest training in painting was under Ōnishi Suigetsu, a pupil of Mochizuki Gyokusen, but at almost the same time he studied *haiku* and Nanga painting under Buson, joining Ōkyo's studio, where he was accepted as an equal rather than a pupil, after Buson's death. In 1788 he established his own studio, with his younger brother Matsumura Keibun (1779–1843) joining him there later, in the Shijō street of Kyoto, which gave its name to the Shijō school supposedly founded by Goshun. The general opinion of Goshun's work is that he combined the styles of Buson and Ōkyo to create the Shijō technique, but it is difficult to believe that Shijō ever existed as a separate school in a meaningful sense. The Shijō artists are normally associated with color flower and bird studies, with less attention given to detail than the Maruyama artists.

Despite a rather individualistic brush technique, Goshun's work is similar to that of Ōkyo, and although he was adept at bird and flower paintings, he was also skilled in landscapes basically in the Nanga style, figure studies and *haiga*. It is true that Goshun's paintings were more abstract than those of Ōkyo and Buson, and Japanese art historians recognize a distinct Shijō style based on the work of Goshun, but in fact, in book illustration, Shijō never developed into a major art movement and was soon merged with the Maruyama school. Goshun himself made contributions to several albums, but the only book he completely illustrated was the *Shin hanatsumi* (1 vol., 1784, color). It is believed that after Buson's death, Goshun came into possession of a manuscript *haiku* diary written by his master and decided to publish it as a memorial with illustrations of his own added to the text, which was reproduced from Buson's handwriting. The illustrations are few in number and are in *haiga* style (Pl. 73) with light colors. All of them are figure studies, including portraits, albeit in impressionistic style, of Buson, and the combination of Buson's calligraphy and Goshun's illustrations make the work one of the most aesthetically pleasing books ever produced in Japan.

Goshun had a number of pupils working in the Shijō style, of whom the most important were Matsumura Keibun, Goshun's younger brother, and Okamoto Toyohiko (1773–1845). Keibun, a painter of pleasant bird and flower pictures, was not solely responsible for any illustrated book, apart from *Keibun gafu* (1 vol., 1830, color), but examples of his work appear in many albums. The very rare *Keibun gafu* is most representative of Keibun's paintings, containing some 20 bird and flower studies in color. Toyohiko first studied under the Nanga artist Kuroda Ryōzan, and the Nanga influence had a lasting effect on his style, but he spent quite a long period in Goshun's studio and acquired a great respect for that artist's work. An able teacher, Toyohiko took in many pupils (very few of whom are significant in book illustration) and enjoyed great popularity, his work appearing in a dozen albums including *Bijin awase*.

Perhaps the most exciting of Goshun's pupils in book illustration, however, was the rather more obscure Satō Suiseki. Very little is known of Suiseki's life apart from the fact that he was Goshun's pupil, but he was active from the early years of the nineteenth century until about 1840, illustrating or collaborating on some 20 books. His best works are *Kachō bunko* (1 vol., c. 1811, bird and flower studies), *Suiseki gafu* (1 vol., 1811, color, designs of various occupations), *Suiseki gafu nihen* (1 vol., 1820, color, his masterpiece of glorious portrayals of plants and birds) (Pl. 82) and *Suzuri no chiri* (1 vol., c. 1819, color, miscellaneous *haiga* illustrations). Through the many followers of Goshun and Toyohiko, in particular, the Shijō tradition in painting continued until well into the Meiji period, and in book illustration was usually associated with poetry anthologies.

KISHI KU (GANKU) (1749–1838)

Kishi Ku (Ganku) was the son of Kishi Michifusa, a samurai serving the lord of Kaga in the city of Kanazawa. Early in his life he is believed to have worked as a textile designer for a dyeing business in Kaga before traveling to Kyoto to study painting. As far as is known, Ganku never received any formal training, but was greatly influenced by Chinese painting, particularly the detailed color bird and flower studies of Shên Nan-p'in. Although he painted many such studies himself, Ganku was at his best with animals, particularly tigers. Later, he was influenced by the Maruyama and Shijō styles, as was inevitable for any artist working in Kyoto at this period, although Japanese art historians recognize the separate existence of a "Kishi" school. This, however, is due more to his relatives, primarily his son Kishi Tai (1782–1865), his son-in-law Kishi (Aoi) Renzan (1804–59), his nephew Kishi Ryō (1798–1852) and his other sons, who all used the Kishi name, giving the impression of a continuity of style. To describe, this style as a combination of the influence of Shên Nan-p'in and Ōkyo is meaningless, as the same could be said of so many artists of the period. It is perhaps too simplistic to talk about any artist in such precise terms in an age when there was so much cross-fertilization of styles. In Ganku's work and that of his followers, however, there are most of the prevailing Kyoto styles. None of Ganku's immediate family worked much in book illustration, but examples of their works exist in albums such as *Meika gafu*.

A pupil of Ganku who did work with great distinction in book illustration and who provides a fine example of the crossbreeding of styles was Kawamura Bumpō (1779–1821), who also studied *haiku* and the Nanga artists, Buson in particular. He was a capable figure painter, but showed marked preference for landscapes and his best illustrations are in the latter genre. His ability with figures, however, is shown in his earliest book, *Bumpō soga* (1 vol., 1800, light colors), a collection of sketches of popular life, and *Bumpō kanga* (1 vol., 1803, light colors), small sketches of Chinese figures probably designed as a companion volume for the former work. His most successful books, however, were on landscapes in a modified Nanga style, where the structure and composition followed Nanga models, but with a strong Maruyama strain particularly in later works. The best of these were *Kanga shinan nihen* (3 vols., 1811, light colors, a collection of Chinese landscapes designed as a manual for landscape painting with advice on the use of figures), *Teito gakei ichiran* (4 vols., 1809–16, light colors, views of Kyoto with shrines and temples as focal points), *Bumpō gafu* (3 vols., published in 1807, 1811 and 1813, light colors, figures and landscapes, of ten volumes originally planned) and *Bumpō sansui gafu* (1 vol., 1824, color, "mountain and water" landscapes in modified Nanga style) (Pl. 78). Bumpō's most capable pupil was his adopted son Kawamura Kihō (1778–1852), whose major illustrations are in *Kihō gafu* (1 vol., 1827, light colors, miscellaneous sketches in the style of Bumpō, especially the color) (Pl. 84). It is noteworthy that although Kihō was the adopted son of Bumpō, he was a year older and had a much longer working lifetime, gravitating in his later career toward the Maruyama and Shijō styles.

Shên Nan-p'in has been mentioned several times and it is appropriate to deal with him here for he has a significance beyond all proportion to his individual talent. A Ch'ing-dynasty bird and flower painter and a skilled colorist, who enjoyed some fame in China, Shên came to Japan in 1731 at the invitation of the Nagasaki officials. He stayed in Nagasaki for less than two years, where he taught his painting methods to a large circle of pupils before returning to China in 1733. So many Japanese artists studied his works as representative of Chinese painting of the time that Shên had a wide influence outside his own immediate circle. Despite his talents, Shên would not have been chosen as the model for Japanese artists had they been fully aware of developments in Chinese painting, but this lapse occurs often in Japanese cultural history and no harm seems to have come of it. Ultimately, elements of Shên's influence permeated into the major impressionistic schools, but his own circle of pupils and their descendants remained faithful to Shên's highly detailed and realistic style. Rather strangely perhaps, many of Shên's major followers chose, in illustration at least, to adhere to black and white, and even when color was used, it was the lighter hues associated with Nanga and, later, Maruyama, rather than Shên's own rich colors. Virtually all of Shên's pupils, quite naturally, specialized in bird and plant subjects.

The first Japanese artist to study directly under Shên was the Nagasaki-born Kumashiro Yūhi (1713–72), who came from a family of Chinese language interpreters (Nagasaki was the only port open to Chinese and Western commerce). Yūhi showed considerable talent for bird and flower pictures, but was also known for his portrayals of tigers and particularly bamboos, which he tended to paint in ink. He never worked in illustration (the 1814 *Meika gafu* is the only source of his work in printed form), but was the only one of Shên's immediate followers who taught pupils to work with distinction in this medium. Yūhi's most notable followers were Sō Shiseki, Mori Ransai, Ogura Tōkei and, best of all, Tatebe Ryōtai.

Sō Shiseki (1712–86), a native of Edo, went to Nagasaki to study painting first under Yūhi and later under the Chinese artist Sung Tzŭ-yen. Like most of the Shên-Yūhi circle, he devoted his talents to copying the works of earlier masters, and like Yūhi himself, was best in painting birds, flowers, animals and bamboos. In book illustration he concentrated on the reproduction of Shên's paintings and those of other Chinese masters, but he also used the medium creatively to a small extent, and was the leading exponent of Shên's style in Edo. His major productions in illustration were *Sō Shiseki*

101. A Shijō-style bird and flower study, by Mori Ransai, from the *Ransai gafu* (1802), the only major work by this little-known artist.

gafu (3 vols., 1765, copies of Shên's birds and flowers in *sumizuri*, with similar studies of his own in color, and copies of bird, flower, animal and landscape paintings from other Chinese artists in *sumizuri*), *Kokon gasō kōhen* (8 vols., 1771, color, miscellaneous copies including landscapes, bird and flower pictures and figure studies) and *Kokon gasō* (3 vols., 1779, bamboos, orchids, chrysanthemums and plum blossoms in both *sumizuri* and color). The title of this work implies that it should have preceded the previous item in publication date, but apparently this was not so. Other works for which Shiseki was responsible, including *Sō Shiseki gasō sansui* (3 vols., 1770), are extremely rare. Shiseki's own pupils, not prominent in book illustration, included widely divergent figures such as Shiba Kōkan and Sakai Hōitsu.

Virtually nothing is known of the life of Mori Ransai (1740–1801), save what has been gleaned from the preface to his only major work of illustration *Ransai gafu*, and this is confined to his date of birth and artistic lineage. *Ransai gafu* (4 vols., 1802) is a painting textbook with birds, flowers and landscapes (Pl. 101). Less is known about Ogura Tōkei (it is not even certain who his master was), although Yūhi is a reasonable hypothesis. His representative work of illustration is in *Tōkei gafu* (3 vols., 1787, copies of Shên's bird and flower paintings together with original work in the same style; an augmented version of this book may have been published in 1809).

TATEBE RYŌTAI (1719–74)

Perhaps the most talented of Yūhi's pupils was Tatebe Ryōtai, also known as Kanyōsai. The son of a retainer of the lord of Hiromae fief, Ryōtai was sent by an Edo patron to Nagasaki to study painting under Yūhi. By this time Ryōtai was already an authority on Japanese literature, particularly *waka* poetry, on which he wrote more than one book. Despite his inclinations toward native literature, he was enormously attracted to the Chinese painting styles of Shên and Yūhi, and also studied several other Chinese painters including Li Yung-yün while in Nagasaki. He was not a prolific illustrator, but the four works by which he is best known were all of outstanding quality. In subject matter he followed the conventions of the Shên school and concentrated on birds and flowers, with a particular penchant for bamboos. With rare exceptions, most of his illustrations were in black and white, and he was especially skillful at using graded ink washes to achieve effects. In book illustration he was the outstanding disciple of Yūhi. His principal productions were *Kanyōsai gafu* (4 vols., 1762, studies of birds, flowers and animals), *Ri Yōun chikufu* (1 vol., 1771, careful copies of bamboo paintings of the Chinese artist Li Yung-yün), *Kenshi gaen* (2 vols., 1771, copies, primarily of landscapes, by various Chinese artists together with his own bird and flower studies, with an augmented version published in 1775 in 4 vols.), *Mōkyō wakan zatsuga* (5 vols., 1772, copies of landscapes, birds, flowers and animals together with original work, remarkable for the effective ink washes) (Pl. 102) and *Kanga shinan* (2 vols., 1779, an instruction manual for landscape painting, perhaps the inspiration for Kawamura Bumpō's *Kanga shinan nihen*).

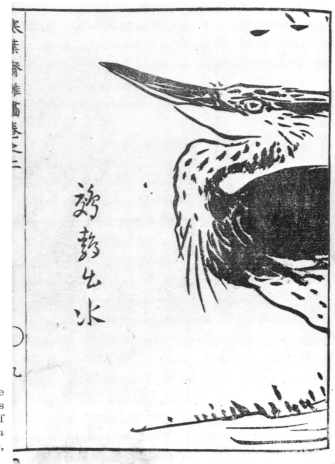

102. This typical example of the work of Tatebe Ryōtai, who was influenced by the Chinese artists of Nagasaki, is from the *Mōkyō wakan zatsuga* (1772), a book of birds, flowers and landscapes.

In this chapter as in those preceding it, it has been impossible to list all the books or indeed all the artists worthy of mention because of limitations of space. Numerous artists such as the Nanga painter Ki Chikudō (d. 1825) produced one or two outstanding books, such as the superb *Chikudō gafu* (2 vols., 1800 and 1815, color), and artists such as the Chō Gesshō group of Nagoya, represented by Gesshō (1772–1832) (Pl. 81) and his pupil Ōishi Matora (1794–1833), made worthwhile contributions to the illustrated book. To describe them all is the province of the specialized catalog rather than this general introduction. As a whole the groups of painters described here as impressionistic, including the convenient categories of Nanga, Maruyama, Shijō and Kishi, were far more individualistic than the Kanō and ukiyo-e schools ever were. Furthermore, they did not use the book as a creative vehicle in the same way as the ukiyo-e artists did. The audience for the illustrated books of the impressionistic schools was far smaller and more discriminating than that for ukiyo-e books, and this in itself is indicative of a different approach to art. This is not to say that all the impressionist amateur painters were of the *bunjin* tradition, but the commercial motive is less evident in their books. The ukiyo-e artists were subject to economic pressures and had to produce a lot of work to earn their living. It is chiefly because of this that the albums of the impressionist schools, whose artists were usually better educated and came from wealthier backgrounds, are of such unfailing high quality, while the masterpieces of the ukiyo-e schools are interspersed with so much mediocrity.

APPENDICES

GLOSSARY

Aka-hon 赤本

Called "red books" on account of their red covers, they were a type of fiction of the *kusa-zōshi* (q.v.) genre, designed for children and the semiliterate. Principally pictorial, the earliest examples were produced in the 1670s. They continued to be published until about 1736.

Ao-hon 青本

"Blue books," stylistically similar to *aka-hon* and aimed at the same audiences, but distinguished by their blue covers. Their principal period of production was c. 1744–74.

Azusa 梓

The catalpa tree, from which printing blocks were made before the more durable *yama-zakura* (q.v.) wood was adopted.

Baren 馬棟

A circular card, wrapped in fine bamboo sheath fiber, used in the printing process for rubbing the paper against the block to achieve the impression.

Beni-e 紅絵

An early to mid-18th century method of printing, where the color *beni* (rouge) was applied by hand to a black and white print.

Bijin-ga 美人画

These "pictures of beautiful women" were prints or paintings usually of either courtesans or geisha.

Bōkoku-bon 坊刻本

"Books printed by popular hands," was the generic name given to "popular" works, often on medicine, which were printed privately in the early 17th century, primarily during the Keichō era (1596–1615).

Bunjin 文人

A term derived from *wên-jên* (literatus), the Chinese ideal of a man of letters and spiritual cultivation. In Japan, its meaning was similar and the term was particularly associated with the scholar painters of the Nanga school who had a keen interest in Chinese literature and who often incorporated themes from Chinese classics in their paintings.

Chō, chōkō, chōshi, chōshu 彫, 彫工, 彫師, 彫手

Terms used to denote the block engraver.

Choku-han 勅版

"Imperial editions," a generic name for books printed by movable type at the express command of Emperor Go-Yōzei between 1593 and 1603. They were lavish in appearance and were typified by the use of a large typeface.

Chōnin 町人

"Townsfolk," the word applied to the artisan and merchant class who lived in the big cities during the Edo period.

Dengyō-ban 伝教版

Editions, now not extant, supposed to have been printed in the 9th century at the command of Dengyō Daishi, founder of the Tendai sect in Japan.

Den Saga-bon 伝嵯峨本

Books identical in style to those printed at the Saga Press but which have not been fully authenticated as Saga Press productions.

Detchō 粘葉

The "butterfly" style of binding (*see* Chapter 1).

E-dokoro 絵所

The Imperial Bureau of Painting set up during the Ashikaga period to superintend affairs relating to painting.

Ehon 絵本

A generic name for "picture books," in which pictures took precedence over text.

E-iri hon 絵入本

"Books with pictures inserted," the name for books that contained illustrations which were secondary in importance to the text.

Emaki, emakimono 絵巻, 絵巻物

"Picture scrolls."

Fudoki 風土記

Eighth-century gazetteers of all the different provinces of Japan, compiled at the command of Empress Gemmei (r. 708–14) and containing descriptions of the region, crops, products and customs. Only the *Izumo fudoki* survives in a more or less complete form.

Fukibokashi 拭暈

A technique of applying color by hand to printing blocks to achieve subtle gradation and used to considerable effect by Toriyama Sekien (1712–88). The resultant colors were pale and aesthetically pleasing.

Fukuro-toji 袋綴

The "bag" style of book binding (*see* Chapter 1).

Fumon-bon 普門品

Usually known as the *Kannon-gyō*, this section of the *Lotus Sutra* tells how the Bodhisattva Kannon comes to help those in distress, and by assuming thirty-three different forms, teaches the law of the Buddha.

Fune 船

The "boat," or trough, into which the paper-mix was poured when making paper.

Fushimi-ban 伏見版

The generic name given to eight books printed at Fushimi near Kyoto by command of Tokugawa Ieyasu between 1599 and 1606. One of the earliest examples of "official" movable type printing.

Gampi 雁皮

A shrub (*Diplomorpha Shikokiana* Nakai), whose inner bark is still used in Japanese handmade paper.

Ganshu 願主

A monk or layman who sponsored the printing of a Buddhist text in fulfillment of a vow.

Gofun 胡粉

A white pigment made from ground seashells used as a means of paper decoration. It was either applied at random to the surface of the paper while still wet, or by stencil or block where patterns were required.

Gōkan-mono 合巻物

A type of fiction of the *kusa-zōshi* (q.v.) genre, they were usually based on historical themes and were produced from the beginning of the 19th century until just after the Meiji Restoration. They are characterized by their garish pictorial covers.

Gorintō 五輪塔

A five-tiered pagoda.

Gozan-ban 五山版

A generic term for the books printed by the Zen monks of the Gozan ("Five Monasteries") temple complexes in Kamakura and Kyoto (particularly the latter) during the Kamakura and Muromachi periods.

Ha 派

A school (of painting, of calligraphy, etc.).

Haiga 俳画

Sketches used to illustrate the themes of *haiku* (q.v.) and *haikai* (q.v.).

Haikai 俳諧

Originally the term for comic *waka*, it is now used almost synonymously with *haiku* (q.v.).

Haiku 俳句

A form of poetry written in the 5-7-5 syllable form popular from the mid-17th century onward. Bashō, Buson and Issa are traditionally regarded as the three greatest exponents of this type of poetry.

Hashibami 端喰

A wooden clamp used to prevent the wood cut for the manufacture of wood blocks from warping.

Hiei-zan-ban 比叡山版

A generic term for any book printed, either by block or movable type, by the Tendai monks of the Hiei-zan temple complex.

Hiinagata 雛形

A small pattern or motif.

Hinoki 檜

The Japanese cypress occasionally used for the manufacture of wood blocks, but mentioned within the context of this book as the wood used for making the pagodas to store the *Hyakumantō darani*.

Hiragana 平仮名

One of the two phonetic scripts of the Japanese language, with *katakana* (q.v.).

Hiragana-majiri 平版名交り

A combination of Chinese characters and the *hiragana* (q.v.) syllabary used in a text.

Hokku 発句

The opening lines (17 syllables) to a *renga* (linked verse) poem which came to be treated as a verse form in its own right in the Edo period.

Honya nakama 本屋仲間

One of three terms (together with *jihondoiya no nakama* [q.v.] and *shorin nakama* [q.v.]) used for the publishers' and sellers' guilds which developed from the 17th century onward.

Hyōban-ki 評判記

Edo-period critiques of courtesans, actors, or famous places.

Imbutsu 印仏

A stamped image of a Buddha or a bodhisattva used in manuscripts and printed books particularly in the Heian and Kamakura periods. It served a devotional purpose at first and later was used simply for decoration.

Intō 印塔

A stamped image of a pagoda used in the same fashion as an *imbutsu* (q.v.).

Jihondoiya no nakama 地本問屋仲間 (*see Honya nakama*)

Jōdo-kyō-ban 浄土教版

Books printed either by block or movable type, produced in the Kamakura, Muromachi and early Edo periods by the temples of the Jōdo (Pure Land) sect.

Jōruri 浄瑠璃

Former name of the *bunraku*, or puppet theater.

Jōruri-bon 浄瑠璃本

Works of fiction whose plots were based on *jōruri* plays and scenarios.

Kabuki 歌舞伎

One of the traditional theaters of Japan, together with *nō* and *bunraku*.

Kachō 花鳥

"Flowers and birds," the most common theme of Kanō and Maruyama artists.

Kakemono 掛物

A hanging scroll.

Kami 紙

Paper.

Kana 仮名

General term embracing both the *hiragana* (q.v.) and *katakana* (q.v.) syllabaries.

Kana-zōshi 仮名草子

A generic term covering novels and other works written in *kana*, but specifically relating to popular fiction of the 17th century written in *kana* to reach a wider audience. The doctrines of Buddhism were frequently explained in works of this sort, where the intention was to instruct as well as entertain.

Kanpan 官版

"Government editions," a generic term for works published in the Edo period specifically under the auspices of the feudal government. Most often these were Chinese classics and other Chinese texts for use in schools.

Kanseki 漢籍

A book written in the Chinese language, but which is not a Buddhist text.

Kansu-bon 巻子本

A book with the earliest form of binding used in Japan, where a wooden or stone rod was attached to the paper roll.

Kara-e 唐絵

"Chinese painting," used to distinguish between early Japanese paintings which imitated Chinese styles and themes, from the native-inspired *Yamato-e* (q.v.) tradition.

Kasa-gami 傘紙

A paper that was normally used for umbrellas (*kasa*) but also widely used in *Kōya-ban* (q.v.) editions.

Kasuga-ban 春日版

Originally this term referred to books that were printed at Kōfuku-ji in Nara and then dedicated at the Kasuga shrine, the family shrine of the Fujiwara family. Strictly speaking, it should only be used in connection with books that were printed at Kōfuku-ji, but it has come to be used for any book or scroll printed in a Nara temple during the Heian, Kamakura and Muromachi periods.

Katakana 片仮名 (*see Hiragana*)

Kentō 見当

A device used in color printing to ensure accurate register.

Kibyōshi 黄表紙

"Yellow cover" books of the *kusa-zōshi* (q.v.) genre of fiction. They flourished in the last quarter of the 18th century and their themes included moral tales, stories for children and humorous *chōnin* (q.v.) adventures.

Kirishitan-ban 吉利支丹版

A generic term used for the books printed by movable type at the Jesuit Mission Press in the last decade of the 16th and the first decade of the 17th century.

Kōetsu-bon 光悦本

One type of *Saga-bon* (q.v.), whose typeface was modeled on Kōetsu's calligraphy.

Kokatsuji-ban 古活字版

A generic term for books printed by movable type in the years c. 1590 to 1650.

Kokkei-bon 滑稽本

Novels depicting humorous adventures of city life belonging chiefly to the early part of the 19th century. Jippensha Ikku's *Hizakurige* series is perhaps the most celebrated example.

Kōwaka-mai 幸若舞

A dramatic dance performed to the accompaniment of flute and drum music, of which 36 different types are generally recognized. The stories on which these dances are based were published and known as *mai no hon* (q.v.).

Kōya-ban 高野版

A generic term for any book printed by the Shingon monks of the Mt. Kōya complex.

Kōya-gami 高野紙

Another name for *kasa-gami* (q.v.).

Kuro-hon 黒本

"Black books," another subdivision of the *kusa-zōshi* (q.v.) genre of fiction produced between about 1740 and 1780 and distinguished by their black covers. Primarily pictorial, the stories were aimed at the same audience as *aka-hon* and *ao-hon*.

Kusa-zōshi 草双紙

A style of fiction that flourished from the late 17th to the late 19th century, where emphasis was placed on illustration. It was basically aimed at children and the semiliterate and includes genres such as *aka-hon, ao-hon, kuro-hon* and *kibyōshi*.

Kushibarai 櫛払

The brush used to sweep cut wood from the block after the engraving is completed.

Kyōgen-bon 狂言本

Theater books containing the stories of *kabuki* plays.

Kyōraku-han 京洛版

A generic term for Buddhist texts printed in the temples of Kyoto.

Mai no hon 舞の本

Book form versions of *kōwaka-mai* (q.v.).

Maki 巻

This term, whose literal meaning was "roll," was originally used for the scrolls that made up the earliest type of "books." Long after codex forms of books became popular, this word was retained to mean approximately "a chapter."

Meisho-ki 名所記

"Records of famous places." This type of book, which evolved from the mid-17th century

233

onward, was designed for pilgrims and travelers, giving descriptions, with illustrations, of famous or beautiful places.

Mitsumata 三椏

A shrub (*Edgeworthia papyrifera* Sieb. et Zucc.) whose fibers were used in the making of paper.

Mokuhan 木版

A wood block.

Naoe-ban 直江版

The movable type edition of *Monzen* produced in 1607 and sponsored by the physician Naoe Kanetsugu.

Nara-ehon 奈良絵本

Manuscripts written in fine calligraphy on high-quality paper that were produced between the late 16th and early 18th centuries. Although the term means "Nara picture book," there was no connection with Nara itself. The illustrations, probably executed by monks, were in late Tosa style, highly colored and often decorated with gold leaf. The contents were usually fiction of either classical, *kōwaka-mai* (q.v.) or *otogi-zōshi* (q.v.) types.

Nara-emaki 奈良絵巻

These were manuscripts exactly similar to *Nara-ehon* (q.v.) except that they were in scroll, rather than book, form.

Nara-han 奈良版

Any pre-Edo-period book that was printed at Nara.

Nomi 鑿

"Chisels," of various sizes, used in engraving a block.

Ōraimono 往来物

Books of social and moral etiquette usually intended for women readers.

Orihon 折本

Concertina binding (*see* Chapter 1).

Oshi-e 押絵

Raised pictures made with cardboard cutouts wrapped in cloth.

Otogi-zōshi 御伽草子

Originally this term was applied to a group of 23 short, anonymous novels of the Muromachi period. Later the meaning was expanded to cover some 500 short stories of the Muromachi period.

Roku 緑

A mineral green obtained from malachite.

Rufu-bon 流布本

Often described as a "popular edition," although it actually means the most widely used variant of a manuscript produced in printed form.

Ryakuga-shiki 略画式

An abbreviated style of painting whereby detail was omitted in an attempt to capture the "spirit" of what was portrayed.

Saga-bon 嵯峨本

Books printed mostly by movable type at the press of Hon'ami Kōetsu and Suminokura Soan in Saga, near Kyoto. There are only 13 "official" *Saga-bon* works, all of which are works of Japanese literature, produced in the years 1608–c. 1624. They are noted for the lavish attention given to the quality of paper, binding, calligraphy and overall appearance.

Saizuchi 小椎

"Mallets" used to drive the chisels in the engraving of a block.

Sansui 山水
> "Mountain and water" landscape.

Satsu 冊
> A volume.

Senryū 川柳
> A comic variation of *haiku* (q.v.) verse associated with the poet Karai Senryū (1718–90) and his followers.

Shakyō 写経
> The practice of copying sutras by hand, particularly associated with the Nara and Heian periods.

Shakyō-sho 写経所
> A scriptorium. A special room within a temple, the court or even, on occasions, the home of a wealthy nobleman, where sutra-copying was undertaken.

Share-bon 洒落本
> A type of novel, often licentious, that flourished from the mid- to late Edo period, portraying the amorous dalliances of courtesans and gallants. Usually disapproved of by the authorities.

Shorin nakama 書林仲間 (*see Honya nakama*)

Sōsho 草書
> The cursive, or "grass form," of the Japanese script.

Suiboku 水墨
> A style of landscape painting imported from China and particularly associated with the Zen monks of the Gozan temple complexes. Effect was achieved not by color but by line, drawn with Indian ink on paper or silk.

Sumi 墨
> Indian ink.

Sumizuri 墨摺
> Black-and-white line drawing.

Suributsu 摺仏
> The same as *imbutsu* (q.v.) except that it was printed from a block instead of a stamp.

Suri-kuyō 摺供養
> The printing of a text in the Heian and Kamakura periods with the specific purpose of commemorating the death of some notable or celebrating his recovery from illness.

Tan 丹
> Red lead, used to make the orange color that was applied by hand to *tanroku-bon* (q.v.).

Tanroku-bon 丹緑本
> A printed book of the first half of the 17th century containing black-and-white printed illustrations that were crudely colored by hand with orange (*tan*) and green (*roku*). Yellow, brown and purple were also often used.

Tendoku 転読
> The Buddhist practice of acquiring merit by reading a sutra, not from beginning to end, but by choosing passages at random. The lengthy *Daihannya-kyō* was often "read" in this way.

Toba-e 鳥羽絵
> A style of caricature painting pioneered by the monk Toba Sōjō (1053–1140).

Torinoko 鳥の子
> A type of handmade Japanese paper that was both sturdy and lustrous, often used for *Nara-ehon* manuscripts. Associated mainly with the Edo period.

Tsukuri-e　作絵
A technique of painting associated with the Yamato-e and Tosa traditions consisting of strong lines filled in with sumptuous colors.

Ukiyo-zōshi　浮世草子
A form of novel that supplanted *kana-zōshi* in the late 17th century. The themes were focused around the townsmen and the stories were often bawdy. Ihara Saikaku was the most famous author working in this genre.

Ummo　雲母
Mica used for decorating the pages of printed books, particularly of Buddhist texts. The mica was applied to the paper when it was still wet during the process of papermaking, or applied by stencil or block when patterns were required, as with *gofun* (q.v.).

Waka　和歌
The classical form of native Japanese lyric poetry consisting of 31 syllables arranged in the 5-7-5-7-7 pattern.

Washi　和紙
A generic term for Japanese handmade paper.

Yakusha hyōban-ki　役者評判記
Critiques of *kabuki* actors.

Yamato-e　大和絵
A style of "Japanese painting," one of the precursors of the Tosa school, which flourished from the 10th century until it merged with the Tosa and other movements. It formed a step in the development of a purely native style of painting that employed Japanese themes as subject matter.

Yamato-toji　大和綴
The only form of native Japanese binding (*see* Chapter 1).

Yamazakura　山桜
The wild cherry tree, whose wood was almost exclusively used in the Edo period for the manufacture of wood blocks.

Yomi-hon　読本
Biographical style novels, usually long and centering around the deeds of famous Japanese warriors. They were greatly influenced by historical works and the Chinese classics, and often contained strong moral overtones. They flourished from about 1750 until the early Meiji period.

Yūsoku kojitsu　有職故実
A general term for matters relating to correct behavior, costume, customs at court and in feudal society.

BIBLIOGRAPHY

The following is a list of some of the major works consulted in the writing of this book, although it is not meant to be exhaustive. There is a scarcity of material published in English on Japanese printing, and readers might find it helpful to consult the bibliographies of the works below. English language sources are listed first, followed by works written in Japanese.

ENGLISH LANGUAGE SOURCES

Brown, Louise Norton. *Block Printing and Book Illustration in Japan*. London: Routledge. New York: E. P. Dutton, 1924.

Cahill, James. *Scholar Painters of Japan: The Nanga School*. New York: Asia House Gallery, 1972.

Carter, Thomas Francis. *The Invention of Printing in China and its Spread Westward*, revised by L. Goodrich Carrington. New York: Ronald Press Co., 1955.

Chibbett, D. G.; Hickman, B. F.; and Matsudaira, S. *A Descriptive Catalogue of the pre-1868 Japanese Books, Manuscripts and Prints in the Library of the School of Oriental and African Studies*. London: Oxford University Press, 1975.

Hickman, B. F. "A Note on the *Hyakumantō Dhāranī*." *Monumenta Nipponica*, Vol. 30, No. 1. Tokyo: Sophia University, 1975.

Hillier, J. *The Uninhibited Brush: Japanese Art in the Shijō Style*. London: Hugh M. Moss, 1974.

Holloway, Owen E. *Graphic Art of Japan: The Classical School*. London: Transatlantic, 1957.

Ishida, Mosaku. *Japanese Buddhist Prints*. English adaptation by Charles S. Terry. Tokyo: Kodansha International, 1974.

Mitchell, C. H. *The Illustrated Books of the Nanga, Maruyama, Shijō and Other Related Schools of Japan: A Bibiliography*. Los Angeles: Dawson's Bookshop, 1972.

Okudaira, Hideo. *Emaki: Japanese Picture Scrolls*. Translated by John Bester and Charles Pomeroy. Tokyo: Charles E. Tuttle, 1962.

Toda, Kenji. *Descriptive Catalogue of Japanese and Chinese Illustrated Books in the Ryerson Library of the Art Institute of Chicago*. Chicago, 1931.

Tsien, Tsuen-hsuin. *Written On Bamboo and Silk: The Beginnings of Chinese Books and Inscriptions*. Chicago: University of Chicago Press, 1962.

Waterhouse, D. B. *Harunobu and His Age: The Development of Colour Printing in Japan*. London: The Trustees of the British Museum, 1964.

JAPANESE LANGUAGE SOURCES

Asakura, Kamezō. *Nihon shōsetsu nenpyō, shinshū* (rev. ed.). Tokyo: Shunyōdō, 1926.

Harigaya, Shōkichi, and Suzuki, Jūzō. *Ukiyo-e bunken mokuroku*. Tokyo: Mitō Shooku, 1962.

Higuchi, Hideo, and Asakura, Haruhiko. *Kyōhō igo shuppan shomoku*. Toyohashi: Mikan Kokubun Shiryō Kankōkai, 1962.

Inoue, Kazuo. *Keichō irai shoka shūran*. Kyoto: Ibundō Shoten, 1916.

Kabutogi, Shōkō. *Hokke hangyō no kenkyū*. Kyoto: Heirakuji Shoten, 1954.

Kawase, Kazuma. *Gozan-ban no kenkyū*. 2 vols. Tokyo: Antiquarian Booksellers' Association of Japan, 1970.

———. *Kokatsuji-ban no kenkyū, zōho*. 3 vols. Tokyo: Antiquarian Booksellers' Association of Japan, 1967 (rev. 1937 ed.).

———. *Nihon shoshigaku gaisetsu*. Tokyo: Kodansha, 1950.

———. *Nihon shoshigaku no kenkyū*. Tokyo: Kodansha, 1943.

———. *Saga-bon zukō*. Tokyo: Isseidō Shoten, 1932.

Kimiya, Yasuhiko. *Nihon ko-insatsu bunka-shi*. Tokyo: Fuzambō, 1932.

Kobayashi, Zempachi. *Nihon shuppan bunka-shi*. Tokyo: Nihon Shuppan Bunka-shi Kankōkai, 1938.

Kokusho sō-mokuroku. 8 vols. Tokyo: Iwanami Shoten, 1963–72.

Makino, Zembei. *Tokugawa bakufu jidai shoseki-kō*. Tokyo: Tōkyō Shoseki-shō Kumiai Jimusho, 1912.

Makita, Inashiro. *Keihan shoseki-shō enkaku-shi*. Osaka and Tokyo: Shuppan Taimusu-sha, 1928.

Mizuhara, Gyōei. *Kōya-ban no kenkyū*. Tokyo: Rinkō Shoten, 1932.

Mizutani, Futō. *Kohan shōsetsu sōga-shi*. Tokyo: Ōokayama Shoten, 1935.

Munemasa, Isoo, and Wakabayashi, Seiji. *Kinsei Kyōto shuppan shiryō*. Tokyo: Nihon Kosho Tsūshin-sha, 1965.

Nagasawa, Kikuya. *Wakanjo no insatsu to sono rekishi*. Tokyo: Yoshikawa Kōbunkan, 1952.

Nakada, Katsunosuke. *Ehon no kenkyū*. Tokyo: Bijutsu Shuppan-sha, 1950.

Nakamura, Kiyomi. *Kinsei shuppan-hō no kenkyū*. Tokyo: Nihon Gakujutsu Shinkōkai, 1972.

Okuno, Hikoroku. *Edo jidai no kohampon*. Tokyo: Tōyōdō, 1944.

Ōsaka Tosho Shuppan-gyō Kumiai. *Kyōhō igo Ōsaka shuppan shoseki mokuroku*. Osaka: Seibundō, 1964.

Ōya, Tokujō. *Nara kankyō-shi*. Tokyo: Naigai Shuppan, 1923.

Sawada, Akira. *Nihon gaka jiten*. 2 vols. Tokyo: Kigen-sha, 1927.

Suga, Chikuho. *Kyōka shomoku shūsei*. Kyoto: Hoshino Shoten, 1936.

Tanaka, Kaidō. *Nihon ko-shakyō genson mokuroku*. Kyoto: Shibunkaku, 1973.

———. *Nihon shakyō sōkan*. Osaka: Sammyō-sha, 1953.

Tanaka, Kei. *Detchō-kō*. Tokyo: Ganshōdō Shoten, 1932.

Tōdō, Sukenori. *Jōdo-kyō-ban no kenkyū*. Tokyo: Daitō Shuppan-sha, 1930.

Tominaga, Makita. *Kirishitan-ban no kenkyū*. Tenri: Tenri Daigaku Shuppan-bu, 1973.

Ueda, Osamu, ed. *Ukiyo-e bunken mokuroku*. 2 vols. Tokyo: Mitō Shooku, 1972.

Uesato, Haruo. *Edo shoseki-shōshi*. Tokyo and Osaka: Shuppan Taimusu-sha, 1930.

Wada, Mankichi. *Kohan chishi kaidai* (rev. ed.). Tokyo: Ōokayama Shoten, 1933.

———. *Kokatsuji-bon kenkyū shiryō*. Kyoto: Seikan-sha, 1944.

Wada, Tsunashirō. *Saga-bon kō*. Tokyo: Shimbi Shoin, 1916.

Yoshida, Teruji. *Ukiyo-e jiten*. 3 vols. Tokyo: Ryokuen Shobō, 1965-71.

INDEX OF ARTISTS

Keiho (*see* Takada Keiho)
Keisai (*see* Kitao Masayoshi)
Kenzan (*see* Ogata Kenzan)
Ki Baitei (1744–1810), 紀楳亭, 213
Ki Chikudō (d. 1825), 紀竹堂, 225
Kishi Ku (Ganku) (1749–1838), 岸駒, 210, 218, 221–22
Kishi (Aoi) Renzan (1804–59), 岸(青井)連山, 221
Kishi Ryō (1798–1852), 岸良, 221
Kishi Tai (1782–1865), 岸岱, 221
Kita Busei (1776–1856), 喜多武清, 214, 215
Kitagawa Shikimaro (act. early 19th cent.), 喜多川式麿, 178
Kitagawa Toyomaro (act. early 19th cent.), 喜多川豊麿, 178
Kitagawa Tsukimaro (d. 1830), 喜多川月麿, 178
Kitagawa Utamaro (c. 1753–1806), 喜多川歌麿, 85, 122, 130, 136, 140, 169, 175, 176–77, 178, 180, 181, 183, 186, 204, 208, 216; Pls. 65, 68
Kitagawa Yukimaro (1797–1856), 喜多川雪麿, 178
Kitao Masanobu (Santō Kyōden) (1761–1816), 北尾政演(山東京伝), 176, 179, 180, 181, 215
Kitao Masayoshi (Sanjirō) (Kuwagata Keisai) (1764–1824), 北尾政美(三二郎)(鍬形蕙斎), 179, 181–82, 184, 187, 188; Pl. 63
Kitao Shigemasa (1739–1820), 北尾重政, 130, 169, 178, 179, 180, 181, 186
Kiyonaga (*see* Torii Kiyonaga)
Kiyonobu (*see* Torii Kiyonobu)
Kiyotsune (*see* Torii Kiyotsune)
Kōetsu (*see* Hon'ami Kōetsu)
Koikawa Harumachi II (Utamaro II) (act. early 19th cent.), 恋川春町二代(歌麿二代), 177–78
Kokan (1653–1717), 古磵, 199, 200, 201
Komai Ki (Genki) (1747–97), 駒井琦(源琦), 217
Kondō Kiyoharu (act. early 18th cent.), 近藤清春, 144
Kōrin (*see* Ogata Kōrin)
Koshū (*see* Hatta Koshū)

Kubo Shunman (1757–1820), 窪俊満, 179, 180–1; Pl. 66
Kumashiro Yūhi (1713–72), 熊代熊斐, 223
Kunisada (*see* Utagawa Kunisada)
Kuniyoshi (*see* Utagawa Kuniyoshi)
Kuroda Ryōzan (act. late 18th–early 19th cent.), 黒田綾山, 221
Kuwagata Keisai (*see* Kitao Masayoshi)
Kuwayama Gyokushū (1746–99), 桑山玉洲, 212

Li Yung-yün, 李用雲, 224

Maki Bokusen (1736–1824), 牧墨仙, 187, 188
"Makie-shi" Genzaburō (act. late 17th cent.), 蒔絵師源三郎, 136, 137
Maruyama (Kinoshita) Ōju (1777–1815), 円山(木下)応受, 217
Maruyama Ōkyo (1733–95), 円山応挙, 181, 210, 216–17, 218, 219, 220, 221; Pl. 85
Maruyama Ōshin (1790–1838), 円山応震, 217
Maruyama Ōzui (1766–1829), 円山応瑞, 217
Masanobu (*see* Kitao Masanobu)
Masayoshi (*see* Kitao Masayoshi)
Matsumura Goshun (1752–1811), 松村呉春, 210, 213, 217, 220, 221; Pl. 73
Matsukawa Hanzan (act. c. 1840–70), 松川半山, 190
Matsumura Keibun (1779–1843), 松村景文, 220, 221
Minagawa Kien (1734–1807), 皆川淇園, 217
Minkō (*see* Tachibana Minkō)
Mitsunobu (*see* Hasegawa Mitsunobu)
Miyagawa Chōshun (1683–1752), 宮川長春, 178
Mochizuki Gyokusen (1692–1755), 望月玉仙, 210, 220
Morikuni (*see* Tachibana Morikuni)
Mori Ransai (1740–1801), 森蘭斎, 223, 224; Pl. 101
Mori Tetsuzan (1775–1841), 森徹山, 217
Moronobu (*see* Hishikawa Moronobu)
Motonobu (*see* Kanō Motonobu)

Nagasawa Rosetsu (1755–99), 長沢蘆雪, 217
Nakai Rankō (1766–1830), 中井藍江, 204
Nakamura Hōchū (act. early 19th cent.), 中村芳中, 206, 207

241

INDEX OF BOOK TITLES

Note: The author regrets that he has not been able to provide the Japanese characters of some of the titles of books no longer extant.

GENERAL INDEX